MW00685137

THE POLITICS OF TRAGICOMEDY

THE POLITICS OF TRAGICOMEDY

Shakespeare and After

Edited by
Gordon McMullan and Jonathan Hope

London and New York

First published 1992
by Routledge
11 New Fetter Lane, London EC4P 4EE

Simultaneously published in the USA and Canada
by Routledge
a division of Routledge, Chapman and Hall, Inc.
29 West 35th Street, New York, NY 10001

Typeset in 10/12pt Bembo by Witwell Ltd
Printed in Great Britain by
Biddles Ltd, Guildford

British Library Cataloguing in Publication Data
The politics of tragicomedy: Shakespeare and after.
1. English drama. History, 1558–1625 2. Shakespeare, William, *1564–1616*
I. McMullan, Gordon II. Hope, Jonathan 822.3

Library of Congress Cataloging-in-Publication Data
The politics of tragicomedy: Shakespeare and after/edited by Gordon McMullan and Jonathan Hope.
p. cm.
Includes bibliographical references and index.
1. English drama—17th century—History and criticism.
2. Politics and literature—Great Britain—History—17th century.
3. Great Britain—Politics and government—1603–1649.
4. Shakespeare, William, 1564–1616—Tragicomedies. 5. Tragicomedy.
I. McMullan, Gordon. II. Hope, Jonathan.
PR678.P65P65 1991
822′.052309—dc20 91–10063
CIP

ISBN 0–415–06403–1

CONTENTS

CONTRIBUTORS

MARTIN BUTLER is a Lecturer in the School of English at the University of Leeds. He is the author of *Theatre and Crisis 1632–1642* (1984) and has co-edited *The Selected Plays of Ben Jonson* (1989).

WALTER COHEN teaches in the Department of Comparative Literature at Cornell University. He is the author of *Drama of a Nation: Public Theater in Renaissance England and Spain* (1985).

MARGOT HEINEMANN taught at Goldsmith's College, London, and New Hall, Cambridge. Her book, *Puritanism and Theatre: Thomas Middleton and Opposition Drama under the Early Stuarts*, was published in 1980. She has several articles forthcoming on politics and patronage in Renaissance drama.

JONATHAN HOPE is Earl Grey Memorial Fellow in the Department of Speech at the University of Newcastle upon Tyne. He is completing a sociohistorical linguistic study of the authorship of the Shakespeare–Fletcher collaborations.

KATHLEEN McLUSKIE is a Senior Lecturer in English at the University of Kent at Canterbury. Her most recent publication is *Renaissance Dramatists* in the Harvester 'Feminist Readings' series.

GORDON McMULLAN is a Lecturer in the School of English at the University of Newcastle upon Tyne. He is completing a study of the plays of John Fletcher.

DAVID NORBROOK is Fellow and Tutor in English at Magdalen College, Oxford, and Lecturer in English at the University of Oxford. He is the author of *Poetry and Politics in the English Renaissance* (1984) and has compiled *The Penguin Book of Renaissance Verse* with Henry Woudhuysen.

LOIS POTTER is Professor of English at the University of Delaware. Her latest publication is *Secret Rites and Secret Writing: Royalist Literature 1641–60*; she has also written on Milton, Shakespeare, and the history of drama, and is now editing *The Two Noble Kinsmen* for the Arden Shakespeare.

ERICA SHEEN is a Lecturer in the Department of English Literature at Sheffield University, where her specializations include film and literary theory as well as Renaissance drama. She has published on Shakespeare and on Hollywood science fiction.

SOPHIE TOMLINSON is a Lecturer in English at Auckland University, New Zealand, and is currently completing a study entitled 'Theatrical women: the emergence of women as actors in English theatre and drama before the Restoration'.

PREFACE

The essays that make up this collection began life as papers given at a conference entitled *The Politics of Drama 1610–1650* which took place at Wadham College, Oxford, in June 1988. The conference was organized by the editors of the present volume when we were graduate students at Oxford and Cambridge respectively. The primary motivation for the conference was our belief that the sustained interest in the politics of Renaissance drama apparent over the last ten years or so could be given a valuable focus by way of the increased attention that has recently been paid to the genre of tragicomedy. We believe, echoing a comment made by Annabel Patterson at the conference, that tragicomedy is best characterized as a genre which is fruitfully 'edgy' and is not to be written off in the traditional way as merely 'bland', and we hope that the original request to consider tragicomedy in preference to other forms encouraged the participants to recognize the value in the shift of focus this entailed. As Nancy Klein Maguire states in the introduction to her recent collection of essays on the genre, the aim is to show that 'tragicomedy is neither a "mungrell" mixture of tragedy and comedy nor a decadent offshoot of tragedy but is rather a genre in its own right' which deserves much more rigorous analysis than it has received to date.

Other motivations for the conference included our shared interest in the work of John Fletcher, as well as a desire to bring together as broad a range as possible of scholars with an interest in the politics of Renaissance drama and thus to promote dialogue and collaboration. The present volume is intended to take its place alongside other recent books in the general subject area. We hope that the gradually increasing quantity of work in this field will encourage those scholars and teachers who have tended to dismiss tragicomedy and writers of tragicomedy to reconsider their position and to recognize the importance of a working knowledge of the genre to the study and teaching of

Renaissance drama. We trust that closer acquaintance with this one crucially important but as yet critically underrepresented genre will permit more informed and sophisticated readings of English drama of the period between the last years of Shakespeare's career with the King's men and the first years of the Commonwealth.

It is worth underlining that the essays included here were not commissioned specially for this volume but were originally presented in the form of short conference papers. We have been unable for various reasons (publication elsewhere, for example) to include several of the conference contributions here. Others have had to be omitted because they represented only preliminary work towards more substantial projects. Contributors to the conference were not restricted to speaking on tragicomic texts alone, and the present collection comprises only those essays which seemed to the editors best to represent the conference's concentration on the relations between politics, romance and tragicomedy in the period 1610–50. The focus of this volume has therefore inevitably been narrower than that of the Wadham conference and by no means all of the conference participants are represented here. The editors would like to thank all those who took part, especially those who chaired sessions or who gave papers which we have not been able to include: Francis Barker, Catherine Belsey, David Bergeron, Julia Briggs, Terry Eagleton, Julia Gasper, Mark Jenner, David Johnson, David Lindley, Willy Maley, Jeremy Maule, Daryl Palmer, Annabel Patterson, Robin Robbins, Frank Romany, Simon Shepherd, Nigel Smith, Geraldo de Sousa, and Peter Womack. We would also like to thank the Warden and Fellows of Wadham for allowing the conference to take place under their auspices. We are grateful to Ken Robinson and to James Knowles for comment on the introduction of this volume. We are grateful, too, to Jane Armstrong for her editorial supervision (and her fondness for lardy cake). The editors' greatest debt by far is to David Norbrook, without whose sustained friendship, support, and encouragement – practical and intellectual – neither the conference nor this volume would have come about.

Gordon McMullan *Jonathan Hope*

University of Newcastle upon Tyne

1

INTRODUCTION: THE POLITICS OF TRAGICOMEDY, 1610–50

Gordon McMullan and Jonathan Hope

I

Tragicomedy was arguably the single most important dramatic genre of the period 1610–50. Yet despite the inroads which contemporary criticism has made into value-judgements based on 'unity', tragicomedy's 'good broken music' still appears to unsettle those who study it. Part of the problem for the critic is that the word 'tragicomedy' itself seems never to have acquired anything akin to a fixed meaning. In the English Renaissance, the term covered an astonishing variety of forms, from formulaic popular drama to courtly romances based on wonder, from formal Italianate pastoral to plays which close with an uneasy combination of marriage and death. To accept Dr Johnson's even-handed definition of the genre as 'a drama compounded of merry and serious events' has never seemed quite adequate in face of this sheer plenitude of forms gathered under one heading.

The closest to a standard survey of the genre remains Marvin Herrick's *Tragicomedy: Its Origin and Development in Italy, France, and England*, which attempts to provide a comprehensive overview from Plautus to Davenant and beyond. The very grandeur of conception of this treatment, however, weakens it, and Herrick concludes by suggesting only that 'English tragicomedy never went far beyond' Florio's 1598 definition of the genre in his *Worlde of Wordes* as 'halfe a tragedie, and halfe a comedie'.[1] Other works, such as Eugene Waith's standard treatment of Fletcherian tragicomedy, attempt somewhat mechanically to define the term according to certain characteristic tenets and themes.[2] But few critics achieve a satisfactory generic understanding, and very few attempt any analysis of the complex relations of tragicomedy and politics in the period. Part of the problem is the tendency of most critics of Renaissance tragicomedy to rely for a working definition of the genre on a short piece of prose by John

Fletcher entitled 'To the Reader', which forms part of the elaborate publication apparatus for his pastoral tragicomedy *The Faithful Shepherdess*, which was published in 1609 or 1610.[3] Fletcher was Shakespeare's successor as chief playwright for the King's Company. He collaborated with Shakespeare on the latest of the late plays, and the stamp of the older playwright was always apparent in his work. Yet Fletcher was as influential as Shakespeare in determining the direction the drama would take up to, during, and beyond the English Civil War, and he is most readily thought of, along with his early collaborator Francis Beaumont, as the playwright who developed the form of tragicomedy in the period. The statement he made early in his career about the form of one of his plays has thus always seemed the best place to begin a study of the genre.

At first glance, Fletcher's 'To the Reader' does indeed appear to provide a succinct description and definition of tragicomedy. As a result it has been rather more widely quoted and discussed than has the play it attempts to 'justifie'. To most critics, 'To the Reader' seems to confirm the consistent reliance of English tragicomedy upon Italianate models from 1610 onwards. *The Faithful Shepherdess* and its defence are quite clearly indebted in various ways to the dramatic theory and practice of Giovanni Battista Guarini, whose *Il Pastor Fido* was first published in 1590 and reappeared with a preface and annotations in 1602 and 1603.[4] The conditions of publication as well as the title and matter of Guarini's and Fletcher's plays demand comparison. *Il Pastor Fido* attracted criticism, and Guarini's justification of tragicomedy, *Il Compendio della Poesia Tragicomica* (1601), was written in response. Fletcher's preface is a similar attempt to justify his work in face of negative public reaction. One crucial feature of *The Faithful Shepherdess*, after all, is its abject failure on the stage when it first appeared. Its subsequent success at court years later in 1634 in completely different political circumstances should not blind us to the initial reaction of the theatre audience in James's day. The publication of the text of *The Faithful Shepherdess* is in fact a literary justification of the play in the wake of its failure on the stage. Chapman's definition of the piece in his dedicatory verse as a '*Poeme and a play too*!' confirms the manoeuvre which is executed in what Beaumont refers to as 'This second publication'.[5] In a move which anticipates Jonson's presentation of his own plays as *Workes* in 1616, print is used to elevate dramatic writing to the level of literature, both because reading is a sign of education (as Beaumont points out with Inn-of-Court arrogance) and simply because print lasts longer than the memories of an audience. The ploy of appealing over the heads of the original audience to the market for printed poetry (and after all, Fletcher claims that the initial failure of the play was due to its being too intellectual for its first audience) was intended to secure Fletcher's reputation as a writer, but it confirms that what we have in 'To the Reader' is a *post hoc* literary justification for a dramatic failure. It seems to have worked. By the time of the *Conversations* with Drummond, Ben Jonson has apparently forgotten all about the play's initial lack of success on the stage.[6] And certainly by 1634, in totally different ideological and theatrical conditions, it had become a spectacular success.

But the specific justificatory context of 1610 makes the assumed value of 'To the Reader' as a considered and coherent definition (or prediction) of tragicomedy across the period to 1650 begin to appear questionable. Critics have not stopped to ask if Fletcher's use of the word 'tragicomedy' in relation to *The Faithful Shepherdess* is relevant to the vast number of plays from the years 1610–50 which we now characterize as tragicomedies, and none has tested what Fletcher says in his preface against his own subsequent practice.[7] To take just one example, Fletcher in 'To the Reader' asserts the 'lawfulness' of the appearance of gods in tragicomedy:

> A tragie-comedie is not so called in respect of mirth and killing, but in respect it wants deaths, which is inough to make it no tragedie, yet brings some neere it, which is inough to make it no comedie: which must be a representation of familiar people, with such kinde of trouble as no life be questiond, so that a God is as lawfull in this as in a tragedie, and meane people as in a comedie.[8]

Fletcher's professional practice, however, appears by and large to ignore this statement. When gods do appear in his subsequent work (and it is very rarely), the tone is often one of burlesque. In *The Mad Lover*, for example, Venus descends to punish the blasphemy of Chilax by kicking him up the behind: 'I'le no more Oracles, nor Miracles,' he cries, 'It gave me on the buttocks, a cruell, a huge bang.'[9] Many of the plays in which Fletcher was involved specifically reject supernatural influences. When Arnoldo in *The Custom of the Country* seeks a miracle cure, Manuel bluntly observes that 'wonders are ceas'd Sir,' and asserts that 'we must work by means'.[10] And the wholesome supernatural influences even in *The Faithful Shepherdess* might be seen to be at least partially circumscribed by recent readings of the play as a satire on sexual mores.[11] On closer inspection, *The Faithful Shepherdess* turns out to be anomalous in several respects in the context of Fletcher's other writing. It is, for instance, wholly unrepresentative of the linguistic style of Fletcher's subsequent plays, none of which repeats the highly artificial, Spenserian diction apparent in this early pastoral.[12] Thus when Cyrus Hoy presented his study of the linguistic determinants for establishing authorship of the various plays within the 'Beaumont-and-Fletcher' canon, he felt obliged to omit *The Faithful Shepherdess* from his statistical analysis as representing the one obvious exception to the rules he had ascertained for the rest of the canon.[13]

The crucial factor about the 'definition' provided by 'To the Reader' is the *ex post facto* reading that critics invariably make of it. Fletcher himself was after all blissfully unaware that he would go on in a few years to become Shakespeare's successor as chief playwright for the King's Company and produce the most substantial dramatic canon of the period. Within a year of the publication of *The Faithful Shepherdess* he was writing in a very different style (perhaps in a way more indicative of his ambitions) in *The Woman's Prize, or The Tamer Tam'd*, a good-humoured comedy which acts as a mock-sequel to *The Taming of the Shrew*. If his aim in this was to attract the attention of Shakespeare, then his collaborations with the older playwright on *Henry VIII, Cardenio*, and *The Two Noble Kinsmen* in 1612 and 1613 would appear to be proof of a certain level of success. But this can only be conjecture. Ascertaining Fletcher's generic intentions in the years between his first collaborations with Beaumont and his work with Shakespeare at the point of Beaumont's retirement remains a critical minefield. What evidence there is, however, suggests that *The Faithful Shepherdess* is perhaps the last place we should look for a working definition of tragicomedy in the Jacobean and Caroline period.

Lois Potter has pointed out the 'inconsistency in the generic descriptions' applied to the various plays in the period 1610–50 that we now group under the general heading of 'tragicomedy'. As she notes, it took until 1679 for Fletcher's 'tragicomedies' to be labelled as such in published form, and the use of the one-word description is decidedly erratic, at least prior to the 1630s.[14] What becomes apparent is that there is a distinction between the very general 'mixed-mood' form denoted by the word 'tragicomedy', and the much more specific, Italianate form signified by 'pastoral tragicomedy'. As Potter observes, 'the evidence suggests that the term "tragicomedy", in the public theatre, never quite lost its sixteenth-century meaning: a play which contained both tragic and comic elements. Dramatists were obviously aware of the genre in its newer, more formal sense, but were curiously reluctant to claim that this was what they were writing.' And she continues: '*De facto* tragicomedy might be written for both popular and courtly audiences, but it appears that to use the term was to make a social as well as an aesthetic statement. What it meant, above all, was a play whose source might be Greek romance or Italian pastoral, but whose immediate context was the court and its circle of gentlemen amateurs.'[15] It would appear thus that in 'To the Reader' Fletcher is writing about 'pastoral tragicomedy', a form derived substantially from Guarini and Italian tradition, and not the mixed-mood form derived from predominantly Spanish romance with which we tend to associate him (the form which Madeleine Doran revealingly referred to as 'the-Beaumont-and-Fletcher-sort-of-thing').[16]

Recent work on Fletcher's context sheds further light on *The Faithful Shepherdess*, making it possible to see quite different motivations from the presumed promotion of this form of Italianate pastoral tragicomedy for a select courtly or gentry audience.[17] There is an irritatingly unspecific reference to the writer's possible future plans in the dedicatory verse to Sir Walter Aston which is part of the *Faithful Shepherdess* apparatus:

> And when I sing againe as who can tell
> My next devotion to that holy well,
> Your goodnesse to the muses shall be all,
> Able to make a worke Heroyicall.

If 'Heroyicall' writing is the next stage in, or after, Fletcher's pastoral project, then it is a pattern redolent of the strategies of Jacobethanism. It is perhaps worth observing that, in terms of publication date, *The Faithful Shepherdess* is bracketed by two other 'pastoral tragicomedies', *The Queen's Arcadia* of 1606 and *Hymen's Triumph* of 1615, both written by Samuel Daniel. No plays are specifically called 'pastoral tragicomedies' prior to *The Queen's Arcadia*, and it is not until *The Shepherd's Holiday* of 1635 and *The Noble Ingratitude* of 1659 that the term reappears on a title-page.[18] There is, however, one play published in 1604 which is described as a *Tragiecomedia* and which quotes extensively from Guarini while yet remaining (to quote G.K. Hunter) 'totally unpastoral': that is, John Marston's *The Malcontent*. Hunter suggests that Marston had recently read the 1602 translation of *Il Pastor Fido* by a relative of Sir Edward Dymock and that the description of *The Malcontent* as *Tragiecomedia* in the Stationers' Register 'refers to Marston's programmatic attempt to reconstruct this genre in English'.[19] If this is true, then Hunter is also correct in suggesting that Marston has opted to concentrate on the specifically non-pastoral branch of tragicomedy's heritage for his reconstruction while none the less acknowledging the importance of Guarini's theoretical contribution. Interestingly, Marston seems not to have been the only English playwright around this time to have attempted a specifically English reconstruction of a version of tragicomedy. Daniel wrote a dedicatory poem for the 1602 version of *Il Pastor Fido* which praises the play and recalls acquaintance with its author but goes on to challenge it with 'England' and 'vertues of the North':

> I do reioyce learned and worthy Knight,
> That by the hand of thy kinde Country-man
> (This painfull and industrious Gentleman)
> Thy deare esteem'd *Guarini* comes to light:
> Who in thy loue I know tooke great delight
> As thou in his, who now in England can
> Speake as good English as Italian,
> And here enioyes the grace of his owne right.
> Though I remember he hath oft imbas'd
> Vnto vs both the vertues of the North,
> Saying, our costes were with no measures grac'd,
> Nor barbarous tongues could any verse bring forth.
> I would he sawe his owne, or knew our store,
> Whose spirits can yeeld as much, and if not more.[20]

Daniel would appear here to be claiming an English right to a form of pastoral drama which Guarini could not disparage. This does not imply slavish imitation of Italianate models, but rather a qualitative equivalence, so that 'now in England' the pastoral 'can/Speake as good English as Italian'.

It is thus possible to suggest that there were at least three playwrights writing in the first years of James's reign who appear to have begun work on ambitious projects for the acquisition of forms of tragicomedy for a specifically English context. In light of patronage and other evidence (Marston, for example, shared patronage connections and milieu with Fletcher), it is difficult to avoid the sense that these efforts, particularly in the form of an English reconstitution of 'pastoral tragicomedy', may in various ways parallel Jacobethan and Spenserian pastoral projects in poetry (Drayton's *Pastorals*, for example) which suggest political motivations for English tragicomedy at this time somewhat different from those usually associated with 'the court and its circle of gentlemen amateurs'.[21] This specific context can only reinforce the inadequacy of a definition based solely on 'To the Reader' for tragicomedy in the period 1610–50.

The use (or misuse) of Fletcher's 'To the Reader' bedevils criticism of tragicomedy because of the mistaken assumption that its precepts can be applied to work as disparate as Shakespeare's 'romances' or 'late plays', Fletcher's early collaborations with Beaumont, his later solo and collaborative work as leading dramatist of the King's Men, and other types of tragicomic drama such as Webster's *The Devil's Law-Case*. Indeed, the evidence of his subsequent dramatic practice suggests that for all his defence of *The Faithful Shepherdess* as literature, Fletcher realized it was not drama. This certainly seems to have been the opinion of the audience – and the supposedly 'sophisticated' private theatre audience at that. Immediately after the fiasco of *The Faithful Shepherdess*, Fletcher abandoned his abortive project for pastoral tragicomedy and began, in his collaborations with Beaumont, to forge other versions of the genre which were to determine the course of mainstream tragicomedy for the next forty years.

II

Rejecting, or at least marginalizing, Fletcher's 'To the Reader' thus opens up a much wider range of possibilities for the study of tragicomedy in the period, from popular-theatre plays in the Elizabethan tradition to the circumscribed romances of Ben Jonson's last phase, from the resonantly political late plays and collaborations of Shakespeare to the pastoral drama written especially for the feminocentric court of Henrietta Maria. During the Wadham conference it became very clear that the participants held diverse views on the nature and quality of tragicomedy. It was universally recognized that work to date on the genre has by and large been mediocre and conservative, and that the time was right for substantive interventions to reassert the possibility of a critically productive politics of Renaissance tragicomedy. The essays in this volume thus represent a series of exploratory approaches to the tragicomedy of the period. As Walter Cohen observes, it is the explorations and the conflict *en route* to tragicomedy's resolutions, rather than the edgy certainties of the plays' conclusions, that offer the primary possibilities for valuable political criticism of the genre. Perhaps more to the point, the 'politics' which the contributors seek or find in the tragicomic texts that interest them varies considerably, and there is no consensus on an ideology-of-form for tragicomedy. For some, the genre has a revolutionary valence; for others it is irredeemably defined by revisionary strategies. Such interpretative alternatives are, we would suggest, entirely appropriate in a volume which aims to represent a chief element in literary–political development in the first half of the seventeenth century.

Certain questions and problems inevitably recur in the study of tragicomic texts, and one major area of critical dialogue is historiographical. After decades of debate, the argument over the origins of the English Civil War continues. In the last ten years there has been a resurgence of different kinds of historicism in both historical and literary–historical circles. This collection, as perhaps the forthright title of Cohen's essay, 'Prerevolutionary Drama', most clearly suggests, belongs predominantly (though not solely) within an historicist framework. But this framework is one which is not always wholly in line with the recent critical phenomenon in Renaissance studies known as New Historicism: aims are at times shared, but strategies can differ. The New Historicism was effectively inaugurated by Stephen Greenblatt's introduction to the collection of essays he edited under the title *The Power of Forms in the English Renaissance*, and the movement's flagship is Greenblatt's own ground-breaking book, *Renaissance Self-Fashioning*, published in 1980.[22] Though Greenblatt retains his commanding position, others have since become key New Historicist names, including Jonathan Goldberg, Louis Adrian Montrose, Stephen Mullaney, and several others. Their characteristic strategy takes them from historical anecdote to wide-ranging analysis of the underlying political motivations of discourse and finally to close reading of certain literary texts, more often than not by Shakespeare. Texts are played off one another in a process which attempts to avoid privileging the literary over other cultural forms. Old historicisms are thus given a new lease of life in the wake of the death of the author and the poststructuralist demolition of the monolithic text. Rejecting the critical dryness too often associated with medieval and Renaissance studies, New Historicists seek accessible if at times oblique ways of approaching the familiar and unfamiliar in literary history.

Writing within the broad remit of this project is of course not restricted to the United States. A number of British critics, united by a shared heritage in the work of Raymond Williams and other British Marxists, offer a parallel discipline which they have christened Cultural Materialism; significantly, the manifesto for this approach – a volume of essays edited by Jonathan Dollimore and Alan Sinfield with the title *Political Shakespeare* – includes one of Stephen Greenblatt's best-known essays.[23] Other critics, including Leah Marcus and Annabel

Patterson in the United States and David Norbrook in the United Kingdom, among others, have been at various times incorporated under the general New Historicist heading by commentators. Yet there are crucial strategic differences between their work and that of critics who concentrate almost solely on court and king and who follow Foucault in seeing subversion as inevitably (if paradoxically) involved in repression and containment. For New Historicists, as one recent commentator has put it, 'every act of unmasking, critique, and opposition uses the tools it condemns and risks falling prey to the practice it exposes'; for some, however, this formulation needlessly limits the possibilities for an autonomy of political consciousness within artistic production and can subordinate subject to structure in an excessively deterministic way, thus failing to account for the agency of individuals or less powerful social groups.[24] Critics such as Norbrook and Patterson are wary of an exclusive focus upon the court and court culture, and look not just for the inevitable contradictions within royalism but for historical alternatives to court politics which enable the recognition of a certain political continuity from Elizabethan writers of militant protestant persuasion such as Sidney right through to the outright republicanism of Milton. These critics thus reject what David Norbrook has called the 'most radically antihumanist and Nietzschean current in recent criticism', preferring to retain the possibility of a certain level of individual political agency within literary texts.[25]

In a number of ways, this perspective enables closer relations with historians such as Thomas Cogswell, Richard Cust, Derek Hirst, Peter Lake, and others, who seek ways of promoting broadly historicist readings of the period 1610–50 which can both recognize some of the harmful oversimplifications of 'Whig' historiography and still capitalize upon the local concentrations of revisionism without losing the possibility of a certain degree of historical overview.[26] These historians share with many of the writers in the present collection a wish to look somewhere other than the court for the threads and motivations of political life as early as 1610. The critical gaze thus transfers to the margins: to the country, to the female audience and the female participant, to popular rather than courtly traditions in the drama, and to 'edgy' genres such as tragicomedy itself. And because of its marginal critical and generic status, tragicomedy can provide a central case for what Walter Cohen calls a 'symptomatic' reading of the drama. Lois Potter has observed that, from the standpoint of the Restoration, history itself (recent history at least) took the shape of a romantic tragicomedy with its characteristic motifs of wandering, loss, and eventual regeneration. It seems appropriate in several ways, then, to make tragicomedy the generic focus of a collection of essays which formulate new readings of drama in the first half of the seventeenth century.

In planning both the conference and this volume, we settled on the dates 1610–50 rather than the more usual 1603–42 for two reasons. First, we wished to limit Shakespeare's inevitably powerful presence in a collection of this nature to only a handful of his late and collaborative plays, partly in order to look towards the relatively uncanonical and away from residual Elizabethan dramatic strategies, and partly as a reaction to the New Historicist tendency to depend excessively on analysis of Shakespeare despite recognition of the politics of his critical dominance. Second, we wished to give a certain amount of space to the examination of drama written in the decade after 1642, material which has traditionally been ignored because of the presumption that the closing of the theatres signified the complete absence of theatrical writing and activity. Thus we aimed to weight our chronological focus in a way somewhat marginal to customary expectations. Some of the best writing in this collection does concentrate on Shakespeare, but it sets up certain questions of agency and of intertextuality, particularly with both classical and contemporary 'republican' writers, that can usefully inform readings of drama later in the period in question. This, we accept, may leave us at least partially susceptible to our own criticisms of the New Historicism with respect to the question of textual, generic, and authorial privileging.

Locating a politics for tragicomedy remains a complex task. Walter Cohen, for example, finds it 'difficult – indeed impossible – to break entirely with the tradition of assigning a conservative valence to romance and tragicomedy' (pp. 125–6). Yet we must be careful, as Margot Heinemann suggests, to find an appropriate definition of 'conservatism' in this context. Certainly, romantic tragicomedy appears conservative in the sense that it is driven by certain forces of reconciliation and regeneration. Yet such regeneration frequently comes in the form of a displacement of the political status quo, the regeneration of a political nation away from tyranny. David Norbrook mentions a good example of this in his brief discussion of the concluding sequence of Fletcher and Massinger's *The Double Marriage*, a play which reworks certain features of *The Tempest* and finishes when 'the hero brings in the head of a tyrannical king of Naples to cries of "Liberty"'.[27] As we have seen, recent work by Philip Finkelpearl and others suggests that Fletcherian tragicomedy, the dominant mode of the period 1610–50, can in fact be characterized more accurately as anti-court drama rather than courtly. Tragicomedy can, it would appear, be anything but conservative in its immediate political impact. But our problem remains precisely that: to find ways to recover the 'immediate political impact' (as well as what Margot Heinemann in this volume problematically calls 'the real material history') of the plays in question.[28]

III

One of the problems faced by the student of 'prerevolutionary' tragicomedy is the sense of some kind of intimate connection between the genre and the royalist cause during and after (and therefore, by inference, before) the English Civil War. Several of the contributors to the present volume, however, can be seen to seek contexts for Renaissance tragicomedy which are clearly at odds with any attempt to assign the genre to royalism or proto-royalism. David Norbrook's essay, for example, with which the collection begins, examines the interrelations of utopia and language in Shakespeare's best-known romantic tragicomedy, *The Tempest*, seeking a way out of the apparent dead end produced by the various forms of critical absolutism that have been applied to the play. Thus, he observes, 'so dominant have courtly readings [of *The Tempest*] become that radical and anti-colonialist critics have tended to accept their historical premisses even while contesting their political outlook' (p. 22). But, he says, 'there is no need for twentieth century readings to be more royalist than the King's Men', and he proceeds to elaborate upon his premiss that 'there is room . . . for a reading that would remain open to utopian perspectives in a way that poststructuralist methodologies cannot allow, taking account of the cogent criticisms of blandly transcendental views of the subject which recent theory has been able to make, but without surrendering some notion of the possibility of the subject as rational agent' (p. 24).

In elaborating upon the question of the subject as agent and in demonstrating aspects of 'the emergence of a literary public sphere which prepared the way for the formation of a political public sphere' (p. 25), Norbrook seeks the sublimated political voices beneath the surface of *The Tempest*, from Guicciardini to Montaigne. Erica Sheen's contribution to the collection, '"The agent for his master": political service and professional liberty in *Cymbeline*', has an equivalent focus on underlying political voices and on the writer's agency as an alternative to models of containment. She seeks to question the almost universal assumption of the political conservatism of *Cymbeline* by way of analysis both of the resonances of the term 'agency' in the play and of one of Shakespeare's sources, Seneca's *Hercules furens*. For Sheen, Shakespeare disturbs 'conventional perceptions of roles of agency and gender' and develops 'a notion of action which has more in common with the resistance to absolutism [in] the period than with absolutism itself' (p. 56). In an earlier version of her essay, Sheen observed that 'historicist criticism is notoriously possessive about the political self-conscious: its discussions of Shakespeare are frequently concerned to discredit the suggestion that his work could offer responsible political reflection or articulate a personal position.' The problem, then, is that certain methodologies automatically deny the value of those techniques of analysis, such as the source-study, which appear to endorse the possibility of agency. Her interpretation of *Cymbeline* suggests that the presence of a major literary text from the Roman imperialist period is evidence of an historicism which does in fact reflect deeply on its own ideological position, and is a reading which is part of her larger project to develop a pragmatics of theatrical communication for the period. Thus by means of close and perceptive source-analysis, she suggests a prerevolutionary undercurrent in *Cymbeline*, rejects the image of Shakespeare as a '"dutiful servant" of his culture's orthodoxies' (p. 74), and in the process moves towards a better critical understanding of Shakespeare's collaborations with both the living and the dead.

Collaboration with the living is the primary focus for Lois Potter, whose essay on *The Two Noble Kinsmen* represents initial work towards her forthcoming Arden edition of the play. She discusses the issues both of the relations of theatre and politics and of the relations of collaboration within the drama, and she demonstrates that 'political meaning is . . . a matter of context', adding that 'the context of *The Two Noble Kinsmen*, for us, is the politics of literary criticism' (p. 90). Thus she examines the problems criticism has found in the play's 'doubly double focus of attention: two heroes, two authors' (p. 77), and she sets the notion of 'topical meaning' against that of 'political meaning', suggesting normally subsumed differences between these terms. She examines the possible topicalities of the play, thus effecting one of the closest historical analyses of the collection, and concludes by echoing concerns already broached: 'When we set Shakespeare and Fletcher against each other, as if the result of their combat could at least give us an answer to this curious play', she suggests, 'we are colluding with precisely the same destructive absolutism whose consequences *The Two Noble Kinsmen* has so vividly depicted' (pp. 90–1).

Kathleen McLuskie's essay in this volume is also to be found as a chapter in her recent book on *Renaissance Dramatists* in the Harvester 'Feminist Readings' series. Although the Harvester volume had appeared by the time we submitted this collection it seemed important to retain McLuskie's piece, concentrating as it does on the plays of John Fletcher, and depending as it does on an historical feminist methodology. Her paper is designed to take issue with Linda Woodbridge's suggestion that women in the audience influenced the representation of sexual relations in Jacobean drama.[29] She proposes instead that discussions of theatre audiences in the period construct women as objects of consumption rather than consumers of theatrical production and that this model of production and consumption informs the play around sexuality evident in Fletcher's drama. For McLuskie, Fletcher's tragicomedies 'offered their urban audience an image of a world where sex was significantly more important than honour and where relations with women had to be renegotiated, unfettered by older conventions of chastity and service and the smooth passage of women from fathers to husbands' (p. 119). Yet this release from restricting conventions was 'only a release into patterns of wit and urbanity in which women could as often be the victims as the heroines of the action' (p. 119).

The position of women in society in the period 1610–50 is Walter Cohen's starting-point for his essay on the drama he calls 'prerevolutionary'. He argues bluntly that 'the English Revolution constitutes the crucial reception' (p. 122) of the tragicomedies and of all the dramatic writing composed in the period, and thus raises the fundamental questions of text and context, historicism and revisionism, that have formed the basis of critical and historical argument over the last decade. In an earlier draft of his paper, he observed of the Wadham conference that it 'simply assumed what would have been seriously contested not long ago, that there *is* a politics of English drama between 1610 and 1650', yet he struggles at times with his sense that 'tragicomedy does not seem to provide the most fertile ground for identifying a prerevolutionary tradition' (p. 124–5). This, however, he treats as a challenge, since if tragicomedy 'can be plausibly connected to the upheavals of the midcentury, the same conclusion holds for the entire spectrum of dramatic forms in the three decades before 1642' (p. 125). His primary wish to oppose 'a monolithically absolutist reading in which Renaissance drama always ends up serving the interests of the monarchy' echoes throughout this collection, and he elaborates on the need to locate this emphasis on non-absolute historical readings within a feminist framework, examining the extent to which the 'failed radical revolution' of the 1640s and 1650s was 'distinctively a woman's revolution' and the ways in which romantic and tragicomic drama of the period gesture towards this linkage.

Margot Heinemann's way of avoiding such absolutism is to direct the focus of her study to the popular theatre. Her approach clearly shares much with Cohen's, and her essay serves in the present volume as something of a bridge between the preoccupations of older and newer historicisms. She suggests that 'to focus solely on the drama of the court and the more expensive and socially exclusive indoor theatres would make it difficult to understand the connections between early Stuart tragicomedy and the "real material history" of the times' (p. 151). She relates popularity, tragicomedy, and utopianism in a way which amplifies the concerns of David Norbrook's essay, proposing Stuart Foxeian history plays as 'one of the most successful kinds of tragicomic theatre in the popular playhouses' (pp. 153–4), and briefly examining utopia and dystopia as modes of popular expression. For Heinemann, utopian endings offset the harsh social criticism she finds in popular tragicomic writing in the period, and she acknowledges that audience and censor alike would have found such endings satisfactory. None the less, she concludes, there is little sense in these plays of any 'general confidence that the existing aristocratic and royal order can be relied upon to right the wrongs of the people' (p. 164).

This unease with the utopian endings tragicomedy can provide requires our recognition of its radical ambivalence and open-endedness as a genre. The ease with which tragicomedy can be appropriated for apparently different ideological ends has led to critics with shared interests finding evidence for diametrically opposed readings of the same tragicomic texts. Martin Butler's essay, for example, replies to the work of Anne Barton and David Norbrook on the late plays of Ben Jonson and rejects their claims that Jonson's politics had radically altered by the late 1620s.[30] Butler's careful reading focuses upon Jonson's 'circumscribed and circumspect' response to the genre of romance in the later part of his career, suggesting that 'however far Jonson went in his rapprochement towards romance . . . he continued to be wary of the form's structural openness and moral indeterminancy' (p. 167). He examines Jonson's output and patronage towards the end of his career, and gives a close account of the Caroline context, showing, for example, the echoes of parliamentary language in the court-of-love scene in *The New Inn*, and relating the play to its political context in the wake of the assassination of Buckingham. He suggests that *The New Inn* 'attempts to reconstruct an aristocratic ideology after the removal of Buckingham, but that it does so by conciliation, not confrontation' (p. 175), and he shows the way certain themes (nostalgia, relationship of the people to the land, social structure, and reconciliation) are dealt with in a tangential drama, themes which lead here too to a politicization of the drama which reflects the increasing politicization of English society at this time. Butler's essay thus acknowledges that, while Jonson was clearly exploring 'new forms, conventions, and motifs' in these late plays, he was none the less 'still concerned to construct fables which reaffirmed rather than called into question the social and political hegemony of the court' (p. 185).

The concluding essay, by Sophie Tomlinson, returns our focus to the question of the role of women in the development of the drama. She extends McLuskie's interest in the representation of women in the drama and the ways in which audiences responded to this representation by addressing the broader question of what she calls the 'staging of women', a staging which involves women not just as auditors but as doers and performers. Beginning with the shocked reaction of the audience to Queen Henrietta Maria's involvement, along with other courtly women, in the performance of a pastoral masque at court in 1626, she plots the effect of the introduction of the actress into Caroline culture. She examines several plays in this light, including William Cartwright's tragicomedy *The Lady-Errant*, which, she claims, legitimates 'the theatrical notion of the woman-actor who keeps to her part, specifically so as to silence her symbolic threat' (p. 199) to male order and power. Thus, 'appropriate female acting' offsets 'the more serious active transgression within the text' (pp. 200–1), and acts as implicit criticism of those women-actors who impersonate men in the court performance of Walter Montagu's pastoral, *The Shepheard's Paradise*, in 1633. For Tomlinson, none the less, the involvement of women in the performance of pastoral and other plays at court in the late 1620s and 1630s might paradoxically have spurred on the greater social, cultural and political activity of women during the revolutionary period.

It will by now have become apparent that the contributors to this volume have widely divergent attitudes to the various forms of tragicomic writing in the period 1610–50, and that their sense of a politics of tragicomedy in the period is complex and at times quite at odds. There is no sense in which this collection is intended as a monolithic statement on the nature of the genre: it is to be hoped that the issues raised here will stimulate further investigation into the least treated of dramatic genres. Quite clearly, however, there are certain questions which can be seen in various guises to intrigue each of the contributors. We have already suggested ways in which a number of contributors differ in their strategies if not their broad aims from those critics grouped under the heading of New Historicism and in which they might be seen to share interest with post-revisionist historians. The central concern is theoretical, and lies with the question of agency. To what extent does culture predetermine the artistic production of individuals and groups? It is possible to see in the tragicomedy of the period in question the enactment of issues other than those subsumed and legitimated by the dominant culture? Answers offered here obviously vary. Yet there is a desire to look further, and an unhappiness with presumed determinisms. Another key concern lies with the nature of history, and the relationship of literature and history. Lois Potter's differentiation between 'topicality' and 'politics', for example, raises somewhat different problems from Margot Heinemann's assertion that there is such a thing as 'real material history'. Yet each viewpoint demands a close understanding of what is required in the historical interpretation of texts.

At least one other major thread can be detected in several of the essays included here: the relationship between gender and genre. It is clear that connected concerns in these fields have puzzled and excited many of the contributors for a variety of reasons. Kathleen McLuskie and Sophie Tomlinson together show the importance of women – as audience, actress, and actress-doer – which is an increasingly strong feature of tragicomic discourse in the Jacobean and Caroline periods, and they elaborate upon ways in which women's participation in political affairs is both enabled and disabled in tragicomedy. Moreover, Walter Cohen, discussing the influence of class tensions on gender issues in tragicomedy, claims that in tragicomic writing there is an overt equation of the 'crisis of sexuality with the crisis of monarchical rule' (p. 142). He observes that 'English tragicomedies between 1610 and 1642 presuppose the analogy between family and state, deploying the love-and-honour code to produce a series of homologies and articulations that make women integral, even central to the fate of the nation', and he points out that 'the plays characteristically raise and resolve interdependent fears about women and monarchs', thereby demonstrating 'the irreducibly political character of gender relations perhaps in the period and certainly in tragicomedy' (p. 128). It is thus possible to see in an historical feminist reading of these plays a way out of the determinisms of current criticism, a way which allows concerns of class and gender to be treated on an equal footing.

By way of conclusion, it is perhaps appropriate to return to one recurrent but somewhat sublimated theme of the contributions to this collection: that of collaboration. Lois Potter's reading of *The Two Noble Kinsmen* is, for example, dependent in large part upon the play's nature as a collaborative text. In rejecting the critical tendency to set collaborative authors against one another she is simply responding to her playwrights' practice. For us, since the wartime appropriation of the term to a thoroughly negative connotation, collaboration seems a deadening of individual ability, a compromise at best. Yet it was, as G.E. Bentley and others have demonstrated, an habitual mode of production in the theatre in the period 1610–50; moreover, the writers most readily associated with the development of one form of tragicomedy in the period, Beaumont and Fletcher, are also those usually thought of first in discussion of Renaissance collaboration.[31] It is perhaps no coincidence that tragicomedy, with its uneasy juxtaposition of apparently opposed dramatic modes, should have a certain affinity for collaborative production. A volume such as the present collection is also of course the product of a collaborative process, as a result both of its multiple authorship and its dual editorship. The process is not always an easy one, yet the result can be the simple but valuable admission of the inadequacy of the single viewpoint. Moreover, a critical awareness of collaboration is perhaps the clearest route to an adequate understanding of the tensions within political drama in the Renaissance. As David Norbrook observes of the epilogue to *The Tempest*, 'authority is transferred to the process of dramatic production in which the company collaborates with the audience – or the reader' (p. 46). Perhaps this is the most relevant aspect for the contemporary critic of the politics of tragicomedy in the early modern period.

NOTES

1 Marvin T. Herrick, *Tragicomedy: Its Origin and Development in Italy, France and England* (Urbana: Illinois University Press, 1955), 317.
2 Eugene M. Waith, *The Pattern of Tragicomedy in Beaumont and Fletcher* (New Haven: Yale University Press, 1952).
3 Quotations are taken from *The Faithful Shepherdess*, ed. Cyrus Hoy in Fredson Bowers (gen. ed.), *The Dramatic Works in the Beaumont and Fletcher Canon* (Cambridge: Cambridge University Press, 1976), vol. III, 483–612. *The Faithful Shepherdess* was written in 1608/9 and published probably in 1610: 'Limits for its date of publication are suggested by the relatively brief

partnership of its publishers, Richard Bonian and Henry Whalley, which is traceable from December 1608 to January 1610. The Q1 text was certainly in print by 3 May 1610 when Sir William Skipwith, to whom Fletcher had addressed an Ode among the quarto's prefatory verses, died' (Hoy (ed.), 485).

4 Giovanni Battista Guarini, *Il Pastor Fido, Tragicommedia Pastorale . . . Con un Compendio di Poesia* (Venice, 1602). For an English translation of parts of the *Compendio*, see Allan H. Gilbert, *Literary Criticism: Plato to Dryden* (New York: American Book Co., 1940), 504–33.

5 Francis Beaumont, 'To my friend Maister *John Fletcher* upon his Faithful Shepheardesse', line 40; George Chapman, 'To his loving friend M. *Jo. Fletcher* concerning his Pastorall, being both a Poeme and a play', line 3, in Hoy (ed.), 491, 492.

6 But then Jonson also seems to have forgotten precisely who wrote the play: 'Flesher and Beaumont ten yeers since hath written the Fathfull Shipheardesse a Tragicomedie well done.' See 'Conversations with William Drummond', in C.H. Herford, Percy Simpson, and Evelyn Simpson (eds), *Ben Jonson* (Oxford: Oxford University Press, 1925–52), vol. I, 138.

7 Philip J. Finkelpearl, in his recent *Court and Country Politics in the Plays of Beaumont and Fletcher* (Princeton: Princeton University Press, 1990), acknowledges that 'the notions of genre developed for *The Faithful Shepherdess* have a limited usefulness for later plays by Beaumont and Fletcher [*sic*]' (104), but does not discuss the wider context of the preface's misuse as an ubiquitious definition of tragicomedy.

8 See Hoy (ed.), 497.

9 John Fletcher, *The Mad Lover*, ed. Robert Kean Turner in Fredson Bowers (gen. ed.), *The Dramatic Works in the Beaumont and Fletcher Canon* (Cambridge: Cambridge University Press, 1983), vol. V, 1–149, V. iv. 1.5.

10 John Fletcher and Philip Massinger, *The Custom of the Country*, in Arnold Glover (ed.), *The Works of Beaumont and Fletcher*, (1905), vol. I, V. i. 374.

11 See Annabel Patterson, *Censorship and Interpretation: The Conditions of Writing and Reading in Early Modern England* (Madison: Wisconsin University Press, 1984), 172–4, amplifying aspects of W.W. Greg's reading in his *Pastoral Poetry and Pastoral Drama* (London: A.H. Bullen, 1906); see also Finkelpearl, *Court and Country Politics*, 101–14.

12 A possible exception to this rule is *The Prophetess* (1622), where the appearance of gods and the pastoral setting are, however, circumscribed by the changing valences of 'country' politics at the beginning of the 1620s.

13 See Cyrus Hoy, 'The shares of Fletcher and his collaborators in the Beaumont and Fletcher canon (I)', *Studies in Biblography* (1956), vol. VIII, 142.

14 The word 'tragicomedy' creeps into the first Folio of 1647 only as a marginal gloss, in minuscule type, to a poem by Lovelace (b2–3).

15 See Potter, '"True Tragicomedies" of the Civil War and the Commonwealth', in Nancy Klein Maguire (ed.), *Renaissance Tragicomedy: Explorations in Genre and Politics* (New York: AMS Press, 1987), 196–7.

16 Madeleine Doran, *Endeavors of Art: A Study of Elizabethan Drama* (Madison: Wisconsin University Press, 1964), 186.

17 See Finkelpearl, *Court and Country Politics*, esp. chapter 1.

18 The first instance of 'tragicomedie' (as one word) in the Stationers' Register comes in the entry of 1598 for Samuel Brandon's 'tragicomedie of the Virtuous Octavia', but plays were not regularly published as tragicomedies until 1630. In the sixty-two years from 1567 to 1629, there are four so-called on their title-pages; in the next thirty years, to 1660, there are forty-eight.

19 John Marston, *The Malcontent*, ed. George K. Hunter (Manchester: Manchester University Press, 1975), lxii–lxiv. The editors are grateful to James Knowles for discussion of Marston and tragicomedy.

20 Samuel Daniel, 'To the right worthie and learned Knight, Syr *Edward Dymock*, Champion to her Maiestie, concerning this translation of *Pastor Fido*', in Giovanni Battista Guarini, *Il Pastor Fido, or The Faithfull Shepheard. Translated out of Italian into English* (London, 1602), A1v.

21 Marston and Fletcher seem to have shared patrons – the Earl and Countess of Huntingdon – and a context – Ashby Castle in Leicestershire, the Huntingdons' seat – and while Daniel seems to have had no primary connection with this circle, he quite clearly has much in common with the 'country' attitudes apparent at Ashby. See Finkelpearl, *Court and Country Politics*, 25–39, but with the reservations noted above. Again, the editors are grateful to James Knowles for discussion about the Ashby milieu.

22 Stephen Greenblatt (ed.), *The Power of Forms in the English Renaissance* (Norman, Oklahoma: Pilgrim Books, 1982); Stephen Greenblatt, *Renaissance Self-Fashioning: From More to Shakespeare* (Chicago: Chicago University Press, 1980).

23 Jonathan Dollimore and Alan Sinfield (eds), *Political Shakespeare: New Essays in Cultural Materialism* (Manchester: Manchester University Press, 1985).

24 See H. Aram Veeser, *The New Historicism* (London: Routledge, 1989), xi. This *caveat* applies with equal validity, of course, to the critic, who is trapped within a deconstructive economy which accounts for the regular appearance of metaphors of circulation and commerce in New Historicist writing.

25 See David Norbrook's essay 'Life and death of Renaissance man', *Raritan* 8 (2) (1989), 89–110. For examples of such criticism, see also Norbrook, *Poetry and Politics in the English Renaissance* (London: Routledge, 1984); Annabel Patterson, *Censorship and Interpretation*; Patterson, *Pastoral and Ideology: Virgil to Valéry* (Berkeley: California University Press, 1988); Patterson, *Shakespeare and the Popular Voice* (Oxford: Blackwell, 1989); Leah Marcus, *The Politics of Mirth: Jonson, Herrick, Milton, Marvell and the Defense of Old Holiday Pastimes* (Chicago: Chicago University Press, 1986); and Marcus, *Puzzling Shakespeare: Local Reading and its Discontents* (Berkeley: California University Press, 1988).

26 See, for example, Richard Cust and Ann Hughes (eds), *Conflict in Early Stuart England: Studies in Religion and Politics 1603–1642* (London: Longman, 1989).

27 See Norbrook, p. 35 below.

28 See Heinemann, p. 151 below.

29 Linda Woodbridge, *Women and the English Renaissance* (Urbana: Illinois University Press, 1984).

30 See Anne Barton, *Ben Jonson, Dramatist* (Cambridge: Cambridge University Press, 1984), and David Norbrook, *Poetry and Politics*.

31 See G.E. Bentley, *The Profession of Dramatist in Shakespeare's Time, 1590–1642* (Princeton: Princeton University Press, 1971), chapter VIII.

2

'WHAT CARES THESE ROARERS FOR THE NAME OF KING?': LANGUAGE AND UTOPIA IN *THE TEMPEST*

David Norbrook

I

'Where's the Master?'[1] That is the question that comes instinctively to King Alonso's lips as his ship is buffeted by the tempest. But the master has left the stage: the work on this ship is impersonally structured and does not need the direct presence of a figure of authority. So little respect does the boatswain have for traditional hierarchies that he refuses to answer. When Antonio repeats the question, the boatswain dismisses the king and all the courtiers with a summary 'You mar our labour . . . What cares these roarers for the name of king?' 'Roaring' connotes misrule and rebellion, roaring boys or girls. In a remarkably defiant gesture, the boundless voice of the elements and of social transgression is pitted against the name of king, the arbitrary language of power. *The Tempest* is structured around such oppositions between courtly discourse and wider linguistic contexts. Throughout the play there is a tension in Ariel between the subordination of his[2] highly wrought fusion of music and poetry to Prospero and the desire to become 'free/As mountain winds', to liberate a purified poetry from the constraints of domination (I.ii. 499–500).[3] Utopian discourse pervades the play, most notably in Gonzalo's vision of a world where nature would produce all in common and '[l]etters should not be known' (II.i. 148). But every figure on the island has some kind of vision of a society that would transcend existing codes and signs: 'Thought is free,' sing Stephano and Trinculo (III.ii. 121).

That libertarian impulse in the play is doubtless why it appealed so strongly to Milton, who rewrote it in *Comus*, transferring Caliban's less attractive qualities to the aristocratic Comus, giving a more rigorous utopian discourse to the lady, and assigning the agency of the resolution not to the aristocrats but to the Ariel-figure and a nature goddess.[4] Continuing that utopian tradition, Shelley found in *The Tempest* a central instance of the utopian power in poetry which 'makes familiar objects be as if they were not familiar'.[5] Ariel had for him the same utopian implications as the egalitarian spirit Queen Mab. Shelley was also alert to the claims of Caliban, as we can see from the significant parallel he draws in his preface to *Frankenstein* between Mary Wollstonecraft Shelley's novel and Shakespeare's pioneering science fiction.[6]

Walter Cohen has recently noted Shelley's perceptive reading of the political implications of romance and has proposed a revised utopian reading of *The Tempest*.[7] But twentieth-century criticism has tended on the whole towards the dystopian, assuming that Gonzalo's ideals are held up for ridicule. Mid-century 'neo-Christians', to use Empson's term, made a sharp distinction between modern political ideas with their sentimental utopianism and the traditional orthodoxy which held that man was a fallen Caliban and therefore needed strict hierarchical order to keep him in line.[8] Coleridge has been a dominant influence in twentieth-century readings of Shakespeare, and Coleridge's interpretations were marked by a revulsion against the radicalism of his age. Hence while Coleridge claims, with reference to *The Tempest*, that Shakespeare 'is always the philosopher and the moralist', without political partisanship, he goes on to present him as a 'philosophical aristocrat' for whom the mob is 'an irrational animal'.[9] With this frame of reference established, accounts of Shakespeare's impartiality had a heavy weighting. Again in the Coleridge tradition, this political conservatism was linked with a turn towards language: Shakespeare's plays were valued for their concreteness as opposed to the etiolated abstractions of Enlightenment egalitarianism. These conservative readings have been strengthened by more recent historical work linking the masque scene with court entertainments; Shakespeare's late turn to romance can be seen as marking a rejection of popular taste for an elite aristocratic genre.[10] So dominant have courtly readings become that radical and anti-colonialist critics have tended to accept their historical premisses even while contesting their political outlook.[11] The best recent readings have indeed drawn attention to contradictions and complexities in the play which open themselves to a radical interpretation.[12] But the general assumption is that these openings would have been unconscious effects of discourse, while Shakespeare and his audiences would have belonged to Prospero's party and seen the play as celebrating the restoration of monarchical legitimacy as a return to a transcendent natural order.[13] Terry Eagleton sees Shakespeare as subordinating language, as signified by Ariel, to a conservative discourse of the body: the plays 'value social order and stability', and in seeking an organic unity of body and language *The Tempest* propagates a 'ridiculously sanguine ideology of Nature'.[14]

Some recent developments in literary theory have tended to reinforce these dystopian readings. Contemporary deconstructionists, like the neo-Christians, oppose the abstract utopianism of the Enlightenment to the need for a turn towards language (there are important linking factors, as in the continuing influence of Heidegger). Language and utopia still go together for Jürgen Habermas and other theorists of universal pragmatics, for whom the 'utopian perspective of reconciliation and freedom . . . is built into the linguistic mechanism of the reproduction of the species'.[15] But poststructuralists have argued that this quest for undistorted communication implies an ultimately fixed and essentialist notion of human nature, which can become repressive and mystifying, prematurely suppressing the particularities of gender and class in the name of a false universality of a subject that is held to be free of the constraints of discourse.[16] Utopia, it can be argued, is utropia, it suppresses rhetoric and hence must fail to recognize its ineluctable basis in the materiality of language and power.[17] In a celebrated essay, Derrida attacked Lévi-Strauss for idealizing the Brazilian Indians as a people blessed in the absence of writing. Such idealization can be seen as belonging to a humanist tradition that goes back to Rousseau's – and, one might add, Montaigne's and Gonzalo's – idealization of letterless primitives. The logocentric analysis, Derrida argues, in repressing writing represses also the materiality of discourse.[18] A simple opposition between language and nature would in effect reinforce the ideology of the western colonization. And it could then be argued that *The Tempest*'s utopianism is complicit in the ideology. Prospero's ideal spirits dance 'with printless foot' (V.i. 34), and Ariel may represent a vision of pure thought breaking free from the material embodiment of language and time, operating between two pulsebeats (V.i. 102). Ariel's utopian vision seems pathetically illusory by the standards of Lacanian psychoanalysis, a dream of return to an androgynous state before the name of the father or king, an unmediated sucking at the place of the bee's being (V.i. 88); thus Eagleton can see him as a 'closet aesthete'.[19]

The more it is insisted that the individual subject cannot escape the specificities of language or discourse, the more the subject may seem to be inexorably determined by existing power structures from which it cannot escape. Foucault has reminded us of all kinds of ways in which thought is not free. While the classic utopian impulse to a transcendent critique is branded as totalitarian and essentialist, immanent critiques are often seen as inexorably contained. And indeed the play itself may seem to undermine idealist bids for an emancipated poetry. The roarers that the boatswain evokes turn out to have been controlled by Prospero with his power to work up the elements to 'roaring war' (V.i. 44, cf. I.i. 2, 204), and the rebellion of those seditious roarers Stephano, Trinculo, and Caliban will be evoked by the very power that then contains it. The roars that pervade the play are those of the tormented bodies of Prospero's enemies: 'I will plague them all,/ Even to roaring' (IV.i. 192–3, cf. I.ii. 369); and Ariel's triumphant cry of 'Hark, they roar!' (IV.i. 262) is underscored by Prospero's threat to return his servant to the howling agony of captivity in the tree. Music in the play may seem not so much emancipatory as deceitful and manipulative, plunging Ferdinand and Alonso into mourning and guilt which the facts do not quite merit, making the wind sing legitimism.[20] The whimsical refrain of barking dogs to Ariel's first song turns nasty when the dog Tyrant bears down on the conspirators. Prospero commends Ariel's performance as the harpy in terms that sinisterly conflate aesthetics and violence: 'a grace it had, devouring' (III.iii. 84).

These newer anti-humanisms, then, may tend to confirm the dystopian perspectives of the neo-Christian anti-humanists. There is room, however, for a reading that would remain open to utopian perspectives in a way that poststructuralist methodologies cannot allow, taking account of the cogent criticisms of blandly transcendental views of the subject which recent theory has been able to make, but without surrendering some notion of the possibility of the subject as rational agent. Such a reading could lay no more claim than its adversaries to being final and exhaustive, but it would, I believe, be more genuinely historical than those which offer the play as absolutist propaganda, for it would take fuller account of the discursive and social contexts. There is no need for twentieth-century readings to be more royalist than the King's Men. A theoretical interest in language was part of the social and intellectual context of Shakespeare and his company – provided that the context is not narrowed down too specifically to courtly discourse but takes account of the immense linguistic curiosity stimulated by Renaissance humanism.

If the term 'humanism' in current discourse tends to connote an abstract resistance to the materiality of language, then Renaissance humanism was a very different phenomenon. It had made its own sharp linguistic turn, an exaltation of rhetoric against scholastic metaphysics, and thus can be seen as paralleling contemporary anti-humanisms in refusing to take for granted a fixed human essence; the attack on abstract generality gave the drama a heightened epistemological status.[21] But Renaissance humanism also had a generalizing, philosophical impulse, an advanced sociological and historical consciousness which looked forward to the Enlightenment.[22] While old arguments about monarchy's being part of the order of nature came to look increasingly feeble, more rationalistic theories of natural law could have a strong critical element. More's *Utopia* plays the transcendent social blueprint of the second book against the immanent critique of courtly language in the first book; More says that it would be pointless for a humanist at court to start reciting the speech in the pseudo-Senecan play *Octavia* which prophesies an egalitarian society.[23] As Erica Sheen has shown, Seneca's plays were very much in Shakespeare's mind when he wrote the last plays.[24] Seneca's prose writings opened up an egalitarian discourse of natural law. His plays, however, made him the very type of the compromised court intellectual, writing for a small elite, and More could still feel an affinity with this status. But by Shakespeare's time the possibilities for a politically critical drama had been transformed by the emergence of professional repertory companies which despite their residual status as royal servants derived their economic strength from a far wider public. Shakespeare's career reflects not just individual genius but the excitement of a whole collective institution at the possibilities of what amounted to a cultural revolution: the emergence of a literary public sphere which prepared the way for the formation of a political public sphere. That excitement, however, was certainly manifested in individuals, and recent radically anti-intentionalist readings have given too little credit to the possibility that the writer as agent could achieve a degree of independence from the prevailing structures of power and discourse.

On this account of the context, it is not surprising that *The Tempest* manifests an acute and sophisticated awareness of the relations between language and power. The play is not overtly oppositional or sensationally 'subversive'; but it subjects traditional institutions to a systematic, critical questioning. The play does not consider language and power as timeless absolutes; rather than counterposing an unmediated, presocial nature to a deterministically conceived language, it is concerned with language in specific social contexts, with the effect of political structures on linguistic possibilities. All of the play's utopian ideals, not excepting Ariel's, come up for ironic scrutiny in the course of the play, precisely because they tend to an idealism that refuses to recognize the material constraints of existing structures of power and discourse. But that awareness need not imply a pessimistic determinism. A sceptical relativism about claims to an unproblematic 'human nature' is played against a searching, universalizing quest for a more general notion of humanity. The play gives the effect at once of tremendous constriction and specificity, manifested in its rigorously classical form, and of the immense expansion through time and space characteristic of the romance mode. Critics have often counterposed romance to realism as the mode of aristocratic escapism. But *The Tempest* is a hard-headed play, rigorous in following through its own logic once the initial supernatural postulates are granted. As several critics have noted, it is not so much that the play is a romance as that it stages, and in the process distances itself from, the romance scenario of dynastic redemption that Prospero is staging.[25] And yet the play also recognizes a certain congruence between a narrowly aristocratic romantic impulse and a broader utopian project. As Shelley, Fredric Jameson, and Raymond Williams have argued in their very different idioms, such imagination of alternatives may be an essential mode of a radical politics in resistance to a world-weary empiricism.[26]

The magic island of Shakespeare's play is at once an instance and an allegory of the players' project of opening up new spaces for discourse. It is a place where no name, no discourse, is entirely natural; language and nature are neither simply conflated nor simply opposed to each other. Prospero abandons the island without leaving behind a colonial force, nor does he refute Caliban's claim that 'this island's mine'. But if Caliban's matrilineal claim may seem to subvert patriarchal authority,[27] it is itself called in question by his own recent arrival. The only figures who can be said to have some natural claim to priority, Ariel and his fellow-spirits, are, precisely, not natural but supernatural, and they do not seem to think of land as something to be possessed; the spirits' history too is left open, and it is possible that Ariel has accompanied Sycorax to the island. At two points in the play the exchanges between Prospero and Ariel focus on uncertainty about what that word 'human' really means, implying that it is an open rather than a fixed category (I.ii. 284; V.i. 20). Arriving on the island makes all conventional codes unfamiliar. Prospero sets up a dizzying relativization of the human by claiming that Ferdinand is a Caliban to most men and they are angels to him (I.ii. 481–2). Similarly, Caliban will say that Miranda surpasses Sycorax as greatest does less; in each case, the hyperbolical comparison is at the same time undercut by the awareness that there is nothing else to compare them with – as long as she is on the island Miranda has no rival to prevent her being Prospero's 'nonpareil' (III.ii. 98). Having asked Miranda a question, Ferdinand is none the less astonished when she answers it in his own language (I.ii. 429). Miranda cannot believe that Ferdinand is 'natural' (419), and describes him as 'it' (412). In a parallel episode Stephano is astonished that Caliban speaks his language (II.ii. 65), though this is not surprising to us as the play has explained that Miranda taught it to him. The Italian Trinculo scornfully observes that in England the monster would be taken for a man (II.ii. 29–30).[28] When the courtiers finally wake out of their trance, they 'scarce think . . . their words/ Are natural breath' (V.ii. 155–7). In a remarkable alienation effect at the end, Miranda turns to the newly-arrived courtiers – and implicitly the audience – and hails them as a 'brave new world' (V.i. 183). A world which seems to Gonzalo itself a utopia looks out at the old world and finds in it a utopia, only to be greeted with Prospero's weary ' 'Tis new to thee'. This repeated defamiliarization makes it very hard to see the end of the play as no more than the restoration of a natural social order. At the same time, it reminds us that when characters project an image of a new world they cannot escape the conceptual apparatus they have brought from the old.

II

This is certainly true of Gonzalo's utopian discourse, his vision of a world where all things will be in abundance:

> Had I plantation of this isle, my lord . . .
> I'th' commonwealth I would by contraries
> Execute all things, for no kind of traffic
> Would I admit; no name of magistrate;
> Letters should not be known; riches, poverty,
> And use of service, none; contract, succession,
> Bourn, bound of land, tilth, vineyard, none;
> No use of metal, corn, or wine, or oil;
> No occupation, all men idle, all,
> And women, too, but innocent and pure;
> No sovereignty . . .
> All things in common nature should produce
> Without sweat or endeavour. Treason, felony,
> Sword, pike, knife, gun, or need of any engine
> Would I not have, but nature should bring forth
> Of it own kind all foison, all abundance
> To feed my innocent people . . .

I would with such perfection govern, sir,
T'excel the golden age.

(II.i. 141–66)

Gonzalo's speech contains many stock topoi, but most scholars agree that it derives particularly from Montaigne's 'Of Cannibals' – with the interesting additional specificity of the reference to women.[29] Montaigne's highly primitivistic essay with its vision of an ideal community may seem to be innocent of More's sophisticated analysis of discourse, an epitome of the idealist repression of writing which poststructuralism has condemned.[30] Gonzalo's speech is often seen as reducing that primitivism to absurdity. But a closer reading of Montaigne's essay suggests a more complex intertextuality.

On one level, certainly, Montaigne's essay privileges the immediacy of experience over writing and representation. A servant of his, he says, had spent some time in the recently discovered continent of South America. The fact that this continent had remained so long unknown prompts Montaigne to say that perhaps we should be more sceptical about the writings of the ancients who obviously did not know everything. The nearest they came to suspecting the existence of the new continent were Plato's legend of Atlantis (which Bacon was to revise for his utopia, the *New Atlantis*) and Aristotle's account of a journey by some Carthaginians beyond the pillars of Hercules. We may recall here the ambiguous suspension of Shakespeare's island somewhere between Carthage and Bermuda. Montaigne goes on to say that he prefers to trust this traveller before all the ancients, precisely because he is the kind of man who is 'so simple that he may have no invention to build upon'. Such people are more reliable witnesses than the learned who 'never represent things truly, but fashion and mask them according to the visage they saw them in, and to purchase credit to their judgement and draw you on to believe in them they commonly adorn, enlarge, yea, and hyperbolize the matter' (229).[31] Montaigne learns from his servant that the Indians live a life purely according to nature, with 'no kind of traffic' and 'no knowledge of letters'. He contrasts this idyll with Plato's 'imaginary commonwealth': the ancients just 'could not imagine' a society like the Indians' (230–1).

But this portrait of a natural world without letters is framed by references to the inescapability and relativity of representation. The essay opens with an account of King Pyrrhus, who was leading a Greek army against the newly emergent Roman state. To the Greeks, non-Grecians were termed barbarians; Pyrrhus declared that this army did not seem at all barbarous. Montaigne comments: 'Lo how a man ought to take heed lest he overweeningly follow vulgar opinions, which should be measured by the rule of reason and not by the common report' (227). Categorizing a foreign nation as barbaric may be pure prejudice; the wise reader is sceptical about assuming a natural correspondence between names and reality. The relations between nature and art deconstruct themselves further in the course of the essay. We learn that the cannibals write very fine poetry: Montaigne quotes an epigram that reminds him of Anacreon, and says that their language resembles ancient Greek in its sound and inflections (237). The poem is in praise of the adder, a transgressive hymn to the beauty of a creature so ominous in conventional Christian terms; Prospero, we may recall, uses the adder merely to hiss the nature-loving Caliban into madness (II.ii. 13). Montaigne concludes with an account of his meeting some native Americans, and at this point the discourse turns round on itself: instead of observing the strangers Montaigne is being observed by them. When asked what has most struck them about France, they reply that they find it strange that the people should submit themselves to a beardless child – the king was then a minor – rather than choosing a ruler themselves. It further puzzles them that the poor, surrounded by conspicuous consumption, do not rebel and set fire to the rich men's houses. It seems so strange because 'they have a manner of phrase whereby they call men but a moiety of men from others' (237). As Montaigne clearly notes (in anticipation of modern anthropologists), South Americans classified their social groups vertically, in terms of diverse but equal 'moieties' rather than horizontally, in hierarchically stratified estates and classes; it is not clear how much he understood of the details, but he emphasizes that they had no conception of hierarchy as part of the order of nature. When he went on to ask them questions, he was frustrated because he had to rely on an interpreter who 'through his foolishness was . . . troubled to conceive my imaginations' (238). A further twist in this tale of distorted communication is that in Montaigne's view the visitors were becoming corrupted by the very fact of engaging in 'commerce' with Europeans: the power relations involved in the conversation undermined the 'facts' it was intended to convey.

Montaigne's essay, then, is not a simple exercise in linguistic primitivism. There is a very sharp awareness of the relations between language and power. At the same time, there is a strong confidence in the power of reason, which is constantly invoked against custom, to break through conventional cultural stereotypes, to go far beyond the cultural achievements of antiquity. That rationalism is, however, in turn qualified by the way the essay encourages a suspicion of its own authority. At the beginning we are told to trust the servant because he gave us direct and unmediated access to the truth about the Indians, but by the end we are left with an awareness of the enormous difficulty of breaking out of discourse, of translating imaginations from one world to another. The problem is foregrounded when Montaigne recalls that in addition to the two questions that were posed to the visitors and gained such politically provocative replies there was a third 'which I have forgotten and am very sorry for it'. His essay's own forgetting thus runs parallel to the ideological forgetting which the visitors probed.

Montaigne's essay had a powerful influence in England. The Leveller William Walwyn was to declare it as one of his favourite texts. This does not prove that Shakespeare was a proto-Leveller – the political conditions of the 1640s were very different from those of the 1610s, and Walwyn was only about ten when *The Tempest* was first performed. But the sources of Leveller ideas were available much earlier, and we need to allow more generous intellectual horizons for Shakespeare and his audience than some critics have been prepared to grant.[32] The scene in which Gonzalo outlines his utopia parallels Montaigne in illustrating the process of ideological forgetting: 'The latter end of his commonwealth', Antonio points out, 'forgets the beginning' (II.i. 155). He is so used to commanding that his own social status is simply invisible to him, and he can see himself as king of an egalitarian society. The scene builds up a very complex interaction between a generalizing aspiration and a reminder of the limits of specific social contexts, and in particular of courtly discourse. The context of Gonzalo's utopian speech resembles the situation imagined by More, where a Senecan prophecy of a golden age is recited at court. Gonzalo imagines a world with no letters, 'no name of magistrate': unmediated nature is pitted against the name of the king. And as Lowenthal has argued, he has a somewhat more rationalistic cast of mind than the more conservative courtiers.[33] But the speech-act he is performing in evoking this utopia is strongly hierarchical, its aim is to console the king, and Gonzalo's soft primitivism bears the stamp of someone used to euphemizing awkward social realities. The immediately preceding scene has ended with an image of a ruler commanding silence: Prospero says to Miranda 'speak not for him' – an injunction which in later scenes she consistently disobeys, but at this point we are left with courtly discourse as repression. The new scene opens with courtly discourse as euphemism.

Gonzalo immediately sets up his discourse in class terms:

> Our hint of woe
> Is common: every day some sailor's wife,
> The masters of some merchant, and the merchant
> Have just our theme of woe; but for the miracle –
> I mean our preservation – few in millions
> Can speak like us.
>
> (II.i. 3–8)

If Alonso grieves too much for the loss of his son he will be debasing himself to the level of common people like the master of a merchant vessel – Gonzalo had of course been anxious enough for the master's help during the storm.[34] Instead, he should enjoy a sense of social superiority which will come from the exclusiveness of his delivery. There emerges a careful counterpoint between two linguistic groups. The discourse of Gonzalo, Adrian, and Francisco is idealizing: Francisco is brought into the scene only to give a hyperbolizing set-piece invoking the pathetic fallacy to express his confidence in Ferdinand's safety (111–20). To use Montaigne's phrase, they 'hyperbolize the matter': 'What impossible matter will he make easy next?' asks Antonio, whose discourse by contrast seems radically materialist. Sebastian and Antonio stress the bodily origins of the spirit: 'He receives comfort like cold porridge' (10); 'he's winding up the watch of his wit' (13); 'what a spendthrift is he of his tongue!' (25); they compare Adrian and Gonzalo to cocks crowing out their words; they are confident that the others will 'take suggestion as a cat laps milk' (286). Gonzalo's '[t]he air breathes upon us here most sweetly' meets a materialistic retort: 'As if it had lungs, and rotten ones' (48–9). By defamiliarizing words into things Sebastian and Antonio draw attention to the speech-acts themselves and their social context, rather than passing through to their content; and when Ariel has put the others into a trance they satirically represent their rebellion as an eruption of the political unconscious, if not a roaring then at least a snoring: 'It is a sleepy language . . .', says Sebastian, '[t]here's meaning in thy snores' (209, 216). The prevailing scepticism about discourse extends even to Alonso: 'You cram these words into mine ears against/ The stomach of my sense' (104–5). In reproaching Antonio, Gonzalo himself comes to see his own discourse in material terms:

> The truth you speak doth lack some gentleness,
> And time to speak it in – you rub the sore

When you should bring the plaster.

(135–7)

Gonzalo's utopia is thus marked as another plaster for the king. But Alonso has no interest in such speculations: 'Prithee no more. Thou dost talk nothing to me.' Utopia is of course nowhere, nothing; and there may be a further sly pun in 'no More'.[35] Gonzalo ruefully retreats and says that he was only talking in order to give mirth to Antonio and Sebastian – his utopian vision was no more than the fantasy of a court jester.

Gonzalo's facile idealism, then, is undercut by a materialist critique. One might even see Antonio as anticipating certain kinds of Foucauldianism, seeing all attempts to change society as the installations of ever greater apparatuses of surveillance and domination. It is Antonio who first introduces the utopian theme at line 85, when Gonzalo is speaking; of the parallels between ancient Carthage and modern Tunis:

ANTONIO: His word is more than the miraculous harp.
SEBASTIAN: He hath raised the wall, and houses too.

The story of Amphion whose music raised the walls of Thebes had become a familiar commonplace, signifying that poetry had a central part to play in politics by instilling civil order and harmony. In their reductive reading, the myth becomes a rather ridiculous example of the way court poets use hyperbole to blow up their own achievements.

Antonio's own viewpoint, however, is hardly beyond criticism; the play does not endorse his cynicism. But its criticism of courtly discourse remains sharp. One point that Gonzalo adds to Montaigne is that his utopia would have no treason, felony, sword, pike, knife, gun, or need of any engine – that is, instrument of warfare or political violence. This is a characteristic emphasis, for behind his euphemizing discourse he is shown to be acutely conscious of the need for violence to maintain monarchical power, and a chain of allusions links the utopian speech with his relations with the sailors at the beginning and end of the play. Gonzalo's sample of a decorous compliment is:

It is foul weather in us all, good sir,
When you are cloudy.

(139–40)

This is a direct inversion of the boatswain's comment to Alonso at the beginning: for Gonzalo the king's very name will of course control the roaring elements. During the storm, however, he was less confident; the boatswain acidly commented that the courtiers' howls of fear were 'louder than the weather or our office' (I.i. 36–7). If Gonzalo's authority could command the roaring elements to silence, he would not handle a rope more (I.i. 21–3). Gonzalo had then taken up the reference to a rope, not as a means of work but as an instrument of punishment – and a socially indecorous one at that, as opposed to the aristocratic beheading: 'Stand fast, good Fate, to his hanging, make the rope of his destiny our cable . . . If he be not born to be hanged, our case is miserable' (I.i. 30–3). Antonio simply makes this reference to hanging more brutally literal: 'hang, cur, hang' (43).

Such a situation had a strong sociopolitical charge. The figure of the ship of state had a greater appeal for seventeenth-century radicals than the traditional figure of the body politic because it viewed the state as an artificial construct rather than part of the order of nature, and implied progress towards a new destination. The figure of the pilot daringly wresting control of the ship of state from its commander was to be used to justify the Puritan Revolution.[36] In this scene, the artisanal connotations are pushed further in that tenor and vehicle have become detached: the aristocrats stand around ineffectually while the real business goes on without them. But they still want overall control. Gonzalo has not forgotten the rope at the end of the play. Even so acute a critic of sentimental readings as Harry Berger describes that much-cited passage where Gonzalo says that they have all found themselves as his 'closing speech';[37] but in fact Gonzalo's 'all of us' (V.i. 212–13) turns out to exclude the sailors who had tried to save his life. In his actual last speech he returns to the storm scene:

> I prophesied if a gallows were on land
> This fellow could not drown. (*To Boatswain*) Now, blasphemy,
> That swear'st grace o'erboard, not an oath on shore?
> Hast thou no mouth by land? What is the news?
>
> (V.i. 217–20)

This is a striking piece of forgetting: it was the courtiers who were swearing, the boatswain gave orders to the courtiers but did not abuse them directly; and his response now is to ignore Gonzalo's taunts and give a precise account of recent events. In fact Gonzalo swears, however mildly, more than anyone in the play except Sebastian.[38] This is not to deny that he is a genial man, who has been very kind to Prospero. The trouble is that such genial goodness may itself become complacent at court; moral qualities need to be seen in a political context.

III

The same applies to Prospero himself. It has been tempting to allegorize him as a figure of Shakespeare or James I. But these readings too easily assume that the play identifies with Prospero as a natural source of authority; and that Shakespeare engages with politics only at the level of direct topical allegories. While the original audience might well have picked up some resonance with the contemporary hopes over the Palatine marriage, there is also a more generalizing sociological consciousness at work in the plays, which means that we need to pay some attention to the discourse in which Shakespeare situates Prospero. The later Shakespeare, and Jacobeans in general, were tending to give more and more sociological specificity to Italian settings by drawing on the discourses by which Italians represented their own history. Particularly influential were Machiavelli and Guicciardini, who offered a radically sceptical analysis of political power which undercut any claim by monarchy to be natural.[39] In the later Renaissance many republican city-states had been taken over by *signon*, rulers with little sense of communal responsibility and sought legitimacy in noble connections, in a kind of refeudalization (or what Sebastian terms '[h]ereditary sloth') (II.i. 221), rather than in popular consent. Guicciardini opens his history with a lament for the monarchical harmony of late fifteenth-century Italy before the foreign invasions in the 1490s, which led eventually to Spanish absolutist hegemony. But even though Guicciardini himself favoured the Medici dynasty, he presented at length the constitutional debates about differing forms of democratic rule; and what gradually emerges is that beneath that superficial harmony there were deep-rooted republican resistances, which meant that the people were often glad to welcome foreign armies against their ruling houses. The unpopular King Alphonso of Naples, who 'knew not (with most Princes now a dayes) how to resist the furie of dominion and rule', abdicated in favour of his son Ferdinand but the people refused to allow him into the city; the precedent was to be used by supporters of the execution of Charles I.[40] Guicciardini places the immediate blame for the foreign invasions on the ambition of Giovan Galeazzo Sforza, the *de facto* ruler of Milan who was anxious to gain legitimacy for his line, but ended up by sacrificing Milan's political autonomy altogether to his personal dynastic vanity.

What sign is there in *The Tempest* of a possible republican subtext? It may seem unduly literal-minded to imagine Shakespeare as considering the precise political status of his Italian states; but there is clear evidence that this was done by his collaborator in his last plays, John Fletcher. About 1621 Fletcher wrote with Philip Massinger a tragicomedy, *The Double Marriage*, which echoed *The Tempest*, with an exiled duke and his daughter as central characters. The play glorifies 'the noble stile of Tyrant-killers'; at the climax the hero brings in the head of the tyrannical king of Naples to cries of 'Liberty'.[41] The political climate in 1621 had become more sharply polarized, and Shakespeare certainly does not undercut monarchical legitimacy in the same way. Nevertheless, it is worth remembering that his audience would have contained people who were far from taking an absolutist dynastic perspective for granted, and the play does permit a certain detachment from the courtly viewpoint. Prospero assures us that his people loved him (I.ii. 141); but he does belong to this political world. He speaks of 'signories' (I.ii. 71) and he sees his power purely in personal terms, as a matter of safeguarding his dynasty: he talks familiarly of 'my Milan' (V.i. 310), while for Ferdinand 'myself am Naples' (I.ii. 435). Though Prospero condemns Antonio for allowing Milan to stoop to Naples (I.ii. 112–16), by the end of the play he has handed the dukedom over to Naples in order to secure his line. His words as he reveals Ferdinand and Miranda to the courtiers at the end scarcely escape banality: 'a wonder to content ye/ As much as me my dukedom' (V.i. 170–1). His tone is echoed by Gonzalo's breathless 'Was Milan thrust from Milan that his issue/ Should become kings of Naples?' (V.i. 205–6). The union between Milan and Naples is a strikingly representative instance of the social processes by which the *signorie* sought legitimacy; the upstart Milanese has definitely made good.

The characteristic genre of such dynastic triumphs was the romance, whose aristocratic closure predominates in Prospero's world over utopian openings; Miranda and Ferdinand are stranded within a very narrow courtly discourse. For Prospero, making Ferdinand do manual work is a punishment degrading him to the level of his slave. He lost his dukedom because the element of work in the public life, as valorized in the republican ethos, seemed to him too degrading, he preferred a private retreat into Neoplatonic contemplation which 'but by being so retired,/ O'er-prized all popular rate' (I.ii. 91–2).[42] His language and that of the courtiers generally reflects the growing class-bound stratification urged by Castiglione and courtly theorists: the rhetoric of courtly praise and dispraise rather than republican persuasion.[43] Ferdinand observes rather clumsily that on his father's death 'I am the best of them that speak this speech': language is the king's (I.ii. 430). Idealizing compliments are directed to the noble, though always with an underlying political pragmatism – Miranda is learning to let Ferdinand wrangle for a score of kingdoms and call it fair play (V.i. 174–5). The base are abused – Caliban is given plenty of opportunity to learn how to curse. Martines has noted that sixteenth-century political discourse in Italy reveals a growing polarity between an abstract aristocratic utopianism and a dark view of the populace as irredeemably base; as Berger has shown, such polarities are characteristic of Prospero's discourse.[44] He reminds Caliban six times in less than seventy lines that he is a slave (I.ii. 308–73) and Caliban fears that his art could make Setebos a vassal (I.ii. 373): Prospero extends feudal relations of service and bondage. Prospero's irascibility has come to the fore in recent productions; idealizations of Prospero require a certain suppression of the play's language. Miranda has to protest that 'My father's of a better nature, sir,/ Than he appears by speech' (I.ii. 497–8). These points remain relatively inconspicuous in the play, which certainly is not a satire of Prospero; nor are the elements of romance cynically dismissed as mere aristocratic fantasy. Shelley's sense of the play as utopian would have involved a recognition of the political importance of a sense of wonder, of defamiliarization, which even a narrowly class-based romance could project. As with Gonzalo, the point is not that Prospero is an evil man but that his political position entails a limited perspective.

Shakespeare's questioning of legitimacy extends even to the genre *par excellence* of the naturalization of authority, the court masque.[45] Prospero's betrothal masque is the richest expression of his ideal society; and whereas in Gonzalo's utopia all things are in common, in Prospero's golden age there is a hierarchical structure in which the labour of the reapers is ultimately motivated by the transcendent gods and goddesses who are figures of the leisured aristocracy. As Berger has noted, however, there are signs of tension even within the masquing speeches, reflecting Prospero's tendency to oscillate between idealistic and radically pessimistic views of man. This tension in the end cannot be sustained and the masque collapses; recent criticism has rightly drawn attention to the ways in which the resolution is very different from the Stuart norm – forming an interesting parallel with *Cymbeline*, as Erica Sheen shows in her essay (p. 55). The aim of the masque was to naturalize the king's name, to turn courtiers into gods and goddesses; Prospero dissolves his masque and its courtly language melts into air, leaving (according to a perhaps non-authorial stage direction) 'a strange hollow and confused noise', an undifferentiated roaring that undercuts the confident marks of social difference. The pageants are 'insubstantial'.

Prospero's 'revels' speech has given rise to a great deal of critical banality, but it is as well to be wary about taking it as a statement of Shakespeare's view of life in general; it needs to be read rather less transcendentally. The two other most celebrated comparisons of life to a play are those of Jacques in *As You Like It* and Macbeth's 'poor player' speech, and neither is unequivocally endorsed: Shakespeare seems to have been wary about generalizations about Life. Prospero is in fact in no mood to say farewell to the world, he wants his dukedom back and in a previous scene he has had Ariel disguised as a religious spirit tell lies about Ferdinand's death in order to facilitate his ends. In a political context, the specificities of the 'revels' speech become more evident. At the climax of the Jacobean masque, these alleged gods and goddesses would come down into the dancing area and mingle with the audience. Court masques were in many ways very substantial things, giving the necessary concrete presence to the royal name by elaborate scenery; their fabric was definitely not baseless. There were clear sacramental overtones: the substance, the body, of the king became divinely transformed. Jonson's preface to *Hymenaei* highlights this physicality with characteristic ambivalence. On the one hand the '*bodies*' are transitory and inferior in comparison to their conceptual souls; on the other hand, Jonson as a firm defender of religious and secular ceremony fiercely disputes the 'fastidious *stomachs*' of rivals like Daniel whose 'ayrie tasts' lay too little emphasis on the external body.[46] As Jonson noted, it was the custom at the end of masques to 'deface their *carkasses*': in the spirit of *potlatch*, courtiers would tear down the scenery, the whole point being the physical concreteness of the manifestation of honour so that its destruction was all the more potent a sign of the donor's greatness.

Prospero's speech, and the whole episode, then highlight the ways in which his spectacle is unlike a court masque. His masque really is insubstantial, because as prince in exile he does not have any actors, musicians, and set-designers. There is something almost ludicrous in the contrival of this spectacle for an audience of just three, even if Ferdinand dutifully declares that there are enough of them for paradise (IV.i. 123–4). Prospero's situation on the island parodies the top-heavy social structure of late Renaissance despotisms, with the aristocracy syphoning off more and more wealth to expend in conspicuous courtly consumption, while representing the people as a mere grumbling margin to the transcendent centre of the court. But in Prospero's case the situation is pushed to the point of absurdity by the absence of any subjects at all apart from Caliban; and in an ideological forgetting directly parallel to Gonzalo's, Prospero's masque can last only as long as Caliban is forgotten. The political point is rubbed home when we learn that Ariel, though intending to remind Prospero about the conspiracy when he was playing the part of Ceres, had 'feared/ Lest I might anger thee' (IV.i. 168–9). The masque cannot reach a climax with the performers mingling with the audience, as was the rule at court, for the performers are spirits. Precisely because they really are what the courtiers pretended to be, supernatural beings, bodiless air, they cannot be taken back with Prospero to Milan. There is an ironic parallel to Stephano's exclamation: 'This will be a brave kingdom to me, where I shall have my music for nothing' (III.ii. 142–3).

IV

The ideal states projected by Prospero and Gonzalo, then, are conditioned by the forms of language and power in which they are constructed, yet also open up utopian possibilities which question complacent celebrations of a natural order. In that context, the notion that the play unproblematically celebrates Caliban's subordination as part of the order of nature needs questioning. The cast-list does describe him as a 'savage and deformed slave'; and Kermode has argued that this means he is to be taken as Aristotle's 'natural slave', incapable of civility.[47] But the cast-list may derive from Ralph Crane rather than Shakespeare; and it would by no means have been taken for granted that slavery was natural. It is not true, as some recent accounts may suggest, that 'colonial discourse' was a monolithic entity which Shakespeare would have been incapable of consciously challenging. In a powerful pioneering essay, Stephen Greenblatt offered a more complex view but still saw the situation in terms of an almost inescapably repressive double bind: a potentially imperialistic logocentrism beset both those who argued that the native Americans were so degenerate that they lacked a proper language and the essentialists who denied the existence of a serious language barrier: both camps naturalized linguistic and social conventions.[48]

As Anthony Pagden has shown in a more recent study, however, the bind was not quite so tight as Greenblatt implies: humanist linguistic theory could help to problematize theories of natural slavery. A vein of linguistic nominalism undermined attempts to see babarism as 'natural'. After all, even the vernacular tongues of Europe were still in the process of shrugging off the stigma of barbarism as opposed to Latin the universal tongue.[49] José de Acosta made the point, which still has a political edge, that the general word 'Indian' mystified the immense variety of different cultures in the New World.[50] Acosta argued that when Aristotle formulated the theory of the 'natural slave' he was 'adulating rather than philosophizing', flattering Alexander's imperial schemes.[51] Such comments hinted that the reformulation of the theory of natural slavery to justify Spanish conquests also reflected the subjection of true philosophy to the name of the king. At the same time, they did imply the possibility that a universalizing philosophy could on occasion move beyond the rhetoric of power. And against the sceptical undermining of simple notions of human nature, an awareness of the universality of language could lead not just to an oppressive levelling of distinctions but to attempts to construct a broader and less constricted theory of human potentiality, to found what Pagden terms a 'comparative ethnology'. Several writers argued that the virtual universality of language was a sign that all people were capable of civility. Some languages might be considered richer than others, but there was no rigid linguistic determinism: if 'language in the postlapsarian world was thought to create power, it was still man who created language'.[52]

Critics have on the whole been remarkably reluctant to admit that Shakespeare the practical man of the theatre could have been interested in contemporary European intellectual debates. But even if we limit him to a more local context, he would have been made aware of complexities in the ideology of colonization. First of all, the champions of colonization in Jacobean England did not have things all their own way. Samuel Daniel had recently directed a verse letter to Prince Henry, a favourite patron of colonists, specifically advising him against supporting overseas colonial projects. Like Montaigne, Daniel had condemned the stigmatization of other cultures as 'barbarous' with a reference to the story about Pyrrhus.[53] Daniel, Shakespeare, and Montaigne's translator John Florio all had contacts with the Earl of Southampton, one of the leading supporters of the Virginia Company, but that did not mean that they shared all the earl's views.[54] And even within the Virginia Company there were divergent emphases. Revisionist historians have effectively scotched the older view that early colonizers like Southampton and Sir Edwin Sandys were trying to turn

Virginia into a laboratory for republicanism and religious toleration.[55] But it is misleading simply to invert that argument, as Greenblatt effectively does, by seeing the colonies as laboratories for the repressive machine of total domination and thought control which in Foucauldian terms is the real agenda of modernity. The Southampton–Sandys group (who were already members of the council though they did not take control until after Shakespeare's death) did face contradictions in their positions. They were suspicious of aggrandizements of royal power at home and their followers represented a politically marginalized group of lesser merchants. They were ready to invoke universalizing theories of natural law against King James, and this could make it difficult for them to deny some kind of natural rights and civility to the native Americans.[56] Sandys's friend John Selden seems also to have been an admirer of *The Tempest*. Selden became involved with the Virginia Company and was interested in natural law theory; he was involved in opposition politics and sided with Parliament in the Civil War. It is said that when discussing the play with his friends Viscount Falkland and John Vaughan, he declared that 'Shakespeare *had not only found out a new Character in his* Caliban, *but had also devis'd and adapted a new manner of Language for that Character.*'[57] Though Selden was no democrat or primitivist, it is possible that he would have heard Caliban's calls for freedom with at least a degree of ambivalence. Noel Malcolm has suggested that Thomas Hobbes's ultra-hard primitivism, his reduction of all social conventions to languages whose meaning was arbitrarily dictated by the sovereign, may to some degree represent a revulsion against ideas he had encountered in his early years of association with the company; his friend Sir William Davenant rewrote *The Tempest*.[58] Shakespeare was writing in an intellectual milieu in which the questions of nature and language were the subject of intense debate.

Prospero and Miranda themselves certainly show no awareness of such complications; their hard primitivism presents Caliban as a natural slave. Miranda claims that

> When thou didst not, savage,
> Know thine own meaning, but wouldst gabble like
> A thing most brutish, I endowed thy purposes
> With words that made them known.
>
> (I.ii. 354–7)

If Caliban's mother died before he was of the age to speak, this claim may be literally true; but it may also reflect the standpoint of those colonialists who argued that Indian languages were intrinsically debased.[59] Caliban may seem to accept Miranda's terms:

You taught me language, and my profit on't
Is I know how to curse.

We have seen how much opportunity Caliban has had to learn to curse. But we should not abstract his words too easily from the speech-act they perform: Caliban is taking up her words for the sake of a polemical retort, and her and Prospero's view of Caliban is not fully borne out by the play as a whole. Nor is the relation between Caliban's language and his possibilities of agency as rigidly deterministic as Miranda's almost Althusserian formulation seems to suggest. Miranda says that he 'deserved more than a prison', and if all that language can teach him is cursing, then perhaps the master's language is itself a prison-house. It is true that there is an implicit material analysis of language as dulling resistance to power as Stephano holds out a bottle to Caliban: 'here is that which will give language to you, cat' (II.ii. 78–9). And Caliban's intense linguistic curiosity to some extent keeps him enslaved. For all his protests to Prospero, he has listened intently to his language and enjoys showing off his knowledge of his vocabulary – 'He has brave utensils, for so he calls them' (III.ii. 94); he notes that he calls Miranda a 'nonpareil' (III.ii. 98). Prospero has taught him 'how/ To name the bigger light and how the less,/ That burn by day and night' (I.ii. 334–6), Miranda has taught him about the man in the moon, and this means that even as his imagination expands towards a wholly new world he is made ready to accept Stephano as a god and subordinate himself to him (II.ii. 134–5); he has internalized and naturalized their myths.[60] In trying to free himself he abases himself to someone less worthy.

But Caliban's subjectivity is not just passively determined by discourse. However limited his alliance with Stephano may be, it is a consciously formed project to change his situation, to construct a 'good mischief' (he too has learned to euphemize).[61] And Caliban is able to make his own linguistic choices – a fact which struck contemporaries, as we have seen. His opening exchanges with Prospero enact his resistance by means of a grammatical rebellion. Sociolinguists have pointed to the distinction made in many languages between the pronouns of power and those of solidarity, those which take subordination for granted and those which initiate a dialogue between equals. In early modern English, such a distinction had emerged, with the plural forms 'ye' and 'you' being addressed to social superiors. Prospero almost always addresses Miranda as 'thou' and she always responds with the plural of respect: thus far, the play falls in with the rules of a rigidly hierarchical society. But linguistic models based on a static, rule-bound *langue* may miss the opportunities for pragmatic innovation in *parole*. In fact there is evidence that the situation in early modern England was fluid and contradictory. On the one hand, in language as well as in other areas of social life such as costume and ornamentation, there was a process of downward drift in which usages theoretically reserved for the artistocracy were imitated by those lower down the social scale: the process which ended in the unmarked, universal, singular 'you' of modern English may have been under way. On the other hand, there was a certain current of humanist and Protestant criticism of the plural pronoun of power, a practice which had emerged in Latin discourse under the Empire and could thus be seen as a symptom of decadence: Cicero would never have abased himself in such a way. By the mid-seventeenth century, the Quakers were causing social panic by insisting on addressing social superiors as 'thou', anticipating the pronoun of fraternity in the French Revolution.[62]

Caliban too challenges the normal grammatical rules:

> This island's mine by Sycorax my mother,
> Which thou tak'st from me. When thou cam'st first,
> Thou strok'st me and made much of me; wouldst give me
> Water with berries in't, and teach me how
> To name the bigger light and how the less,
> That burn by day and night; and then I loved thee,
> And showed thee all the qualities o'th'isle,
> The fresh springs, brine pits, barren place and fertile–
> Cursed be I that did so! All the charms
> Of Sycorax, toads, beetles, bats light on you!
> For I am all the subjects that you have,
> Which first was mine own king, and here you sty me
> In this hard rock, whiles you do keep from me
> The rest o'th'island.
>
> (I.i. 331–44)

Caliban opens the speech by disputing the validity of Prospero's claim to authority; and he enacts this validity challenge linguistically by addressing him as 'thou'. When he moves into the past tense, however, to recall the early days when Prospero treated him as an equal, his 'thou' takes on overtones of a recollected solidarity and mutuality.

Caliban wants to receive the kind of treatment that Prospero continues to give to Ariel. Prospero has absolute power over the spirit, but Ariel is in some sense a being outside secular hierarchies and makes claims to personal intimacy and affection. Thus Prospero's 'thou' when addressed to Ariel flickers between power and solidarity, and Ariel feels able on occasion to answer him back with 'thou' (I.ii. 190). Ariel's use of the word is always insecure, however: in the plaintive 'Do you love me, master; No?' (IV.i. 49) the 'you' and the 'love' cancel each other out in a question that cannot decide quite how rhetorical it is. All the same, there is some room for dialogue in the relationship, and in the retrospective part of his speech, Caliban looks back to a time when he could engage in dialogue with Prospero. When he reverts to cursing himself and Prospero at line 390, he is reproaching his ruler for that loss of intimacy: the 'you' therefore itself becomes a reproach to him. The grammar is now socially correct but the speech-act is rebellious. Caliban addresses Stephano consistently as 'thou', constructing such radically unconventional forms as 'thy honour' (III.ii. 22). This can perhaps be considered as an archaizing form directed to a deity: the 'thou' form could oscillate between intimacy and enormous distance.[63] But Caliban's earlier deviance gives the usage a political charge.

Grammar may have been termed the 'instrument of empire',[64] but it could be turned against empire. Caliban is able to resist the dazzling theatre of power: where Stephano and Trinculo are seduced by the courtly wardrobe, Caliban sees that 'it is but trash' (IV.i. 223). And he is fortified in his resistance by his empathy with his natural surroundings, his sensitivity to the blind mole's hearing (IV.i. 194): he listens as well as roaring. Yet the dialectic of nature and language is complex, and his language is not presented as a transparent window on nature. As Greenblatt notes, his discourse contains words like 'scamel' which are resistantly unnaturalizable in European terms.[65] His lyrically charged speeches are normally printed in verse in modern editions. Interestingly, in the Folio his exchanges with Stephano and Trinculo are in prose: that would be the more conventional decorum, the prose of the base set against aristocratic verse. But Caliban's discourse cuts across those boundaries. Early readers might even have expected Caliban to be revealed according to a popular romance convention as an aristocrat in disguise; but this never happens. Leslie Fiedler has suggested that the end of his song – 'Freedom, high-day! High-day, freedom! Freedom, high-day, freedom!' (II.ii. 181) has the ring of Whitman and is 'the first American poem'.[66]

So far is Caliban from accepting conventional stereotypes that he warns his allies against reducing themselves to the way their masters might want to construct them:

> We shall lose our time,
> And all be turned to barnacles, or to apes
> With foreheads villainous low.
>
> (IV.i. 248–50)

Ironically enough, later polemicists have misread this speech as a self-description and have portrayed republicans, Irishmen, blacks, and other enemies of the natural order as low-browed Calibans.[67] But Caliban's history could be taken to show that 'monstrous' behaviour, rather than being natural, is the result of imitating distortions in traditional linguistic and social forms; and that while language may determine conduct it also empowers change. That, certainly, is the moral Mary Shelley tried to draw in her presentation of Frankenstein's monster, who was partly conceived as a challenge to conventional counter-revolutionary sterotypes of the masses as fallen Calibans.[68] Like her monster, Caliban does not accord with simpler idealizations of a wholly pacific natural man – he never repents of his attempted rape of Miranda – but the effect is to complicate moral and political issues rather than to reinscribe a simplistic notion of natural good and evil.

The complications extend, of course, to the question of Caliban's cultural origins: he is little more 'natural' to the island than Prospero, having been born to a citizen of Algiers. As Peter Hulme has pointed out, there is a dual topography in which Mediterranean and American features are kept in unstable interaction, preventing an easy naturalization of the play even as an allegory of colonization – Milan after all had limited opportunities of becoming a great naval power since it lacked a coast. The instability is registered in the gap between 'Caliban' and 'cannibal'. Alonso's daughter has married a prince from Caliban's native land, and 'Caliban' also echoes in 'Claribel'; there was a town called Calibia in North Africa, and Barbary was considered to be the original home of barbarians.[69] The instability extends in time as well as place: as Hulme puts it, the 'handful of miles between Carthage and Tunis balances our reading on a knife-edge'.[70] In identifying ancient Carthage with modern Tunis, Gonzalo wants to construct an unproblematic, naturalizing genealogy in which the Neapolitans will directly inherit the glories of the ancient world; but the dispute opens up a gap between the worlds, reminding us that the same piece of land has been claimed as a natural possession by many different cultures over the process of time. Montaigne's essay had opened at a time when southern Italy was occupied by Greeks for whom the Romans were mere barbarians; the Dido reference may function as a reminder of the time when Carthage itself was a newly-founded city, long before it became a victim of Roman imperialism and the faithful widow Dido was reconstructed as a seductive deviation from the path of political duty. Montaigne's essay also noted that the Carthaginians had at one time tried to colonize a new world beyond Gibraltar. The buried classical references partake of the Renaissance humanist recognition that the old world of classical antiquity was itself a new world, a new set of texts whose resistance to being translated directly into feudal discourse could become a point of purchase for a political critique. *The Tempest* registers the necessary slippage between Carthage and Tunis, the historic discontinuities belied by Gonzalo's courtly euphemizing but recognized by critical textual analysis. But humanism also had a generalizing impulse that did acknowledge the possibility of reviving and reshaping the texts and political projects of the past in new ways. John Pitcher has argued that the allusions to Carthage help to set up a complex intertextuality with Virgil's *Aeneid*, and in particular with the scene where the Trojans see the new city under construction, including the foundations of theatres. Pitcher argues that Shakespeare could have read these lines as prophetic of his own art, of the new theatrical medium that would be born out of the epic just as Tunis is born out of Carthage.[71] Antonio's reductive attitude to Gonzalo's antiquarianism is not entirely justified; new futures can be built out of a restructured past.

Shakespeare's own drama, in its little Globe, its island of relative autonomy, was part of that process. Prospero's masque dissolves because its actors were not natural aristocrats but spirits; but 'spirit' was a familiar term for 'actor', reminding us that the real agency involved was that of a professional repertory company.[72] Despite their royal label, the King's Men owed most of their revenue to public performances; Shakespeare's plays were thus able to pit different discourses against each other with far greater freedom than courtly literature.[73] Prospero may have staged the storm, but the common players staged Prospero. Greenblatt notes that as a joint-stock company the King's Men had the same kind of autonomy as the Virginia Company, whose members, as we have seen, did distance themselves from the royal viewpoint.[74] As Erica Sheen has pointed out, the play frequently alludes to the company's own repertorial self-consciousness: Prospero may dismiss his spirits as a 'rabble' of 'meaner fellows' (IV.i. 37, 35), but he depends on their work.[75] The link between language and work recurs throughout the play. Even Ariel's more visionary language is the product of work, of careful crafting, and has a material, bodily aspect: the spirits' feet may be printless, but they still '[f]oot it featly' (I.i. 378). Prospero's feet may indeed be his tutor (I.ii. 470). To return for a moment to the opening scene, the boatswain complains that the courtiers' panicking howls and curses are 'louder than the weather or our office' (I.i. 36–7): courtly discourse is contrasted not only with natural sounds but with the sailors' practically oriented work-language under the absent master's directing whistle.[76] To Sebastian's 'A pox o' your throat,' the boatswain bluntly replies: 'Work you, then.' Shakespeare researched the sailors' language with great sociolinguistic precision.[77] The master's whistle may seem to be merely a figure for the playwright's authority, the sovereign author displacing the sovereign prince in a valorization of an individualistic bourgeois work-ethic. But there is a parallel between the master's disappearance at the beginning of the play and Prospero's renunciation at the end: in each case authority is transferred to the process of dramatic production in which the company collaborates with the audience – or the reader. Prospero's epilogue thus gives a final twist to the confrontation between the king's name and the public air:

> Gentle breath of yours my sails
> Must fill, or else my project fails.
>
> (V.i. 329–30)

NOTES

1 For comments on earlier drafts I am grateful to W.R. Elton, Margot Heinemann, Frank Romany, and Erica Sheen.

The edition used for quotations is the New Oxford, edited by Stephen Orgel (Oxford and New York: Oxford University Press, 1987). This edition is sharper politically than Kermode's New Arden edition, which has, despite its great merits, tended to fix authoritarian readings of the play.

2 Ariel's gender is not specified in any of the play's speeches, and from the eighteenth century through to the early twentieth century the part was regularly played by a woman (see Orgel's edition, 70). The indeterminacy arises in the first instance from the fact that Prospero shields his relationship with Ariel from the other characters, so that there are no third-person references in the dialogue. A stage direction in III.iii does define Ariel as male, however, and the part was a male one in the Davenant-Dryden version. Nevertheless, the text itself is open to a large degree of indeterminacy in the question of a spirit's sexuality.

3 On Ariel as language, see Terry Eagleton, *William Shakespeare* (Oxford: Blackwell, 1986), 94–5. Some recent critics have been drawing attention to

utopian elements in the play: see Annabel Patterson, *Shakespeare and the Popular Voice* (Oxford: Blackwell, 1989), 154ff; Kiernan Ryan, *Shakespeare* (Hemel Hempstead: Harvester Wheatsheaf, 1989), 97ff; and Graham Holderness in a forthcoming piece which he kindly showed me.

4 On language and utopia in *Comus* see my *Poetry and Politics in the English Renaissance* (London: Routledge & Kegan Paul, 1984), 259ff. The relations between *The Tempest* and *Comus* have recently been studied by Mary Loeffelholz, 'Two masques of Ceres and Proserpine: *Comus* and *The Tempest*', in Mary Nyquist and Margaret W. Ferguson (eds), *Re-membering Milton: Essays on the Texts and Traditions* (New York and London: Methuen, 1987), 25–42, and Christopher Kendrick, 'Milton and sexuality: A symptomatic reading of *Comus*', Ibid., 43–73.

5 'A defence of poetry', in *Shelley's Prose or The Trumpet of a Prophecy*, ed. David Lee Clark, with a preface by Harold Bloom (London: Fourth Estate, 1988), 282. On the Shelleys and *The Tempest* see Christopher Small, *Ariel Like a Harpy: Shelley, Mary, and 'Frankenstein'* (London: Victor Gollancz, 1972), 123ff.

6 *The Letters of Mary Wollstonecraft Shelley, vol. 1: 'A Part of the Elect'*, ed. Betty T. Bennett (Baltimore and London: Johns Hopkins University Press, 1980), 263 n. 9, 292, 334.

7 Walter Cohen, *Drama of a Nation: Public Theater in Renaissance England and Spain* (Ithaca and London: Cornell University Press, 1985), 384ff, notes Shelley's readings of Calderón; Shelley was interested in parallels between Shakespeare and Calderón.

8 William Empson, 'Hunt the symbol', *Essays on Shakespeare*, ed. David B. Pirie (Cambridge: Cambridge University Press, 1986), 231–43 (first published in *The Times Literary Supplement*, 23 April 1964).

9 *Coleridge's Shakespearean Criticism*, ed. Thomas Middleton Raysor, 2 vols (London: Dent, 1960), vol. I, 122.

10 Gary Schmidgall, *Shakespeare and the Courtly Aesthetic* (Berkeley, Los Angeles, and London: University of California Press, 1981), continues the authoritarian tradition and sees the play as defending 'the Tudor theory of obedience' against 'an increasingly obstinate Parliament' (171 n.13). See my review in *English* 31 (1982), 247–52. More directly topical readings have been offered by Glynne Wickham, 'Masque and anti-masque in *The Tempest*', *Essays and Studies* 28 (1975), 1–14; Frances A. Yates, *Shakespeare's Last Plays: A New Approach* (London: Routledge & Kegan Paul, 1975); David M. Bergeron, *Shakespeare's Romances and the Royal Family* (Lawrence: Kansas University Press, 1985), 111; and, most fully documented, Michael Srigley, *Images of Regeneration: A Study of Shakespeare's 'The Tempest' and its Cultural Background* (Acta Universitatis Upsaliensis. Studia Anglistica Upsaliensia 58, Uppsala: Almqvist & Wiksell International, 1985). As Orgel points out (Orgel (ed.), 1ff), the evidence scarcely warrants calling *The Tempest* a 'court play', but I would not rule out the possibility of the play's having some connection with enthusiasm for the Palatine match of 1613. That would not, however, make the play absolutist given that the strongest supporters of the Palatine match were those most anxious about the growing hegemony of counter-Reformation absolutism both abroad and potentially in England.

11 Readings of the play as treating colonialism go back at least as far as Jack

Lindsay and Edgell Rickword (eds), *A Handbook of Freedom* (London: Lawrence & Wishart, 1939), 103; see also Bruce Erlich, 'Shakespeare's colonial metaphor: on the social function of theatre in *The Tempest*', *Science and Society* 41 (1977), 43–65; Thomas Cartelli, 'Prospero in Africa: *The Tempest* as colonialist text and pretext', Jean E. Howard and Marion F. O'Connor (eds), *Shakespeare Reproduced: The Text in History and Ideology* (New York and London: Methuen, 1987), 99–115; Rob Nixon, 'Caribbean and African appropriations of *The Tempest*', *Critical Inquiry* 13 (1986–7), 557–78; Ania Loomba, *Gender, Race, Renaissance Drama* (Manchester: Manchester University Press, 1989), chapter 6.

12 For readings that align the play with colonial discourse but are in differing degrees alert to unconscious complexities and contradictions, see Paul Brown, ' "This Thing of Darkness I Acknowledge Mine": *The Tempest* and the discourse of colonialism', in Jonathan Dollimore and Alan Sinfield (eds), *Political Shakespeare: New Essays in Cultural Materialism* (Manchester: Manchester University Press, 1985), 48–71; Francis Barker and Peter Hulme, 'Nymphs and Reapers Heavily Vanish: the discursive con-texts of *The Tempest*', in John Drakakis (ed.), *Alternative Shakespeares* (London and New York: Methuen, 1985), 191–205; Peter Hulme, 'Prospero and Caliban', in *Colonial Encounters: Europe and the Native Caribbean, 1492–1797* (London and New York: Methuen, 1986), 89–134; Stephen Greenblatt, 'Martial law in the land of Cockaigne', in *Shakespearean Negotiations: The Circulation of Social Energy in Renaissance England* (Oxford: Clarendon Press, 1988), 129–63. Deborah Willis, 'Shakespeare's *Tempest* and the discourse of colonialism', *Studies in English Literature 1500–1900* 29 (1989), 277–89, questions monolithic accounts of colonial discourse.

13 E.g. Leonard Tennenhouse, *Power on Display: The Politics of Shakespeare's Genres* (New York and London: Methuen, 1986), 177–8.

14 Terry Eagleton, *William Shakespeare* (Oxford: Blackwell, 1986), 1, 93, 99. In support of Eagleton's claim that Shakespeare seems to have read Derrida, it can be pointed out that Caliban's ' 'Ban, 'Ban, Ca-Caliban' seems to echo the old refrain 'Da, da, da – Deridan': *A New Variorum Edition of Shakespeare, The Tempest*, ed. Horace Howard Furness (Philadelphia and London: J. B. Lippincott 1892), 141.

15 Jürgen Habermas, *The Theory of Communicative Action*, trans. Thomas McCarthy (Boston: Beacon Press, 1984), vol. 1, 598.

16 Mary Louise Pratt, 'Linguistic utopias', in Nigel Fabb *et al.* (eds), *The Linguistics of Writing: Arguments Between Language and Literature* (Manchester: Manchester University Press, 1987), 48–66. Pratt identifies the ideal speech situation with ideals of homogeneous patriarchal nationhood; she is acute on the blindness to gender and other inequalities often found in pragmatics, but the overall identification of Habermasian rationalism with organicist nationalism may be questioned.

17 But for a rhetorical analysis of utopian discourse see Louis Marin, *Utopics: Spatial Play*, trans. Robert A. Vollrath (New Jersey: Humanities Press, 1984).

18 Jacques Derrida, 'The violence of the letter: from Lévi-Strauss to Rousseau', in *Of Grammatology*, trans. Gayatri Chakravorty Spivak (Baltimore and London: Johns Hopkins University Press, 1976), 101ff. For

extensive discussion of this issue, often with reference to *The Tempest*, see the special issue of *Critical Inquiry*, vol. 12 (Autumn 1985) on ' "Race", writing and difference', and responses in vol. 13.

19 Eagleton, *William Shakespeare*, 95.

20 David Lindley, 'Music, masque, and meaning in *The Tempest*', in David Lindley (ed.), *The Court Masque* (Manchester: Manchester University Press, 1984), 47–59, sees the music of the masque as pragmatically rhetorical rather than unproblematically retaining older symbolic values.

21 Victoria Kahn, 'Humanism and the resistance to theory', in Patricia Parker and David Quint (eds), *Literary Theory/Renaissance Texts* (Baltimore and London: Johns Hopkins University Press, 1986), 373–96; cf. Jonathan Dollimore, *Radical Tragedy: Religion, Ideology and Power in the Drama of Shakespeare and his Contemporaries* (Brighton: Harvester Press, 1984), 10ff.

22 The best discussion of this topic is Graham Holderness, *Shakespeare's History* (Dublin: Gill & Macmillan, New York: St Martin's Press, 1985). For an instance see my '*Macbeth* and the politics of historiography', in Kevin Sharpe and Steven N. Zwicker (eds), *Politics of Discourse* (Berkeley, Los Angeles, and London: California University Press, 1987), 78–116. I now think that I overstressed the degree of Shakespeare's reaction against this politically rationalistic vein in humanism.

23 Cf. my *Poetry and Politics in the English Renaissance*, 26.

24 See Erica Sheen's essay below (chapter 3). In his adaptation of *The Tempest* Aimé Césaire has Prospero banished by the Inquisition, among other crimes, for reading Seneca's tragedies: *Une Tempête* (Paris: Editions du Seuil, 1960), 21.

25 On the unusual generic complexities of *The Tempest* see Cohen, *Drama of a Nation*, 390ff; R.S. White, *'Let Wonder Seem Familiar': Endings in Shakespeare's Romance Vision* (New Jersey: Humanities Press; London: Athlone Press, 1985), 159ff; Brown, ' "This Thing of Darkness I Acknowledge Mine" ', 61ff; Hulme, 'Prospero and Caliban', 115ff.

26 Fredric Jameson, *The Political Unconscious: Narrative as a Socially Symbolic Act* (Ithaca: Cornell University Press, 1981), 103ff; cf. Raymond Williams, 'The tenses of writing', in *Writing in Society* (London: Verso, 1983), 267–8.

27 See Orgel's edition, 37–8.

28 In a stimulating analysis of such twists Terence Hawkes none the less flattens out one complexity by assuming that all the characters are imagined as speaking English: *That Shakespeherian Rag: Essays on a Critical Process* (London and New York: Methuen, 1986), 54.

29 Margaret Hodgen, 'Montaigne and Shakespeare again', *Huntington Library Quarterly* 16 (1952–3), 23–42, argues that some details of the speech may have been taken from other writers on the New World; if he did consult further sources the hypothesis that he read Montaigne's essay closely and critically would be strengthened. See also Valentina P. Komarova, 'Das Problem der Gesellschaftsform in Montaignes *Essays* und Shakespeares *Sturm*', *Shakespeare Jahrbuch* 122 (1986), 75–90.

30 Michel de Certeau, 'Montaigne's "Of Cannibals" ', in *Heterologies: Discourse on the Other*, trans. Brian Massumi, foreword by Wlad Godzich (Manchester: Manchester University Press, 1986), 67–79.

31 Page numbers in the text refer to the modernized-spelling version of Florio's translation in Orgel's edition of *The Tempest*.

32 See 'Walwyns just defence', in *The Writings of William Walwyn*, ed. Jack R. McMichael and Barbara Taft (Athens and London: University of Georgia Press, 1989), 399–400: 'Go . . . to these innocent Cannibals, ye Independent Churches, to learn civility.'

33 Leo Lowenthal, *Literature and the Image of Man: Sociological Studies of the European Drama and Novel, 1600–1900* (Boston: The Beacon Press, 1957), 71, 75. Lowenthal, however, sees the courtiers as relics of feudalism, whereas the sociological situation is more complex.

34 The word 'masters' was socially equivocal and appears in the sense of 'servants' in Prospero's later 'Weak masters' (V.i. 41); the multiple usages are part of a process of problematizing power relations.

35 John X. Evans, '*Utopia* on Prospero's island', *Moreana* 18 (1981), 81–3.

36 Michael Walzer, *The Revolution of the Saints: A Study in the Origins of Radical Politics* (Cambridge, Mass.: Harvard University Press, 1965), 179–82; John M. Wallace, *Destiny His Choice: The Loyalism of Andrew Marvell* (Cambridge: Cambridge University Press, 1968), 131–2.

37 Harry Berger Jr, 'Miraculous harp: a reading of Shakespeare's *Tempest*', *Shakespeare Studies* 5 (1969), 253–83 (264).

38 Frances A. Shirley, *Swearing and Perjury in Shakespeare's Plays* (London: George Allen & Unwin, 1979), 148. Bergeron, in his highly courtly reading, finds it necessary to transfer the 'gallows-style humour' from Gonzalo to the boatswain: *Shakespeare's Romances and the Royal Family*, 111. Lowenthal, *Literature and the Image of Man*, 226–7, finds parallels between Gonzalo and the boatswain, both of them being more directed to rational goals than the courtiers and both cursing in a nominalist, self-expressive vein in contrast to the almost realist cursing of the courtiers (on cursing see also 73ff); Lowenthal even argues that the boatswain 'speaks as if he had read Montaigne, and Gonzalo answers as if he were Montaigne' (227).

39 On Guicciardini and Machiavelli respectively see G.K. Hunter, 'English folly and Italian vice: the moral landscape of John Marston', in *Dramatic Identities and Cultural Tradition: Studies in Shakespeare and his Contemporaries* (Liverpool: Liverpool University Press, 1978), 103–32, and William W.E. Slights, 'A source for *The Tempest* and the context of the *Discorsi*', *Shakespeare Quarterly* 36 (1985), 68–70. On Italian cultural history see Lauro Martines, *Power and Imagination: City-States in Renaissance Italy* (London: Allen Lane, 1979); on Guicciardini's discourse see J.G.A. Pocock, *The Machiavellian Moment: Florentine Political Thought and the Atlantic Republican Tradition* (Princeton: Princeton University Press, 1975), 114–56, 219–71 (and on Milan, 55, 150). Shakespeare would probably have known the essay 'Of books' (II, x) in which Montaigne praised Guicciardini's accuracy, though he censured him as too cynical. Guicciardini's history was translated into English in 1579 by Geoffrey Fenton, and become a source for political theory: see e.g. Robert Dallington's *Aphorismes Civill and Militarye* (London, 1613).

40 *The Historie of Guicciardin*, trans. G. Fenton (London, 1579), 28, 64ff; Wallace, *Destiny His Choice*, 83. Speaking in support of the Virginia

Company in the 1614 Parliament, Richard Martin, a friend of Christopher Brooke and other Jacobean poets with an interest in Virginia, said that the colony would become a bridle for the Neapolitan courser if the youth of England were able to sit him (*Commons Journals*, I, 488).

41 *The Double Marriage*, I.i, V.i in *The Works of Francis Beaumont and John Fletcher*, ed. A.R. Waller, 10 vols (Cambridge: Cambridge University Press, 1908), vol. VI, 325, 405. For parallels with *The Tempest* see especially II.i. The play notes that the rulers of Naples in fact came from Spain, hence the Spanish names of Shakespeare's dynasty. The major source was Comines: see E.M. Waith, 'The sources of *The Double Marriage* by Fletcher and Massinger', *Modern Language Notes* 64 (1949), 505–10; the English translation had frequent cross-references to Guicciardini. Montaigne praises Comines in 'Of books'.

42 On work in *The Tempest* see Lowenthal, *Literature and the Image of Man*, 62ff, and Hulme, *Colonial Encounters*, 131ff. Hawkes, *That Shakespeherian Rag*, 3ff, offers a more critical view of the play's work-ethic than Lowenthal; but it is worth remembering that in its context the play's valorization of work criticizes the neo-feudal ethos (cf. Berger, 'Miraculous harp', 257).

43 Cf. Peter Burke, 'Language and anti-language in early modern Italy', *History Workshop* 11 (Spring 1981), 24–32.

44 Martines, *Power and Imagination*, 452ff, 'The lure of utopia'; Berger, 'Miraculous harp', 262, notes the parallel with More's itself rather academic utopianism which had its roots in Florentine Neoplatonism.

45 I cannot here do justice to the text of Prospero's masque, which has been discussed by Lindley, 'Music, masque and meaning in *The Tempest*', 51ff, and Ernest B. Gilman, ' "All eyes": Prospero's inverted masque', *Renaissance Quarterly* 33 (1980), 214–30; Glynne Wickham, 'Masque and anti-masque in *The Tempest*', *Essays and Studies* 28 (1975), 1–14; Irwin Smith, 'Ariel and the masque in *The Tempest*', *Shakespeare Quarterly* 21 (1970), 213–22; Berger, 'Miraculous harp', 270ff; and Hawkes, *That Shakespeherian Rag*, 5–7. John Gillies, 'Shakespeare's Virginian masque', *English Literary History* 53 (1986), 673–707, argues that the masque in *The Tempest*, far from glorifying the ideology of colonization, goes directly against the court masques on that theme.

46 *Ben Jonson*, ed. C.H. Herford and Percy and Evelyn Simpson, 11 vols (Oxford: Clarendon Press, 1925–52), vol. VII, 209–10. Catherine M. Shaw, '*The Tempest* and *Hymenaei*', *Cahiers Elisabethains* 26 (October 1984), 29–40, notes similarities but not differences between these works. Bergeron, *Shakespeare's Romances and the Royal Family*, 197–8, notes possible similarities with Daniel's *Vision of the Twelve Goddesses*, which lays more emphasis on the masque's insubstantiality. It is possible that Shakespeare was indeed aligning himself more with Daniel than with Jonson: the two poets were contesting the political implications of the masque (see my *Poetry and Politics in the English Renaissance*, 201).

47 William Shakespeare, *The Tempest*, ed. Frank Kermode, New Arden edn (London: Methuen, 1954; reprinted with corrections, 1970), xliii.

48 Stephen J. Greenblatt, 'Learning to curse: aspects of linguistic colonialism in the 16th century', in Fredi Chiappelli (ed.), *First Images of America: The Impact of the New World on the Old*, 2 vols (Berkeley: California University Press,

1970), vol. II, 561–80. On language and communication in relation to colonization see also Tzvetan Todorov, *The Conquest of America: The Question of the Other*, trans. Richard Howard (New York: Harper & Row, 1984), 28-33, 77ff.

49 See Stephen Mullaney, 'Strange things, gross terms, curious customs: the rehearsal of cultures in the late Renaissance', in Stephen Greenblatt (ed.), *Representing the English Renaissance* (Berkeley, Los Angeles, and London: California University Press, 1988), 66–92 (80).

50 Anthony Pagden, *The Fall of Natural Man: The American Indian and the Origins of Comparative Ethnology* (Cambridge: Cambridge University Press, 1982), 162. For a reading of Caliban in the context of defences of the Indian as natural man, see Sister Corona Sharp, 'Caliban: the primitive man's evolution', *Shakespeare Studies* 14 (1981), 267–83.

51 Pagden, op cit., 165.

52 ibid., 128.

53 'To Prince Henrie', in John Pitcher, *Samuel Daniel: The Brotherton Manuscript: A Study in Authorship* (Leeds: University of Leeds School of English, 1981), 131–7; Samuel Daniel, *Poems and A Defence of Ryme*, ed. Arthur Colby Sprague (Cambridge, Mass.: 1930), 139–40.

54 Florio was tutor to Southampton: see H.C. Porter, *The Inconstant Savage: England and the North American Indian 1500–1660* (London: Duckworth, 1979), 137ff. I am indebted to Margot Heinemann for this reference and for showing me an unpublished paper on Southampton's patronage.

55 Noel Malcolm, 'Hobbes, Sandys, and the Virginia Company', *Historical Journal* 24 (1981), 297–321, revising the model put forward by such scholars as Charles Mills Gayley, *Shakespeare and the Founders of Liberty in America* (New York and London: Macmillan, 1917). Gayley's book itself imparts a new emphasis to the older republican interpretations by seeing Shakespeare as a strong opponent not only of absolutism but also of communism (3, 41, 63ff); the date of the book's publication may be significant here.

56 Malcolm, 'Hobbes, Sandys, and the Virginia Company', 302–4.

57 The story goes back to Rowe; although late, it is interestingly specific. See Brian Vickers (ed.), *Shakespeare: The Critical Heritage, 1693–1753*, 6 vols (London and Boston: Routledge & Kegan Paul, 1974–81), vol. 2, 197. Selden was interested in literature as well as in theories of natural law; he was a close friend of Jonson and composed notes for the first part of Drayton's *Poly-Olbion*, published about the time *The Tempest* was composed. He, Vaughan, and Falkland were members of the Great Tew circle which had a cult of Shakespeare; another friend, Suckling, imitated *The Tempest* in his play *The Goblins*.

58 Malcolm, 'Hobbes, Sandys, and the Virginia Company', 318, provides some hints on Hobbes's development, though the identification of the Hobbes of the Virginia Company with the philosopher is not certain. On the Davenant–Dryden *Tempest*, see Katharine Eisaman Maus, 'Arcadia lost: politics and revision in the Restoration *Tempest*', *Renaissance Drama* N.S. 13 (1982), 189–209. A poem by Davenant seems to link the nautical language of *The Tempest* with the ship-of-state figure: 'Song: The Winter Storms', in *Sir William Davenant. The Shorter Poems, and Songs from the Masques and Plays*, ed. A.M. Gibbs (Oxford: Clarendon Press, 1972), 130–2. Dryden, taking an

unfavourable view of Caliban, none the less noted the linguistic specificity: his 'language is as hobgoblin as his person': *Essays of John Dryden*, ed. W.P. Ker, 2 vols (London, 1900), vol. I, 220.

59 As Greenblatt, 'Learning to curse', 566, points out, there is also a conflation of Caliban with the speechless 'wild man' of European folklore.

60 These exchanges gain a retrospective irony from the fact that the subsequent technological dominance of Anglophone culture has led to heavenly bodies being named after Shakespearian characters, with Miranda giving her name to a moon of Uranus.

61 Or, perhaps, to recognize the political elements in moral vocabulary: compare the exchange in *Coriolanus*, I.i. 12–13: 'One word, good citizens.' – 'We are accounted poor citizens, the patricians good.'

62 On pronominal politics see R. Brown and A. Gilman, 'The pronouns of power and solidarity', in T.A. Sebeok (ed.), *Style in Language* (Cambridge, Mass.: MIT Press, 1960), 253–76. On the opposition of Erasmus and other humanists to the formal 'vos', see Thomas Finkenstaedt, *You und thou: Studien zur Anrede im Englischen* (Berlin: Walter de Gruyter & Co., 1963), 98ff.

63 E.A. Abbott, *A Shakespearean Grammar* (new edn, London: Macmillan, 1876), 154; Abbott notes that Caliban 'almost always *thou's unless he is cursing*' (159). Sister St Geraldine Byrne, *Shakespeare's Use of the Pronoun of Address: its Significance in Characterization and Motivation* (Washington: The Catholic University of America, 1936), 137–40, classes Caliban's 'thou' as 'coarse'.

64 The grammarian de Nebrija, quoted by Greenblatt, 'Learning to curse', 562, and by Barker and Hulme, 'Nymphs and Reapers Heavily Vanish', 197.

65 Greenblatt, 'Learning to curse', 575. L.T. Fitz, 'The vocabulary of the environment in *The Tempest*', *Shakespeare Quarterly* 26 (1975), 42–7, argues that in an attempt to convey the sparseness of the island Shakespeare strips his language unusually bare of Latinate forms, with the exception of the masque.

66 Leslie Fiedler, *The Stranger in Shakespeare* (London: Croom Helm, 1973), 236.

67 Trevor R. Griffiths, '"This Island's Mine": Caliban and colonialism', *Yearbook of English Studies* 13 (1983), 159–80. It is, however, worth noting that Caliban has also been allegorized in terms of the materialistic and positivisic culture of the United States: José Enrique Rodó, *Ariel*, trans. Margaret Sayers Peden, with foreword by James W. Symington and prologue by Carlos Fuentes (1900; Austin: Texas University Press, 1988).

68 See Lee Sterrenburg, 'Mary Shelley's monster: politics and psyche in *Frankenstein*', in George Levine and U.C. Knoepflmacher (eds), *The Endurance of Frankenstein: Essays on Mary Shelley's Novel* (Berkeley, Los Angeles, and London: California University Press, 1979), 145–71.

69 *New Variorum Edition of Shakespeare, The Tempest* 3; Pagden, *The Fall of Natural Man*, 133.

70 Hulme, *Colonial Encounters*, 108.

71 John Pitcher, 'A theatre of the future: *The Aeneid* and *The Tempest*', *Essays in Criticism* 34 (1984), 193–215.

72 Emrys Jones, *The Origins of Shakespeare* (Oxford: Clarendon Press, 1977), 146 n.

73 The social basis of the drama has of course been much debated. Cohen, *Drama of a Nation*, 388, speaks of the 'subversive contradiction between artisanal base and absolutist superstructure'; I would question whether even

the ideological 'superstructure' needs to be considered unequivocally absolutist.

74 Greenblatt, 'Martial law in the land of Cockaigne', 148, 160.

75 I owe this point to an unpublished paper by Erica Sheen.

76 For a detailed sociological analysis of the storm scene, see Lowenthal, *Literature and the Image of Man*, 221–9.

77 There was a politics in the degree of Shakespeare's sociolinguistic specificity. A.F. Falconer points out in *Shakespeare and the Sea* that he 'has not only worked out a series of manoeuvres, but has made exact use of the professional language of seamanship . . . He could not have come by this knowledge from books, for there were no works on seamanship in his day, nor were there any nautical word lists or glossaries' (quoted by Orgel, 208).

3

'THE AGENT FOR HIS MASTER': POLITICAL SERVICE AND PROFESSIONAL LIBERTY IN *CYMBELINE*

Erica Sheen

I

As far as the critical history of *Cymbeline* is concerned, all roads lead to Rome. However critics approach the play, their point of departure is generally the assumption that its political affiliations are conservative ones. Readings as far apart as those of Emrys Jones and Leonard Tennenhouse[1] converge in the suggestion that the work's fundamental mode is panegyric – thus linking it with the court masque, whose growing influence in the first decade of the seventeenth century is so apparent in the theophany of V.iv. In the composite image of kingship constructed by Cymbeline's triumphant submission to Augustus, Shakespeare endorses the interests of the king who modelled himself on 'the pacific emperor under whom Christ was born'.[2] For such critics, the leading dramatist of the King's Men is definitely a king's man, 'the agent for his master' – as the queen describes Pisanio at I.vi.76. But the complex analysis of agency that underlies this phrase is precisely the issue in this play, and it confounds the ease with which a simplistic identification of political alignment can be made. For the apparent political orthodoxy of this play is haunted by an unruly subliminal presence: *Hercules furens*, one of Seneca's most ironic exposures of the imperial attitude.

The rhetorical use of implicit meaning is a resource which questions the very nature of rhetoric. Typically an almost imperceptible disjunction between dominant and subordinate semantic material, it both sets up and challenges a framework of explicit textual meaning. I shall propose that Shakespeare's use of a canonical text of absolutism in crisis works exactly in this way, and that the challenge it produces should be read in political terms as a professional dramatist's *non serviam*. His rereading of Seneca's analysis of personal and political power juxtaposes Posthumus and Imogen with Hercules and Megara, disturbing conventional perceptions of roles of agency and gender and developing out of them a notion of action which has more in common with the resistance to absolutism within more explicitly political discourses of the period than with absolutism itself.

There is, of course, a connection between a reading of Imogen which is never seriously questioned – the 'earthly paragon'; loyal, faithful, and above all chaste – and traditionalist interpretations of the play's political point of view. Such readings have not been achieved without some methodological strain. The characteristic response to the surprisingly frequent difficulties associated with an idealizing view of Imogen's perfections is to assume textual incoherence, or to displace such an incoherence onto an implied authorial failure in character realization. The Arden editor, J. M. Nosworthy, responds typically to Imogen's pre-empting of her husband's sexual jealousy at I.iv.28–30:

> Imogen lapses, rather unhappily, into the Beatrice or Portia vein. It is not a most pretty thing to say and is quite out of character.[3]

But the greatest difficulties are created by IV.ii – the headless body episode, and the scene on which I shall be concentrating in the first part of this essay. Of the discussions I have read, very few have any response to the unsettling feeling that the lid comes off Imogen here and never really fits afterwards. Leah Marcus acknowledges the problems –

> The scene of Imogen's desolate but misguided grief over Cloten is difficult to read without an uncomfortable admixture of levity . . . there remain awkward moments, perilously close to low comedy.[4]

– but she deals with them by subordinating the meaning of dramatic behaviour to the details of her analysis of the play's topicality. Such manoeuvres might well elicit a response similar to that of Frank Kermode on the editorial difficulties caused by the *Aeneid* material in *The Tempest*:

> It is a possible inference that our frame of reference is badly adjusted, or incomplete, and that an understanding of this passage will modify our image of the whole play.[5]

This observation was vindicated by the extent to which subsequent criticism did indeed identify the particular frame at work here,[6] illuminating a politically significant intertextuality between this late play and *another* canonical confrontation between personal liberty and political service. My suggestion here will be that many of the difficulties of *Cymbeline* fall into place when something surprisingly similar is observed in this play; and that the intertextuality thus displayed is the basis of a structure of implication which would appear to be an important feature of Shakespeare's dramatic discourse during the early reign of his company's patron.

Points of contact between *Cymbeline* and *The Tempest* require attention because they are features of the intellectual context of my discussion. Patronage – in the broad Elizabethan sense that encompasses imaginative relations of romantic tribute as well as economic ones of political tribute – is a concern in both. Within this concern both plays demonstrate an opposition between the real and the ideal in the relations between servants and masters; both represent a movement towards the 'proper praise' [7] of one by the other. In both, our perception of just how 'proper' that praise is, and consequently how appropriate the position of service is, is specifically undercut by the classical narrative.

This is a compressed description of compressed material. However, neither my purposes nor Shakespeare's would be served by rendering it less so since that would suggest that what I am going to discuss is 'available' within the text as a 'theme' or an 'idea'. That is not the status of the type of textual meaning with which I shall be concerned here.

As a partial explanation of such an assertion, I should say that what I am trying to do in the course of this discussion is part of a larger project, which is to describe the pragmatic structure of intentionality in drama of this period; to describe what kinds of social transactions were being made possible, for those working within it, by the development of the characteristic communicative resources of the Elizabethan/Jacobean professional theatre. It seems to me increasingly important for the assessment of our *own* resources of personal and intellectual autonomy to find a response to the characteristic reductiveness of currently dominant critical approaches like New Historicism which tend to see theatre of this period as an ultimately passive re-enactment of relations of power being acted upon it by a 'dominant' ideology.

Although this essay will be very different in method, what I want to do in it has been influenced by the work of Quentin Skinner. My concern will be to describe what a text is 'doing in saying something' – in theatrical texts, of course, the phonocentrism of that Austinian formulation is a material feature of the structure of its speech-act, not an unknowing deconstruction – and how its institutional context helps materialize its performative textual force. The relevance of Skinner's work for literary analysis has possibly been marginalized not only by the domination of text studies by the epistemological pessimism of poststructuralist approaches to the problem of meaning, but also by his own particular interest in political science. It is perhaps a consequence of his understanding of the terms upon which 'historical absurdity'[8] can be created by inappropriate interpretations of writers like Shakespeare – an understanding that I may well be about to violate – that he has elaborated his method through texts that are relatively explicit about their engagement in the sphere of political thought. It is interesting that those literary historians who *are* prepared to address the issue of intentionality do in fact try to find ways of identifying 'ideas' that can bridge the gap between literary and political discourses. What this means is that they have proposed responses to the complex issue of textuality – for long associated with the supposed intrinsic traditionalism of the 'literary' text – which sidesteps the fact of its existence. They do this by providing readings of the intellectual context, rather than of the text as a whole and in particular of its relation to the material basis of its production. No performative theory of meaning can afford to ignore those two elements of signification; it is such a reading that I am going to try to develop here.

Beyond the scope of this limited exercise, my conviction is that a pragmatic approach – the application to textual studies of a historicized model of the Gricean concept of the implicature,[9] for instance – could help find a way out of difficulties that have only been addressed through theories of ideology: those of accounting for the epistemological falsehood of seeing ideas or knowledge as in some way fully present to the people using them. It is this question of use to which I want to give emphasis here. Ideas – even ideology – can be used by people without being controlled by them, particularly when operating within the institutional context of work, in which such a use can become constitutive of the *negotiation* of control. It is such a negotiation that I consider to be articulated in this play. Political discourses current at this historical juncture were typically concerned with the question of use rather than truth: to what extent it was possible, or otherwise, for what kinds of people to use what ideas and in what interests. One of the beauties of Grice's 'conversational maxims' is that, through the concept of the implicature, they provide a model that can describe *degrees* of use, including incapacities, failures, or refusals to communicate, as a legitimate area of the realization of intention. As I shall now try to show, a strategic negative use of this kind is at the heart of one of the most important discourses at work in *Cymbeline* – Senecanism: a discourse, curiously, which has rarely been seen within Renaissance studies as political in any contemporary sense, even though it is one of the most dominant rhetorical registers in drama of the period. I take the fact that critics have not so far commented on its presence in *Cymbeline* – generally acknowledged to be a 'topical' play – to be in some sense a product of this misrecognition. It is a misrecognition which is strikingly echoed in *Cymbeline* itself.

Seneca had a two-fold presence in Renaissance intellectual traditions. Apart from Senecanism, and surprisingly distinct from it in terms of its explicit sense of topical relevance, the personality of Seneca himself figures controversially as the type either of a principled rejection of tyranny or of an ignominious complicity with it. My suggestion will be that one of the most important implications that Shakespeare makes through his use of Senecan material in *Cymbeline* concerns the meaning of the gap between the supposedly non-political theatrical Senecanism and this strand of overt political reflection as focused on a historical political figure. This can be seen as an implication about the very process of implication: a reflection on the conditions available to a dramatist for the construction of meaning through his profession.[10] Seneca was the acknowledged master of the Renaissance tragedian. Polonius – another master's 'agent' – testifies to his pre-eminence in tragedy and to that of Plautus in comedy, articulating it through an evocative generic opposition between the 'law of writ' and 'the liberty'.[11] Politicians can have good reason for policing the proximity of these two conditions for theatrical and social meaning with a barrier of antithesis. Claudius and Polonius treat the presence of the 'tragedians of the city' at the Danish court as an opportunity for what is an essentially *comic* entertainment. Claudius in particular is pleased to hear that Hamlet is preoccupied with drama:

> Good gentlemen, give him a further edge,
> And drive his purpose into these delights.[12]

But as *Hamlet* itself shows, the wall between the two genres was already being dismantled by dramatists working in a theatre increasingly preoccupied with combining these two complementary processes of recognition and exposure. And in *Cymbeline* – a product of the same historical momentum towards tragicomedy – the process is once again negotiated through Seneca and Senecanism.

II

Cymbeline develops broadly a basic and relatively abstract Senecan concern – the destructive effect of anger on nobility: the power vacuum of the king's domestic rage; Posthumus with his initial forbearance and subsequent irascibility; the surprising and dextrous coalescence of the 'comic subplot' of Cloten's bellicosity and Imogen's offhand flash of irritation with him.[13] But as even a brief description suggests, it develops this interest in a complexly symphonic way that should alert us to a process of signification that is striving to go way beyond a literary manner or a style. In the light of such counter-pointing, it is not surprising to find Seneca's own music emerging onto the textual surface. Nor should it be surprising to see at what point it does this. *Hercules furens* materializes within Shakespeare's text in the scene that results directly from that almost casual exchange between Imogen and Cloten – a masterly release of an implicit deep structure by the explicit randomness of the dramatic syntax it has been allowed to generate. There is a direct parallel between Imogen's recognition of the headless body as she wakes from her drugged sleep IV.ii at 291, and Hercules's recovery of his senses after the frenzied madness in which he has slain wife and children. I quote here both texts, giving the Seneca in its 1581 translation by Jasper Heywood[14] because there are specific textual echoes from that version:

> What place is this? What region? or of the world what coasts?
> Where am I? . . .
> What ayre draw we? o weary wight, what ground is underfet?
> Of truth, we are returned from hell. Whence in my house downe bet
> See I these bloudy bodyes? hath not my mynd of cast
> The infernall shapes? but after yet returned from hel at last
> Yet wander doth that hely heape before myne eys to see?
> I asham'de to graunt, I quake. I know not what to me,
> I cannot tell what greevous yll my mynde before doth know . . .
> What mischief do I see?

> Yes sir, to Milford Haven, which is the way?
> I thank you: by yond bush? pray how far thither?
> 'Ods pittikins: can it be six-mile yet?
> I have gone all night: faith I'll lie down and sleep.
> But soft! no bedfellow! O gods and godesses!
> These flowers are like the pleasures of the world;

This bloody man, the care on't. I hope I dream:
For so I thought I was a cave-keeper
And cook to honest creatures. But 'tis not so:
'Twas but a bolt of nothing, shot at nothing,
Which the brain makes of fumes. Our very eyes
Are sometimes like our judgements, blind. Good faith,
I tremble still with fear: but if there be
Yet left in heaven as small a drop of pity
As a wren's eye, fear'd gods, a part of it!
The dream's here still: even when I wake it is
Without me, as within me: not imagin'd, felt.
A headless man? The garments of Posthumus?

The similarities between the two speeches may seem allusive, but as my discussion continues I will suggest that the relationship between them is part of a process of systematic and accumulative semantic focusing, not just one of simple, local reference. It is a process marked by the difference between 'use' and 'mention' – 'mention' being the simple preoccupation of the kind of 'source studies' approach that has until recently dominated the study of Senecanism. I should point out briefly that Shakespeare's speech reproduces the sequence of perception followed by Seneca. First, there is a bleary-eyed reversion to the time before the crisis; second, a sighting of the bodies and the thought that these must be hung-over horrors; third, an admission of fear; finally, the recognition of the bodies. But in the course of this the nature of the parallel between the two changes. To begin with, Imogen, disguised as a man, is identified with Hercules – she is speaking his lines. But compared with Hercules, Imogen is an unlikely 'hero'; she enjoys (and makes use of) her disguise far less than comic predecessors like Rosalind or Viola, so a parallel with this great dramatic 'Worthy' adds professional irony. But it does more than that.

At the fourth stage in the sequence – the recognition of the bodies – 'Hercules' becomes an image within this speech as well as a glance at its source: the name is introduced. There is perhaps more humour here; Shakespearian text pays tribute to Senecan text. But in more significant dramatic terms, identification with Hercules is now with Posthumus, not Imogen:

A headless man? The garments of Posthumus?
I know the shape of's leg: this is his hand:
His foot Mercurial: his Martial thigh:
The brawn of Hercules: but his Jovial face –
Murder in Heaven! How –? 'tis gone. . .

Here, Shakespeare turned to an earlier episode in Seneca's play – Amphitryon's recognition of his son when he first returns to Thebes. As meaning intensifies around the merging of the two texts, details of shared language appear with increasing frequency:

Is this my sonne. . . ?
See I thy body true indeede, or els deceiv'de am I
Mockt with thy sprite? art thou the same? these brawnes of armes I know
And shoulders, and thy noble handes from body hie that grow.

I am not offering a gratuitous proliferation of parallel passages. This collage of reference helps Shakespeare to do several things – first, to develop a tragic potential in two conventional devices of romantic comedy: confusion of gender brought about by disguise, and the recognition scene; and second, to open up an escape-route from this potential. The peculiar, almost surreal narrative compression achieved by this transposition of materal – Hercules's recognition, in effect, of a body he himself has killed as himself returning from the land of the dead – is expressive of a significant circularity in Posthumus and Imogen's relationship, as well as of the release they find from it.

Imogen's identification of Posthumus in a series of mythological metaphors which re-enact the titanic ascent to Olympus is intended as a tribute to his own qualities as an 'earthly paragon'. But the climax of this series is 'Murder in Heaven', and a reference to the purpose of that ascent betrays an ambiguity. Is Posthumus victim, or murderer?

Shakespeare lets Seneca footnote Imogen's soliloquy about Posthumus's magnificence with the story of an insane wife-killer. Murder in Heaven is exactly what Hercules thinks he is doing while actually beheading Megara. Amphitryon records an event which has striking visual similarities with Shakespeare's:

And now likewise his heavy club is shaken towards his wife:
He broken hath the bones, her head from blocklyke body gone
Is quight, nor anywhere it stayes. Dar'ste thou this looke upon. . . ?

The implication that this body could be the wife rather than the husband is of course appropriate: the sleep from which Imogen is waking is a version of the death planned for her by Posthumus. IV.ii is thus counterpointed with II.ii, where Iachimo explores Imogen's sleeping body, as parallel images of the deconstructive complicity between sexual idealization and victimization, praise and power. This gentleman of the bedchamber's response to the apparent failure of his princess's chastity exposes his 'husband's' pride in it as a significant reversal of power relations. In a recent study of Renaissance Senecanism, Gordon Braden[15] has suggested that 'Imperial aggression and Stoic retreat are both informed by a drive to keep the self's boundaries under its own control.' Posthumus's investment in 'the self's boundaries' ('man and wife is one flesh', as Hamlet puts it)[16] is made obvious in the anger with which he seeks to destroy 'the woman's part in me'.[17]

Imogen's behaviour tends to been seen as an ideal and idealistic effort to preserve the integrity of that 'part', but I suggest, on the contrary, that her praise of Posthumus undoes herself as unwittingly it does him.

When Amphitryon recognizes Hercules, he sees him first as a whole being, and then as the sum of his parts – the proof of his haecceity. Imogen thinks she is making a similar identification, but starts from a false sense of wholeness, one derived from externals: 'the garments of Posthumus?' She too then proceeds to a naming of parts, but our sense of that process *as* naming registers self-fashioning rather than otherness – as her false identification of the body then confirms. She works up the body towards the head and reinforces this movement with a climactic progression of classical powers. A predatory imperialism similar to Posthumus's shows itself, as with Iachimo, in an act of rape, its falseness by the fact that language stands in for the real thing. Imogen's exploration of this corpse is a blason – the literary representation of a man making love to a woman. Its characteristic mode of approach is metonymic deconstitution, a form of dissection which reveals its affinity to murder particularly when seen bizarrely from the Senecan perspective of mutilation. So here again there is a sense in which this body is that of a woman, and again it is the object of victimization by a man. We appear to be a long way from the unifying and affirming recognitions of romance. This 'gaze' is a process of self-mirroring: a way of seeing which is narcissistically contained within narratives of the self. Describing Medea's challenge to Jason after killing her own children, Gordon Braden refers to 'a very Senecan kind of recognition scene: the victim's acknowledgement of his conqueror'.[18] Shakespeare presents an even more complexly deconstructive analysis of the bias towards power rather than solidarity in the process of visual address. Braden continues: 'Medea needs to be seen; her triumphant selfhood must be confirmed in the sight of her victim.' Imogen also needs to be seen. Bathing herself in blood and throwing herself on the dead body, she presents a dramatic emblem of the roles in which she is so deeply implicated.

Critics have not recognized the Senecan element in what is generally agreed to be a nasty episode. Most have judged it simply a miscalculation. In fact, it marks with parodically Senecan hyperbole the emergence of this subliminal text onto the surface of the drama. It is impossible not to admire the rhetorical control with which this is achieved: the disruptive impact of hyperbole is contained by the behavioural limits of domestic tragedy, while also deepening their scope. Throughout it, we become aware of the acts of violence of which husband and wife are mutually guilty. Imogen has presented to Posthumus a face of pale cheeks coloured with blood before, and on that occasion too agency was problematic, as Posthumus himself testifies:

Me of my lawful pleasure she restrain'd
And prayed me oft forbearance: did it with
A pudency so rosy, the sweet view on't
Might well have warm'd old Saturn; that I thought her
As chaste as unsunned snow.

(II.iv.161)

The embrace that ends the headless body episode in IV.ii is thus a curiously appropriate climax in their relationship. I.iv, the scene after Posthumus's departure, has already shown to what extent a logocentric moral rhetoric formed the basis of exchange between them. It tells us about a non-event – 'I did not take my leave of him' – as well as what would have happened if she had:

. . .but had
Most pretty things to say: ere I could tell him
How I would think on him at certain hours
Such thoughts, and such . . . or have charg'd him
At the sixth hour of the morn, at noon, at midnight,
T'encounter me with orisons, for then
I am in heaven for him.

(I.iv.25)

Clearly, the location of identity in the *head* is a structural misrecognition in this relationship: its false transcendence is exposed by the fact that the body has never been so important as when the head is missing. Posthumus's description of his wife in II.iv moves from her chaste verbal relationship with himself – where the idealized body colours red and white are realized as moral attributes located on the face – to a silent but physical one with Iachimo. Even here her body is conspicuously absent. Posthumus repeats Imogen's word 'encounter', but he has a different meaning for it, and it is one they both systematically resist:

> perchance he spoke not, but
> Like a full-acorned boar, a German one,
> Cried 'O!' and mounted; found no opposition
> But what he look'd for should oppose and she
> Should from encounter guard. Could I find out
> The woman's part in me.
>
> (II.iv.167)

In the evasiveness of his language Imogen is the absent object of an action, not a subject – just as she has not been a subject in the action of his 'lawful pleasure' earlier in the speech. This missing woman is something they both need to find. She lingers in the background of IV.ii – a silenced, dispossessed textual ghost. It is worth remembering what Seneca's Megara is doing when Hercules kills her: she is trying to embrace him. By contrast, Posthumus and Imogen are locked in the false reciprocity of a reductively linguistic relation which identifies itself as a heroics of masculinity: a competitive, mutually destructive imperialism. This version of what Cloten calls the 'self-figur'd knot' [19] of marriage transforms the bond of mutuality into a destructive double-bind. But in doing so it releases both the 'self' and its potential for mutuality into a process of social redefinition. That process is the subject of the next part of my discussion.

III

A comparison of the organization of agency in these two stories shows how Seneca helps Shakespeare to plot these meanings – to develop the problems they pose, as well as a solution for them.

Hercules kills Megara, but the act is involuntary, performed while imagining himself to be doing something else. This is in itself a challenge to the concept of heroic individualism: the will is the source of agency, but cause and effect are helplessly severed. Shakespeare takes the challenge further, cutting adrift the fundamental connection between will and causation. He presents an action which is complex, extended – a sequence of involved participation. Unlike Hercules, Posthumus intends to kill, but he fails because he needs the services of an intermediary, and because that intermediary sees himself *not* in fact as 'the agent for his master' but as an agent in his own right:

PISANIO: If it be so to do good service, never
Let me be counted serviceable.

(III.ii.14)

– and, as an agent, motivated by shared rather than individualist terms of moral reference:

How look I
That I should seem to lack humanity
So much as this fact comes to?

Notice here that Pisanio's understanding of those terms are expressed in a compression of self as subject of an action and of self as object of a gaze. This sensitization of the basic theatrical resource of acts of seeing will become increasingly important in the discussion that follows.

The challenge to the notion of direct agency does not show something simply failing to happen: as we have seen, Posthumus's actions towards Imogen do take effect. She does 'die'. But the figurative nature of this death means that it can happen again. Posthumus's initial action against Imogen, a voluntary, unsuccessful counterpart to Hercules's involuntary, successful attack on Megara, is re-enacted in V.v, when he attacks her again, this time, like Hercules, unknowingly. This second attack is a contracted, cartoon version of that earlier complex action. It is an example of what John Lyons calls the 'paradigm instance' of the notion of agency – 'physical manipulation'.[20] In a momentary flash, the Hercules story comes strikingly to the surface of the action. At last, Posthumus makes real physical contact with Imogen. But the play stresses the fact that this is a moment of shared rather than individual action: the revelation brought about by the blow to Imogen is as striking for others as it is for her:

POSTHUMUS: How comes these staggers on me? . . .
CYMBELINE: . . . the gods do mean to strike me
To death with mortal joy.

(233)

These reverberations of the actual blow extend the disruption of conventional agency roles: the role of patient – the object of the action – is shared by Imogen with the agent, Posthumus. Even more remarkably, the whole event is shared with the audience. Seneca's play evades the spectacle of Hercules's attack on Megara – and draws attention to the fact that it is doing so: 'Dar'ste thou this looke upon?' says Amphitryon, exploiting the political alienation of Senecan drama's intimacy with the page. In a play consistently cynical about the narcissisms of reading and writing, Shakespeare shows what Seneca will only tell.

Posthumus's blow is replayed and converted into the embrace that follows it. This is a double climax of extreme subtlety. The conversion of competitive violence into the partnership of embrace is a process which characterizes the wider action of the play, one which offers a demonstration of the force of theatrical work. In the course of a preoccupation with images of fighting, the play uses a transition from telling to showing to move from verbal power play towards collective physical action. Cloten's scenes of reported combat and gaming, Posthumus and Iachimo's verbal duels, the princes' daily routine of offstage hunting give way to the real thing. Cloten finally succeeds in picking a fight, and loses his head. Iachimo and Posthumus fight in silent earnest. Belarius and the princes make the 'stand' that changes the course of the battle. Underlying this transition is one from oppositional meanings to collaborative ones. The British victory is not so much the conquest of Rome as the unlikely cohesion of the British army. The replacement of the image of Posthumus striking his wife with one of them embracing encapsulates and restates this change, rather as musical material is restated in a coda. The 'self-figur'd knot' of this embrace, like that of the intertextuality through which Shakespeare brings it about, provides a release from the stalemate of personal agency examined in IV.ii:

IMOGEN: Why did you throw your wedded lady from you?
Think that you are upon a rock, and now
Throw me again.
POSTHUMUS: Hang there like fruit, my soul,
Till the tree die.
(261)

Imogen invites Posthumus to provide the final permutation of the elements of the Hercules story: an attack which is voluntary, successful, and performed at the bidding of its victim. Posthumus accepts the invitation, but transforms its generic momentum from tragedy to comedy. They complete Megara's embrace, as well as the recognition she had hoped to precipitate by it:

MEGARA: Husband spare us, I beseech thee nowe,
And knowe thy Megara.

But there is an important difference between the Senecan and the Shakespearian forms of the knowledge associated with dramatic anagnorisis. The latter is a knowledge not possessed or controlled by any single character; in *Cymbeline* it is one that constructs itself collaboratively through the *coup-de-théâtre* of V.v, not even making itself fully present at that final point, as Cymbeline himself acknowledges:

> When shall I hear all through? This fierce abridgement
> Hath to it circumstantial branches, which
> Distinction should be rich in. . .
> . . .But nor the time nor place
> Will serve our long inter'gatories.
>
> (383)

J. M. Nosworthy is circumspect about the precise force of 'fierce' here, observing that 'The meanings attached to this word by Shakespeare in his final period are not always easy to define.' It is in fact a word more frequently used by Shakespeare at an earlier stage in his career, and generally has at least primary connotations of combative violence. We have seen what the purpose of combat is in *Cymbeline*. The king is right. The time and place offered by theatre of this kind does not 'serve': it masters.

IV

The forcefulness of theatre is perhaps one of the most important recognitions on offer in V.v. Taking in the auditorium as well as the stage, Cymbeline himself offers a complex reformulation of the theatrical gaze which develops the deconstruction of subject and object I noted earlier in Pisanio at III.ii.15:

> See,
> Posthumus anchors upon Imogen;
> And she (like harmless lightning) throws her eye
> On him: her brothers, me: her master hitting
> Each object with a joy: the counterchange
> Is severally in all.
>
> (393)

Notice the violence of this spectatorship. The predatory but passive subject/object gazes of the earlier part of the play give way to physically positive, collective acts of seeing. But notice too how Cymbeline himself interprets this:

> Let's quit this ground,
> And smoke the temple with our sacrifices.
>
> (398)

He attributes what has happened to the agency of a transcendental power. But there is little to encourage us to endorse such an attribution. In fact I would suggest that the king, far from being in possession of a definitive reading of the action, is as unequivocally 'stranded' by the conclusion of the play as is Prospero at the end of *The Tempest*. In this respect the structure of *Cymbeline* subverts another significant romance convention – the framing device of earlier romantic comedies, used also in non-Shakespearian texts like *Gawaine and the Green Knight* (another decapitation story concerned with the British revival of Roman imperium). This is a technique by which a main plot has its action 'read' by characters who appear to be only observing but are in fact in some way controlling its terms of reference (and who are generally figures of political authority). Shakespeare's Elizabethan comedies tested but ultimately endorsed that framework of interpretation. By the end of his career he appears to question it more conclusively.

This challenge to transcendence is nowhere clearer than in the apparently masque-like elements of the theophany. Most critics concerned with the topicality of *Cymbeline* are prepared to see Jupiter in his analogy to James I – as a quasi-monarchical source of transcendent power. If this is the case, then one can only say he is not doing a very good job. Frequently invoked, he is conspicuous by his absence in the earlier stages of the play, and when he comes, it is not of his own accord. A series of namings finally focuses itself into the collective summons of the Leonati at V.iv. I suggest that it is this group – not Jupiter – that constitutes the most important source of agency in the play. Their importance is underlined by the fact that, like Pisanio, their understanding of their position is reinforced by the concept of accountability:

> Help, Jupiter, or we appeal
> and from the justice fly.
>
> (91)

This dislocates the deity as a source of agency precisely at the point at which it would seem to be manifesting itself. Jupiter asserts a control which retrospectively anticipates the Leonati's demands, but not before they have made them. The overriding effect of this exchange is exactly that – of an exchange, and one initiated by the subordinate element. Contrary to New Historicist orthodoxies about theatricality at the service of power, it is hard to avoid the conclusion that this play puts Jupiter on stage *in order* to undermine his authority.

In the Leonati the subliminal presence of *Hercules furens* finds an objective correlative of a suitably Senecan variety: the ghost – but now transformed from the avenging individual (in real terms powerless to produce results, as with the ghost in *Hamlet*) into a group, collectively negotiating its rights through the machinery of law. From this perspective there is an interesting point of contact between the kind of 'law' which articulates the implicit sovereignty of 'the people' and that which negotiates the status of the canonical text.[21] Like the Senecan text, these ghosts emerge from the depths to impose their meaning on the story. Partly actors, partly spectators, the Leonati extend the play's use of the relationship between company and audience to subvert the semiotics of Jonsonian masque. As either, they have a history that qualifies them to intervene rather than acquiesce in the proceedings. In Jonsonian masque the source of power is always located outside the action in a conflation of poet and monarch: a transcendent individualism which never loses overall control. There is sometimes a performative extension of this individualism within the action in the form of the part taken by one of the king's sons or an important courtier, but while this may serve as a device to educate the monarch – the function of Jonson's entertainments as court critique has been made clear in Martin Butler's work – it has little effect on his status: it is if anything an enhancement of the metaphysical terms upon which it is constructed. Shakespeare pays nominal tribute to a transcendent source of authority, but the generative initiative of his action is all with the onstage group. Jonson's aim was to release that authority (in its authorial as well as its political persona) from any real accountability to history by turning it into myth. His observations about poetry's ability to bring so many queens together on stage in *The Masque of Queens* illustrates the effect such power was supposed to have on the structure of time: he typically subordinates its historical necessity to the transcendent 'moment' of the king's presence. But in *Cymbeline* an internal history resubjects present time to its dependence on past and future, and is seen to be both anterior and posterior to the authority it summons. In other words, the play renders active intellectual relativisms of history according to which even the nature of a particular government could turn out to be contingent rather than essential.

Arguably, this is a challenge which finds a material form in the mechanical structures of theatrical performances.[22] The Senecan 'deep structure' to which I referred at the beginning of part II realizes itself in the rearstage trap which could open to allow figures like the Leonati to emerge upwards from beneath the stage. The contrast between this and Jupiter's emergence downwards through the trap in 'the heavens' relates to a contrast between rock and sky that develops around the

British princes and the Milford Haven location, where 'rock' has associations with the political strength of the British people. The most assertive representation of the sky as a location of transcendence comes from Belarius, who suppresses knowledge of his own essentially material challenge to a king's power – depriving him of his sons. But even with them, Belarius's mystification does not count for much. For Guiderius and Arviragus, the sky is simply an inhospitable space above their heads, and they actively seek to replace it with one with which they can have a more direct contact – like that of the enclosed Blackfriars theatre, perhaps:

> their thoughts do hit
> The roofs of palaces.
>
> (III.iii.83)

Cymbeline's transcendental reading of the power of Imogen and Posthumus's reunion is equally an abuse – more seriously, though, it is an abuse of the future it could create, rather than just of the past from which it has derived. His response to their actions is a deferral of the release they bring about. He simply puts back in place the conditions that began the war in the first place, setting the scene for a repetition of events at another remove – during Guiderius's reign, perhaps. Like Prospero, Cymbeline ends by displacing the power that has come into focus around him; but then, it is not really *his* power. His effective absence from the body of the play of which he is titular head is not changed by the last scene. He has 'met the time' [23] *not* because it sought him, but because people did: the attacking Romans, the rescuing Britons. As Posthumus makes clear to the Lord of V.iii, there is nothing transcendent about that:

> Nay, do not wonder at it: you are made
> Rather to wonder at the things you hear
> Than to work any.
>
> (53)

But that is exactly what Cymbeline does. Pardon's the word to all,[24] but thanks are given to the gods. This particular mystification would be a familiar one to a Jacobean audience which, if excluded from the privileged attendance of court masques, could nevertheless wonder at the commemorative texts so carefully issued by Jonson. That such a mystification could be seen as playing with the very fire it was trying to suppress can be seen in the overlap between the rhetorics of privilege and of decapitation. James's famous speech to Parliament in 1603 echoed not only the instabilities of agency and gender that Shakespeare develops in *Cymbeline*, but also the dangers he allows them to precipitate. James referred to Britain as his wife: 'I am the head, and it is my body.' When the body takes upon itself to reorder the orientation of privilege implicit in this metaphor, there is a potential for violence which is far from transcendental.

V

It is one of the great ironies of the humanist intellectualism that gave such status to the Stoic tradition that a wisdom born out of the trauma of political alienation came to be seen as the preparation *par excellence* for Renaissance government. The social roles this wisdom helped to articulate were figured in terms of the same transcendence of history that I have referred to as a feature of the realization of power in the masque. And as with the masque, that transcendence found material form in the book, with its artificial insulation from the society into which it is placed and its seemingly direct relationship with an authorial voice. In 'A Defence of Seneca and Plutarch', Michel Montaigne[25] associates this authorial concept of identity specifically with Seneca. Responding to a challenge to the philosopher's moral nature offered by his compromising intimacy with Nero, he wrote: 'His vertue appeareth so lively, and wisedom so vigorous in his writings . . . that I beleeve no witnesse to the contrary.' This canonization of writer as book looks forward to the personal status aimed at by Jonson, for whom the function of such transcendence was quite definitely to appropriate for the writer the exercise of power, not to detach him from it: he speaks of the poet as 'a master of manners' who 'can alone, or with a few, effect the business of mankind'.[26] Of course, such positions are conservative ones, aimed at mystifying agency *as* power, and thereby effecting what is in social terms a dematerialization of the structures of exchange from which and within which competing positions can be articulated. The relationship between the publication of plays as texts and the development of professional theatre is a complex one, and cannot be schematized simply as either positive or negative with regard to its autonomy as a social institution. But it can be said that, at a certain level of ideological practice, plays that aspire to the condition of book conspire in such a dematerialization, and of course Jonson can be cited as the prime example of a dramatist who more or less consciously identified himself with such interests in his withdrawal from a full collaboration in the professional practices of the public theatre and consequent movement towards an increasingly patronized status as an essentially publishing writer. Conversely, Shakespeare can be cited as the obvious case of a dramatist whose career developed in an almost directly opposite way, choosing to base his identity as a dramatist on an increasingly powerful economic role within his own company at the expense of a clearly defined momentum towards publication. The importance of the fact that Shakespeare wrote himself into contracts of ownership rather than into print as an author should not be underestimated, but invariably has been. Indeed it is disappointing that even Marxist critics like Terry Eagleton have chosen to see such developments retrospectively as a contemptible rapprochement with the bourgeoisie[27] rather than historically as a significant change in the forces of production: the establishment, through a particular form of labour, of the terms upon which space can legitimately be occupied by someone other than a traditional authority, and its ideological 'content' as a consequence redefined. What I have been looking at in this essay is how the basic resources of Elizabethan/Jacobean drama give material form to such a redefinition. In the theatre the basic resource for the production of meaning is at the simplest level the theatrical space itself, and this is quite clearly something that is being defined by this play. But the process of production constitutes itself also in negotiations between discourses, like Senecanism, which *theorize* contesting forms of control in terms that themselves become part of the production. Officially and ideologically under direct court patronage, but financially and materially independent to a remarkable extent, Shakespeare was in an unprecedented position to use theatre to make present within the discourses of his culture relations between political and professional mastery which he was himself helping to unsettle. The figure of Seneca himself, like Shakespeare a 'king's man', seems to focus such a presence in *Cymbeline*: like Megara and Hercules, it certainly haunts the political unconscious of the play. For even as the Senecan text of *Hercules furens* facilitates the overt passage towards the 'harmony' of the *pax romana*, its own historical identity points beyond that to the inevitable crisis of the absolutist ego. The collapse of imperialism under Nero expressed itself in a theatricalism of court power whose aesthetics constituted a grotesque proleptic parody of court masque. Suetonius records how Nero gave new meaning to the phrase 'a captive audience';[28] the political ironies of compulsory entertainment take on the characteristically Jacobean form of masque in *The Tempest*. Like that play, *Cymbeline* appears concerned to retrieve the initiative for the institution within which its producer made his living.

As New Historicism demonstrates, the academic profession still has an enormous investment in resisting the notion that Shakespeare's status as a dramatist could be related to any kind of historically specific personal autonomy. It seems to me crucial, however, that we should be prepared to define his theatrical productions as a significant independence of agency within a culture in which political and professional practices were becoming increasingly closely allied. At a minimal level, it would hardly have been in his dramatist's interests to allow the developing pragmatics of theatrical communication to become subsumed within those of a 'dominant' ideology.[29] From that point of view, those pragmatics are in themselves precisely what a professional like Shakespeare was engaged in producing. Grice's theory of implicatures suggests that the construction of meaning is a process which operates essentially as a contest for mastery of the principles by which meaning is made. According to this view, such a subsumption would constitute an effectively *unthinkable* withdrawal from those essential conditions. And it is indeed mastery that we have seen Shakespeare negotiating in the course of this play. Like Pisanio's relationship with Posthumus, his use of Seneca's *Hercules furens* in *Cymbeline* makes service to one kind of master the terms for liberty within the law of another.

My suggestion has been, then, that the Senecan discourse of this late play effects a deployment of historical and cultural implications that places this drama within the scope of the libertarian practices of the early seventeenth century. If this is the case, we have no alternative but to resist Stephen Greenblatt's assessment of Shakespeare as the 'dutiful servant'[30] of his culture's orthodoxies as itself essentially a resource in New Historicism's own contest for control of the academic space.

NOTES

1 Emrys Jones, 'Stuart *Cymbeline*', *Essays in Criticism* 11 (1961), 84–99; Leonard Tennenhouse, *Power on Display: The Politics of Shakespeare's Genres* (New York: Methuen, 1986).

2 Jones, 'Stuart *Cymbeline*', 90.

3 William Shakespeare, *Cymbeline*, ed. J. M. Nosworthy, New Arden edn (London: Methuen, 1955), I.iv.28–30 n. All subsequent references to *Cymbeline* are taken from this edition.

4 Leah Marcus, '*Cymbeline* and the unease of topicality', in Heather Dubrow and Richard Strier (eds), *The Historical Renaissance: New Essays on Tudor and Stuart Literature and Culture* (Chicago: Chicago University Press, 1988), 147.

5 William Shakespeare, *The Tempest*, ed. Frank Kermode, New Arden edn (London: Methuen, 1954; reprinted with corrections, 1970), II.i.74 n.

6 Significantly, Kermode's comment anticipated an explosion of interest in the presence of *Aeneid* material within *The Tempest*. At the time of writing, *Cymbeline* was being re-edited for the Cambridge and Penguin editions by Martin Butler, whose research into Stuart masque has in its method as well as in its content helped to establish new British approaches to intentionality in Renaissance texts, and by John Pitcher, who himself contributed to the *Aeneid* debate in his essay 'A theatre of the future: the *Aeneid* and the *The Tempest*', *Essays in Criticism* 34 (1984), 193–215. In a recent edition of *The Tempest* (Oxford and New York: Oxford University Press, 1987), Stephen Orgel, the heir to Kermode's mantle of authority over that play, brought that debate together with a survey of this and other recent work. The re-editing of *Cymbeline* may well stand in a similar relation to a similar modification of understanding – and, obviously, the present essay hopes itself to be a contribution to that. But this (in the fullest material sense of the word) *productive* relationship between editing and criticism is worth drawing attention to, because it is an important professional analogue to the process of implication with which I shall be concerned in this essay: a way of working with knowledge which is 'in process' rather than fully present to those seeking to use it. I stress this because an understanding of academic work as pragmatically structured in the same way as the object of its study – in distinction to the curiously omniscient posture of New Historicism – should be understood as a subtext of this essay.

7 Robert Y. Turner uses this phrase to describe the relations between Cymbeline's Britain and Rome in 'Slander in *Cymbeline* and other Jacobean tragicomedies', *English Literary Renaissance* XIII (1983), 182–202.

8 See 'Meaning and understanding in the history of ideas', in *History and Theory* 8 (1969), 3–53, reprinted in James Tully (ed.), *Meaning and Context: Quentin Skinner and his Critics* (Cambridge: Polity Press, 1988), 35.

9 See H. P. Grice, 'Logic and conversation', in P. Cole and J. Morgan (eds), *Syntax and Semantics III: Speech Acts* (New York: Academic Press, 1975).

10 John Pitcher's article (see note 6 above) is suggestive about the way the *Aeneid* – its status as a text, its metaphorical resources – helped Shakespeare consolidate his empowerment as a dramatist by the theatrical apparatus.

11 William Shakespeare, *Hamlet*, ed. Harold Jenkins, New Arden edn (London: Methuen, 1982), II.ii.397.

12 III.i.26. Hamlet and Polonius are not the only people in the play who expose the relationship between contemporary literary theory and political practices. Claudius's concern to divert Hamlet's attention from the situation at court might suggest that he is using the particular notion of 'delight' which Sidney associates with romantic comedy – a theatrical response which shuns the contemplation of deformed realities like those beneath the surface of life at Elsinore. See Sir Philip Sidney, *An Apology for Poetry*, ed. Geoffrey Shepherd (Manchester: Manchester University Press, 1973), 136.

13 II.iii.85–135.

14 *Hercules furens*, trans. Jasper Heywood, from *Seneca: his Tenne Tragedies* (1581).

15 Gordon Braden, *Renaissance Tragedy and the Senecan Tradition* (New Haven: Yale University Press, 1985), 23.

16 *Hamlet*, IV.iii.51.
17 II.iii.118.
18 Braden, *Renaissance Tragedy*, 60.
19 II.iii.118.
20 John Lyons, *Semantics* (Cambridge: Cambridge University Press, 1977), 483.
21 For a discussion of points of contact between canon formation and republican traditions of thought in this period, see David Norbrook's introduction to his forthcoming anthology of Renaissance verse for Penguin. It is a form of contact which suggests that the concept of the canon, itself a product of this period of literary history, cannot be seen as in any essential way conservative, as is often assumed, but rather in more general pragmatic terms as an ideological resource for those seeking a position from which to consolidate selected areas of meaning.
22 The use of the theatrical apparatus itself to materialize ideological meanings in this way, particularly those that are in a critical state of contestation, is a phenomenon worthy of consideration by the culture that could produce *Star Wars*, and experience as meaningful the conversion of the concept of cinematic special effects into defence policy – and the fact that the special effects *came first*.
23 IV.iii.33.
24 V.v.423.
25 Michael Montaigne, *Essays*, 3 vols (London: Dent, 1965).
26 Ben Jonson, 'Epistle to . . . the Two Famous Universities', in *Three Comedies*, ed. Michael Jamieson (Harmondsworth: Penguin, 1966), 41–5.
27 See Terry Eagleton, *William Shakespeare*, Rereading Literature series (Oxford: Blackwell, 1986), 96.
28 Suetonius, *Nero*, 213–22, quoted in Braden, *Renaissance Tragedy*, 9.
29 Postructuralist criticism has made quite obsessive use of the basic structuralist premiss that our capacity to make meaning is contained and determined by a pre-existing linguistic system. As with most applications of linguistic theory to literary studies, it has limited this insight to an abstract rather than a pragmatic concept of language. It seems to me that it would be productive to extend it in such a direction, since this would result in a far more socially and historically inflected notion of linguistic performance and call attention to precisely the kind of contests to which I am referring here. The model of language as a determining, containing 'system' of meaning underpins the whole post-Althusser an approach to ideology. If you dispense with the notion that the contest for meaning is the unequal struggle of language user against language, in favour of one of language user against language user, you can begin to do justice to the historical fact that unequal struggles have in fact been demonstrably fought and won. Particularly in the period in question, the adaptation of principles of negotiation to the interests of an increasingly complex social structure was a process which ensured that a 'court' ideology could never establish itself *as* 'dominant'.
30 Stephen Greenblatt, *Renaissance Self-Fashioning: From More to Shakespeare* (Chicago: Chicago University Press, 1980), 253.

4

TOPICALITY OR POLITICS? *THE TWO NOBLE KINSMEN*, 1613–34

Lois Potter

The Two Noble Kinsmen is a play with an almost embarrassingly long literary past, balanced by a theatrical afterlife which is short even by comparison with Shakespeare's other Fletcherian collaboration, *Henry VIII*. We think of it as a dramatization of Chaucer's *Knight's Tale*, and the prologue invites us to admire it for his sake, but in fact everyone who tells the tale attributes it to someone else. It can be traced, in some form or other, as far back as the earliest Greek legends of Thebes. Antiquity seems to be one of its claims to attention in the first edition of 1634. Not only does the prologue refer to 'Chaucer, of all admired', it also calls Shakespeare and Fletcher (the latter less than ten years dead) 'the Memorable Worthies of their Time'. Despite this pedigree, the play effectively disappears from theatrical history after its revival, heavily adapted by Davenant, in the early years of the Restoration. Subsequent revivals, where they occur, get so little critical attention as to make its stage history almost completely obscure. One reason, I think, is its doubly double focus of attention: two heroes, two authors. Its title, by contrast with that of *Henry VIII*, indicates that there will be no part to serve as a vehicle for a star actor; its dual authorship means that readers can adopt a more critical view than they would allow themselves with a play attributed to Shakespeare alone.

The politics of both theatre and criticism are thus bound up with the history of *The Two Noble Kinsmen*. I shall return to them at the end of this essay, but first it seems important to consider whether the play can be described as inherently political. Normally a story about the love of two men for one woman, when it has no larger dynastic implications, is seen as comic. This play is tragicomic, not in the sense of Shakespeare's late romances, but because its ending is tragic for one hero, comic for the other. Indeed, to call the ending comic at all is possible only if one accepts that marriage is always by definition a happy ending. Arcite's death comes just in time to save Palamon from death, because Theseus has insisted that the conflict shall be all or nothing: the loser and all his friends are to die on the block. In Chaucer's version of the story, Mars and Venus are overridden by the more powerful and sinister figure of Saturn, who provides the solution to the plot by sending the monster which frightens Arcite's horse so that he is killed in the moment of his triumph. But the playwrights omit Saturn and apparently go back to Boccaccio's *Teseida*, where Mars is responsible for Arcite's victory and Venus for Palamon's final triumph. Thus, the gods are left equally balanced, both having fulfilled the letter though not the spirit of their promises. Theseus has to acknowledge that 'the gods have been most equal', but he also recognizes that their decisions do not bear examination:

Let us be thankful
For that which is, and with you leave dispute
That are above our question.

(V.vi.134–6)

This main plot is set against another story, which seems to be original. The Jailer's Daughter helps Palamon to escape from prison because she is in love with him, goes mad in the woods out of frustration, and is finally 'cured', if that is the word, by a doctor who makes her think that her long-suffering suitor, a man of her own class, is Palamon. Her story is kept so completely separate from the rest of the play that Richard Proudfoot has suggested it may be a later addition.[1]

A story which on one level is trivial, yet which is taken immensely seriously by all its characters and expressed in language of tremendous – almost portentous – solemnity, naturally makes one wonder whether it 'means' more than it says. The search for a political meaning is often a last resort when a work seems not to make aesthetic sense. Often, however, finding topical meanings in a Renaissance play is taken to be the same thing as establishing a political meaning. This is obviously too simple: recognizing the resemblance of a fiction to reality is not in itself going to affect one's attitude to that reality. Since we have reasonably good evidence about the dates of some early performances of *The Two Noble Kinsmen* up to its first publication in 1634, I propose to look at some of the ways in which it might have seemed topical at these various dates, and then to consider whether they can be made to add up to a genuinely political statement.

The time-lag between the play's first performance (*c.* 1613) and its publication means that its political meaning was initially controlled by the company which produced it. The approximate period of the play's premiere can be deduced to have been some time after 20 February 1613, that being the date of Beaumont's *Masque of the Inner Temple* from which it apparently borrows its morris dance interlude, and some time before the first performance of *Bartholomew Fair* (October 1614), in which Jonson seems to comment rather sarcastically on the story. A well-known and widely accepted view of the play's first occasion is that, as Richard Proudfoot, Muriel Bradbrook, and Glynne Wickham have suggested, it was a response to the death of Prince Henry in November 1612 and the marriage of his sister Elizabeth to Frederick the Elector Palatine in February 1613.[2] On Wickham's theory, the play would have been taken as an allegory of Elizabeth's reluctance to leave her brother even for the man she loves, and the resolution of her problem by death. Elizabeth is Emilia, Henry is Arcite, and the Palsgrave is Palamon; young Prince Charles has no part in the story according to Wickham, but it would be possible to argue that, whereas the Palsgrave replaces Henry as the object of Elizabeth's love, Prince Charles replaces him in his political role. On this account, then, the play would have had a basically consoling purpose.

Proudfoot and others suggest that *The Two Noble Kinsmen* may have been put together hastily, after the Globe fire of June 1613, either for the Blackfriars season that autumn or for the opening of the new Globe in 1614. Perhaps some of the discontinuities in the play are the result of revisions necessitated by the company's reduced circumstances. The scene in which the combatants are described by Pirithous and an anonymous messenger is one which Gary Taylor thinks shows evidence of revision.[3] It might have replaced a more elaborate pageant-like entry, like those of the knights in *Pericles*, whose shields are described by Thaisa. The final trial by combat is also replaced by description: we experience it, with Emilia, only through offstage shouts. It is true, of course, that other Jacobean plays, like *Bussy d'Ambois*, *Cymbeline*, and *The Winter's Tale*, show a tendency to classicizing and refinement in the replacement of action by messenger scenes; it can also be argued that Emilia's presence alone onstage heightens her role and emphasizes the suspense of the scene. But why bother to reduce Chaucer's enormous tournament to a fight between the two heroes with three friends each, if not to enable it to be performed? *The White Devil* had already displayed fighting at the barriers, and *The Devil's Law-Case* would later include an elaborate trial by combat for several duellists. It is at least arguable that the play, originally envisaged as a spectacular feast for the eyes, was revised, whether before its first performance or in later revivals, into a more small-scale, psychological drama.

Several features of *The Two Noble Kinsmen* might have offered its first audiences visual reminders of the elaborate celebrations for the royal wedding. The most obvious would have been the morris dance, probably using the same costumes and characters as Beaumont's highly successful masque. *The Lord's Masque*, which Campion wrote for the same occasion, includes a woodland setting with a thicket out of which a wild man comes (like Palamon in Act III of *The Two Noble Kinsmen*) and, more interestingly, a final scene in which statues of the bridegroom and bride are seen on either side of a silver obelisk. The obelisk stands for fame, Campion's notes explain, and in Ripa's *Iconologia* an obelisk or pyramid (the two terms were interchangeable) symbolizes 'the glory of princes'.[4] As Theseus describes his projected tournament (III.vi.292–4), its central feature is to be a 'pyramid', but he also refers to it as a 'pillar' and it would make a lot more sense to pin one's opponent against an obelisk than to try and flatten him against a pyramid. It is possible, then, that there may have been some intention of reusing the obelisk from the masque in this final scene.

The fact that 'funerals' and 'nuptials' could be made to rhyme led a number of writers to greet the wedding of Elizabeth and Frederick with reminders of the sorrow that they had just passed through and of the importance of submitting to the will of fate.[5] Thomas Heywood's *A Marriage Triumphe Solemnized in an Epithalamium* (1613) not only links the funeral with the marriage but also recalls that the princess herself has replaced, in her name, the much-lamented Queen Elizabeth.[6] Rather interestingly, he also introduces widowed queens into his poem, complimenting the Palsgrave for defending them against 'the triple-headed *Gerion*'. This idea is borrowed from Spenser, who had already depicted Belgia as a widow in Book V of *The Faerie Queene*. The widowed queen is of course a common symbol for a country without a ruler.

We know of a couple of possible revivals between that first performance and the play's first printing in 1634. There is some evidence – a fragment of a note – that it may have been given a court performance in 1619 or 1620. If this did happen, the three widowed queens might have turned out to be its most important feature. In 1619, Frederick's acceptance of the crown of Bohemia had precipitated the Thirty Years War. His wife pleaded with her father and brother for help, and on 27 May 1620 a letter to the same effect arrived from the Protestant princes of Germany. Prince Charles took part in a special tilt on 20 June 1620, partly to display his skill and partly to lead the recruiting campaign which started almost immediately after the receipt of the message from Germany. To recall the circumstances of Elizabeth's wedding at this time would have been to invoke the warlike sentiments for which Prince Henry had been so much admired and the popular support for the war. By comparison both with Chaucer and with Lydgate's *Siege of Thebes*, which is a sort of *Knight's Tale, Part One*, the authors of *The Two Noble Kinsmen* seem positively in favour of the purifying effect of Mars, who, as Arcite puts it, rids the world of the pleurisy of people. Other topical possibilities may also be noted. The death of Queen Anne in 1619 would provide another example of royal grief to be transcended. The depiction of ideal friendship in Theseus and Pirithous would have been particularly appropriate to the role which Buckingham had assumed by 1619 in his relations with both James I and the Prince of Wales. Whereas Palamon and Arcite fight for a ruler they despise and a country they see as corrupt, Theseus and Pirithous are associated throughout, despite all the legends to the contrary, with pure friendship and just causes. Moreover, Theseus, in his ability to maintain a perfect balance between married love and ideal friendship, might be taken as James's ideal self-image.

The stage directions of the printed text include the names of two actors who are known to have 'overlapped' in the King's Men only in 1625–6, so there seems some evidence that the play had a revival at that time.[7] The play would have been equally topical at this revival. The pattern of death and replacement in the royal family had worked itself out yet again in a particularly spectacular way. James I died in March 1625; Charles was married to Henrietta Maria by proxy on 1 May. Moreover, his marriage was another example of a second choice: as everyone knew, England's negotiations with the French princess had started only after the breakdown of those with the Spanish infanta began to seem inevitable. Henrietta Maria arrived in England on 13 June, when the plague had already taken hold to such an extent that Charles's first Parliament had to move from Westminster to Oxford and was finally adjourned early because fewer and fewer members dared to attend it. The second Parliament closely followed his coronation in early February 1626. The chief business which Charles urged it to perform on both occasions was the voting of subsidies for the Protestant cause in Europe. The defeat of the Bohemian army at the Battle of White Mountain in November 1620 had made Frederick and Elizabeth exiles and their cause was thus even more urgent than in 1619/20.

By the time the play was printed in 1634, some twenty years after its first performance, Elizabeth of Bohemia was not only symbolically but literally a widowed queen, living at The Hague. Following the assassination of the Duke of Buckingham in 1628, Charles and Henrietta Maria had reconciled their differences and begun to lead an exemplary married life. Its most immediate results were the births of the future Charles II in 1630, of Mary (the future Princess of Orange) in 1631, and of the future James II in 1633. Thus the royal family of 1634 precisely duplicated the royal family of 1612, with an elder son, a daughter, and a second son. This is not the kind of fact likely to be overlooked by court poets, always desperate for new things to say on the subject of each royal birth. For instance, William Cartwright's poem on the birth of the Duke of York recalls that his title was also the one by which the present king was known until his brother's death made him Prince of Wales, and hopes, with what seems crashing tactlessness, that there will be 'no imitation of the father here'. Interchangeability had already been the theme of a number of the poems written on Henry's death. Campion's words for Coperario's *Songs of Mourning* (1613) urged Charles to:

Follow, O follow yet thy brother's fame;
But not his fate. Let's only change the name,
  And find his worth presented
  In thee, by him prevented.

The Caroline court, however isolated it may seem from some kinds of reality, was sharply aware of the pattern of death and renewal and could see the threat of the son to the father as already present even on the apparently joyous occasion of childbirth. Henry King begins his poem on the birth of the Prince of Wales by explaining that he has been late in writing it because he felt almost disloyal in rejoicing at an event which, by implication, foretold the death of the king:

  each following Birth
Doth sett the Parent so much neerer Earth:
And by this Grammer, wee our Heires may call
The smiling Preface to our Funerall.[8]

Yet he goes on to reproach himself for his reluctance to accept this lesson, which is also a lesson for the king himself:

  if Fathers should remaine
For ever here, Children were borne in vaine;
And wee in vaine were Christians, should wee
In this world dreame of Perpetuitye.

Decay is Nature's Kalendar, nor can
It hurt the King to think He is a Man:
Nor grieve, but Comfort Him to heare us say
That His owne Children must His Scepter sway.

(II.49–56)

As W. P. Williams has argued, Fletcherian tragicomedy is 'a form which expresses the unity and simplicity of hereditary succession: a happy outcome which cannot occur without the death of a predecessor'.[9] *The Two Noble Kinsmen* is unusual among tragicomedies in that it does not deal with the question of hereditary succession. It is indeed possible that the marriage of Emilia will turn out to have consequences for the succession in Athens, especially if the audience is meant to be aware of what will eventually happen to the son of Theseus and Hippolyta. This possibility is not developed in the play, probably because its medieval sources dominate its classical ones. But the fact that the story deals with replacement on the horizontal rather than the vertical plane would have made it, if anything, still more relevant at the time of its publication in 1634. Its appearance followed closely on two important court performances. One was a revival of Fletcher's *The Faithful Shepherdess*, which has as its title character a woman whose chastity and fidelity to the memory of her dead lover give her a special charismatic power in a world of confused sensuality. The other was a new work, which offers a different view of fidelity: Walter Montagu's famous *Shepheard's Paradise*. Since this play was written for, and specifically identified with, the queen and her ladies, it seems worth looking more closely at what it shows of the Caroline court's self-image in the early 1630s.

Though Montagu's play was privately performed in January 1633, it was not published until 1659. At that time, its publisher, Thomas Dring, prefaced it with an epistle virtually guaranteed to discourage anyone from reading it; the play, he explains, is addressed

> to the inspir'd and more refin'd part of men! Such as are capable to be ravish'd when they find a fancy bright and high, as the *Phoebus* that gave it: Such as have experienced those extasies and Raptures, which are the very Genius of Poetry; Poetry its selfe being nothing else but a brave and measur'd Enthusiasm; such as know, what it is to have the Soul upon the wing (suspending its commerce with clay) reaching a room almost as lofty as the proper Scene of Spirits, till warm'd with divine flames, it melts it selfe into numbers as charming as the Harmony of those Spheres

> it left beneath it: Such as are thus qualified, may here read upon the square; Others will find themselves unconcern'd.[10]

Not surprisingly, readers then and since have decided that they were not refined enough to cope with *The Shepheard's Paradise*. Yet, contrary to what one might expect from Dring's rhetoric, the play is surprisingly balanced in its attitude to the super-refined love it depicts. The character who most completely embodies its principles is the court poet, Martirio. But his verses are greeted with amusement by everyone, including the brilliant Bellesa herself – the part played by the queen and therefore, presumably, the one uncriticizable character. After Martirio has read verses defining the nature of his love for a mistress he refuses to name, she declares that 'they that could understand these verses might know your Mistress, the impossibilities to me seem equall' (IV.95). What the poet's lines most suggest, in fact, is an uninspired equivalent of Marvell's 'Definition of Love', since its point is that the impossibility and the loftiness of the love go together. The play's hero, having heard the poem, cross-examines Martirio about his love: didn't it, he asks, start in the senses and then become platonic only when the lover found that it could *not* be satisfied? Perhaps, he suggests, 'It was necessity, not choice that drew it up so high.' Martirio replies with dignity that 'my love had ne're so low a thought, as hope' (IV.96). Bellesa later tells him that he exists at 'such a transcendent height above all sense' that nothing should surprise him (IV.106). This attitude to 'transcendent' love is not unlike that of some of Chaucer's sophisticated characters, such as Theseus in *The Knight's Tale*. Near the end of the play, an elderly courtier arrives in search of an unusually large number of misplaced princes and princesses. Asked whether he has ever been in love, he replies devastatingly, 'Nevere Sir, I have not known so light a griefe in all my life' (V.141).

Part of Montagu's plot must have struck its courtly audience as remarkably familiar. The hero has obtained his father's permission to travel, with a close friend who is equally dear to both of them, in an effort to forget an unsuccessful love. Under assumed names, they come to a place called the Shepheard's Paradise, which was created specifically as a refuge for unhappy lovers. It is not a totally platonic society; each year, on the day when the new queen is chosen, lovers can ask to be released from their vows and marry. There is a clear sense that both kinds of life are valid. Once he has met Bellesa, who has just been chosen queen of the shepherds because of her exceptional beauty, the prince falls in love with her. She is equally taken with him, though she conceals the fact that she is the woman he was originally supposed to marry and that she had left court in disguise when she learned of his love for someone else, both in order not to create a political scandal and because she didn't fancy being second best. She and the prince discuss his problems as if he were a third party, reaching the conclusion that he is entitled to love a second time, and that the second love may well be more mature than the first. Clearly, the Caroline court was entertaining itself with its own story. As the witty Bellesa, Henrietta Maria is shown to have complete control over the play's interpretation. But Montagu's transformation of the unromantic facts about the royal marriage into a pastoral romance is the more effective precisely because it retains the capacity to laugh at the excesses of love.

The leading actor of the King's Men, Joseph Taylor, was also the director of *The Shepheard's Paradise*, and conducted rehearsals at court from 15 September 1632 until it was finally performed, on 9 January 1633. His fellow-actors must therefore have known a good deal about this play, even if they never saw either of its two private performances. As a reward for Taylor's help, they were given the splendid costumes worn by the aristocratic actors, which they used in their revival of Fletcher's *The Faithful Shepherdess*, played at court on Twelfth Night 1634. The fact that Montagu's play was not published at this time may have been due to its status as a private affair or to the controversy over Prynne's *Histrio-Mastix* in which it became embroiled. However, a new quarto of *The Faithful Shepherdess* appeared in 1634, with a reference to the court performance on its title-page and a new prologue and verses written specially for it.

The publication of the quarto of *The Two Noble Kinsmen* in 1634 can be seen in the context of these events and of other publications of those years: its printer, Thomas Cotes, was also the printer of the second Shakespeare Folio in 1632 and of *Pericles* in 1635. The title-page of the quarto does not mention a court performance, but it explicitly calls the play a tragicomedy, associating it with a type of drama that Fletcher claimed was too refined for its first audiences, and it names Shakespeare and Fletcher ('the two memorable worthies of their age') in terms which appeal to contemporary nostalgia. Even the Chaucerian source would have had both a nostalgic and an elitist appeal. This was a period when he was thought of above all as the poet of courtly love, as is evident, for example, in the references to him in Jonson's *New Inn* (1629).[11] Moreover, the difficulty of his 'antique' language added to his prestige: in 1635, Francis Kynaston published a Latin translation of the first two books of *Troilus and Criseyde*. Both Chaucer and the play based on his story were thus being appropriated by a courtly society sophisticated enough to recognize and enjoy the fact that its values might appear absurd to the uninitiated.

The evidence I have been amassing about the play's several occasions shows, I think, that a plot involving the conjunction of death and marriage in a royal household would rarely have been anything but topical in the early seventeenth century – or, probably, at any other time, except the reign of Elizabeth I, the last of the Tudors. In so far as both Chaucer and the Jacobean dramatists demonstrate the need to accept the fact that human life consists of the processes of death and renewal, they are simply stating, in elegantly tragic language, something with which no one could disagree. The theme can be applied specifically either to the situation of the royal family or to that of the actors themselves, who had lost the Globe in 1613, Burbage in 1619, and Fletcher in 1625. It would probably have had a resonance for most members of the audience. The very abundance of these possible allusions might perhaps reinforce a conservative attitude. '*Plus ça change*. . . .' The play's most famous couplet –

> This world's a city full of straying streets,
> And death's the market-place where each one meets.
>
> (I.iv.15–16)

– expresses its dominant paradox: characters are constantly being urged to choose one road or another (friendship or love, Palamon or Arcite, Venus or Mars, getting married or fighting a war), but all choices are tragic.

The emphasis on the all-or-nothing nature of the decisions which are forced on the characters is something which Chaucer added to Boccaccio, but Boccaccio retains, as Chaucer does not, the sense of the dark Theban legend in the background of the chivalric romance. The harshness of the play may be due to a similar awareness on the part of at least one of the authors. Hippolyta, commenting on the fighters who are coming to the ceremonial fight, says that

> They would show
> Bravely about the titles of two kingdoms.
>
> (IV.ii.145–6)

Symbolically, women and cities are interchangeable, and in the Theban legend it is over Thebes itself that the brothers Eteocles and Polynices destroy each other. Boccaccio's *Teseida* makes the point that Palamon and Arcite are the last of the Theban line, and traces their conflict to the initial curse of the dragon's seed as well as comparing it to the hatred between Polynices and Eteocles (V.lvii–lix). Chaucer seems to think of Thebes as surviving the war and remaining a possible home for the two men – Theseus comments on the absurdity of Palamon and Arcite remaining in Athens when they could be living there in comfort, and Palamon's marriage to Emilia appears to be part of a treaty between the two countries. Boccaccio, however, had made it clear that the city is utterly destroyed by Theseus, and in the play Arcite knows that it is 'but a heap of ruins' (II.iii.20). If neither of the authors knew Boccaccio, one or both might have read Lydgate's *Siege of Thebes*, which was printed in Speght's edition of Chaucer (1598 and 1602).[12] They would also have known the source which he follows, Statius's *Thebaid*, probably the bloodiest of classical epics.

The analogy between fighting for love and fighting for power seems, at least at first sight, to point towards the political absolutism from which both David Norbrook and Erica Sheen are anxious to dissociate Shakespeare. In particular, the equality between the two heroes, which makes it so impossible to choose between them, is depicted as ultimately a source of destruction, not co-operation. Similarly, in *Antony and Cleopatra*, many characters appear convinced that the greatest danger to the peace of the world is not Antony's love for Cleopatra but the absolute equality that exists between him and Octavius, forcing their two stars to 'divide/Our equalness to this' (by 'this', the speaker, Octavius, means Antony's death (V.i. 477–8)). Coriolanus speaks of the confusion which results 'when two authorities are up,/Neither supreme' (III.i.112–13). The danger of absolute equality is not a purely Jacobean theme, however; it can be traced back through other Shakespearian works, at least as far as the 'two households, both alike in dignity' of *Romeo and Juliet*, which, at the end, are raising golden statues, of equal value, to the young people who have been destroyed by the feud. Perhaps the most interesting example of dangerous equality comes in *King John*, where the equation of the besieged city and the woman is particularly clear. The citizens of Angiers react to the armies of England and France much as Emilia does to Palamon and Arcite:

> Heralds, from off our towers we might behold
> From first to last the onset and retire
> Of both your armies, whose equality
> By our best eyes cannot be censured.

Blood hath bought blood and blows have answered blows,
Strength matched with strength and power confronted power.
Both are alike, and both alike we like.
One must prove greatest. While they weigh so even,
We hold our town for neither, yet for both.

(II.i.325–33)

In this case, however, the armies react by rejecting the option of total destruction (either of themselves or of the city) in favour of compromise and a dynastic marriage, and the Dauphin and Blanche suddenly discover a whole vocabulary of courtly love with which to deal with the situation. As in *Antony and Cleopatra* later, this turns out only to postpone the conflict. *King John*, however, ends with the war finely balanced, with defeats on both sides. Only the principle of hereditary succession offers hope of a new beginning in this play. By contrast, *The Two Noble Kinsmen*, which cannot invoke this principle, seems to demonstrate the danger of multiplicity. 'Doubtless/There is a best,' says Emilia (I.iii.47–8), referring to the apparent equality in Theseus's division of his love between Pirithous and Hippolyta. Her words recall the reaction of the Citizen of Angiers to the contending claims of the French and English armies: 'One must prove greatest.' That emotional claims should be as absolutist and irreconcilable as those of warring states explains the more 'tragic' sense of the play in those parts generally agreed to be Shakespeare's – that is, the first and last acts.[13] Absolutism is tragic and Shakespearian; compromise is comic and Fletcherian: this largely summarizes the critical response to the play.

But this is to discuss the Chaucerian plot in isolation. In practice, our sense of the play's politics must depend on how we see the relation of the story of Palamon and Arcite to the story of the Jailer's Daughter. Barry Kyle's RSC production (1986) saw a pattern which made a point about the 'politics of gender': his final tableau juxtaposed Emilia and the Jailer's Daughter, each dressed as a bride, each being tricked or forced into a marriage she did not really want. Alternatively, the two plots can be contrasted in terms not of gender but of class, as exemplified in the Daughter's traditional plebeian obsession with sex and the more refined love of the three aristocratic characters. The distinction is blurred at one point, when Fletcher makes the two men exchange rakish reminiscences of 'the wenches/We have known in our days' (III.iii.28–9), but it holds substantially true. At the one point where Palamon shows any awareness of the Daughter's existence, just before his expected execution, he and his friends offer the Jailer money towards her marriage. Before doing so one of the knights asks the inevitable question: 'Is it a maid?' Palamon says that he thinks so, but in fact he is probably wrong by this time, since her doctor has just given the almost unheard-of prescription of sex before marriage, telling the wooer moreover that as she's probably not 'honest' anyway it doesn't matter what he does to her. The Daughter's final scene can perhaps be described as an example of the 'politics of genre'. When she takes the suitor for Palamon, she asks him whether the doctor is his cousin Arcite, and the doctor, falling in with the role-playing, replies:

> Yes, sweetheart,
> And I am glad my cousin Palamon
> Has made so fair a choice.
>
> (V.iv.91)

This is, surely, the play's alternative ending – what *could* have happened if women were allowed to court men, if the two kinsmen had not been so noble, if the play had been a comedy.

The contrast between the two plots is thus a parallel to the contrasting attitudes frequently set up in Chaucer himself, for instance in *The Parliament of Fowles*, where the noble birds are prepared to die for love whereas the plebeian ones argue, 'But [unless] she wol love hym, lat hym love another!' (line 567). But is one plot being used to ridicule the other? Are the two noble kinsmen fools to commit themselves to an uncompromisingly destructive code of conduct, or is the girl a fool to let herself be tricked into a happy ending which depends on deception and compromise? Critics of the play used to be disgusted by the Daughter's behaviour and, still more, by her cure, but in modern productions it is easily the most touching and successful part of the play. It is possible, I think, that it may even have had this effect in its own time. The play's epilogue, in which the speaker compares himself to a schoolboy who is 'cruel fearful' about its reception, must have been intended for a boy actor, and the obvious choice would be the one playing the Daughter. That the dramatists gave her three soliloquies in a row suggests an astonishing reliance on the abilities of this particular boy. If he scored as great a personal success as Imogen Stubbs did in the 1986 RSC revival, the balance between the two plots, and their apparently opposing attitudes to love, might have remained unresolved. Whether audiences found the Daughter's final situation tragic or comic would depend on whether they wanted to make her story, as Barry Kyle's production did, part of the tragedy of the play. The fact that

Davenant's Restoration adaptation arranged a happy ending for the character who corresponds to her (though only after raising her social status) also suggests another way of making the two stories harmonize generically instead of contradicting each other. Another point about performance, of course, is that the differences between the two actors of Palamon and Arcite will inevitably work against any idea of the interchangeability of the two men. The play may be intended to invite the audience to debate which is the more attractive, just as Chaucer's characters occasionally ask the readers of the *Canterbury Tales* to answer what are really unanswerable questions, such as the one the Knight asks at the end of the first book of his *Tale*: Which is better, to be in prison and see Emily, or to be free and banished from her sight? The impossibility of choice is balanced by the inevitability of the need to choose.

Our sense of uneasiness at the end of the play is not only the result of these various kinds of uncertainty. Political meaning is, as I have tried to show, a matter of context, and the context of *The Two Noble Kinsmen*, for us, is the politics of literary criticism. Our awareness that the play is the work of at least two authors makes nonsense of any attempts to ignore the question of intention. Is the extraordinary balance of forces in the play deliberate, or was there a struggle between the two authors on the level of language, genre, and political meaning, corresponding to the struggle between the two heroes and the gods whom they represent? The fact that we cannot possibly answer this question does not prevent us from asking it. It is uncertainty on this point that makes critic after critic discuss *The Tempest* as 'Shakespeare's last play', in spite of the existence of the two later collaborative works. This is the result of our own politics, which demand commitment and distrust pluralism. To suspend judgement is felt to be irresponsible: we *must* interpret, and this means discriminating between Shakespeare and Fletcher; it means finding a meaning in the play or, if there are more possible meanings than one, giving priority to the one belonging to the dramatist who long since won the trial by combat. Like Theseus, we want a straightforward decision about property: Who has a 'right' to Emilia, who is (as the prologue puts it) the 'breeder' of the play? Like Emilia, we are sure that 'Doubtless/There is a best', even if they are 'both too excellent', and we must destroy one in order to reward the other. Maybe, in view of the recent controversies about Shakespearian authorship, we are afraid of repeating the mistake of the Jailer's Daughter, letting ourselves be led off by a false Palamon. But when we set Shakespeare and Fletcher against each other, as if the result of their combat could at last give us an answer to this curious play, we are colluding with precisely the same destructive absolutism whose consequences *The Two Noble Kinsmen* has so vividly depicted.

NOTES

Shakespeare's plays are quoted from *The Complete Works*, ed. Stanley Wells and Gary Taylor (Oxford: Oxford Univesity Press, 1986).

1 Richard Proudfoot, 'Shakespeare and the new dramatists of the King's Men, 1606–1913', in J. R. Brown and B. Harris (eds), *Later Shakespeare*, Stratford upon Avon Studies (London: Arnold, 1966), 250–1.
2 John Fletcher and William Shakespeare, *The Two Noble Kinsmen*, ed. Richard Proudfoot, Regents Renaissance Drama Series (London: Arnold, 1970); M. C. Bradbrook, 'Shakespeare as collaborator', in *The Living Monument: Shakespeare and the Theatre of his Time* (Cambridge: Cambridge University Press, 1976); Glynne Wickham, ' "The Two Noble Kinsmen" or "A Midsummer Night's Dream, Part II"?', in G. R. Hibbard (ed.), *Elizabethan Theatre* (London: Macmillan, 1980) vol. VII, 167–96.
3 See Stanley Wells and Gary Taylor, with John Jowett and William Montgomery (eds), *William Shakespeare: A Textual Companion* (Oxford: Oxford University Press, 1987), 633.
4 Walter R. Davis (ed.), *The Works of Thomas Campion* (New York: Norton, 1967), 259 and n.
5 See, for example, Augustine Taylor, *Epithalamium upon the All-Desired Nuptials, etc.* (London, 1613), a collection of poems by divers hands on the wedding of Princess Elizabeth and the Palsgrave.
6 Thomas Heywood, *A Marriage Triumphe. Solemnized in an Epithalamium* (London, 1613).
7 See Proudfoot's edition of *The Two Noble Kinsmen*, xii.
8 Henry King, 'By Occasion of the young Prince his happy Birth. May 29. 1630', ll.23–6, *The Poems of Henry King*, ed. Margaret Crum (Oxford: Clarendon Press, 1965), 73–5.
9 William Proctor Williams, 'Not hornpipes and funerals: Fletcherian tragicomedy', in Nancy Klein Maguire (ed.), *Renaissance Tragicomedy: Explorations in Genre and Politics* (New York: AMS Press, 1987), 143.
10 Walter Montagu, *The Shepheard's Paradise. A Comedy. Privately Acted before the late King Charles by the Queen's Majesty and Ladies of Honour* (London, 1659; misprinted as 1629).
11 Caroline F. E. Spurgeon, *Five Hundred Years of Chaucer Criticism and Allusion 1357–1900*, 2 vols (Cambridge: Cambridge University Press, 1925).
12 Geoffrey Chaucer, *The Workes of our antient and learned English Poet, Geffrey Chaucer, newly Printed. In this Impression you shall find these Additions: 1. His Portraiture and Progenie shewed. 2. His Life collected. 3. Arguments to every Booke gathered. 4. Old and obscure Words explaned. 5. Authors by him cited, declared. 6. Difficulties opened. 7. Two Bookes of his neure before printed* (London, 1598).
13 See, for example, Ann Thompson, *Shakespeare's Chaucer: A Study in Literary Origins* (Liverpool: Liverpool University Press, 1978), 172.

5

'A MAIDENHEAD, *AMINTOR*, AT MY YEARES': CHASTITY AND TRAGICOMEDY IN THE FLETCHER PLAYS

Kathleen McLuskie

I

'A maidenhead, *Amintor*, at my yeares!' (II.i.193–4). Evadne's show-stopping line from *The Maid's Tragedy*, addressed to her bewildered husband on their wedding night, presents a paradigm case of the difficulties involved in offering a feminist reading of the plays of Fletcher.[1] The line's arch sarcasm throws down a challenge to all the assumptions of Elizabethan writing from poems to coy mistresses to handbooks on conduct, to tragedies, often by Beaumont and Fletcher themselves, in which the loss of maidenhead is enough to shake the very foundations of the family and the state. The line brings to a halt all Amintor's coyly expressed assumptions about the behaviour of brides, throwing into question both the narrative and the social conventions which assume that marriages will achieve the happy and automatic conjunction of social form and sexual pleasure.

In response to Evadne's line, Amintor articulates quite clearly the implications for the sexual politics of future ages:

Hymen keepe
This story (that will make succeeding youth
Neglect thy ceremonies) from all eares.
Let it not rise up for thy shame and mine
To after ages, we will scorne thy lawes,
If thou no better bless them; touch the heart
Of her that thou hast sent me, or the world
Shall know, there's not an altar that will smoke
In praise of thee; we will adopt us sonnes,
Then virtue shall inherit, and not blood;
If we do lust, we'le take the next we meet,
Serving our selves as other creatures doe,

And never take note of the female more,
Nor of her issue.

(II.i.214–27)

In this speech Amintor quite clearly acknowledges the political connection between the sexual control of women and the maintenance of social order. Amintor is evidently appalled at the prospect of such anarchy but the connection itself can be (and has been) seen as evidence of a subversive and radical sexual politics in these plays.[2] However the argument over the precise ideological import of such scenes demonstrates the dangers of readings which are 'readings' and no more. In the case of this scene, all its radical potential, the acceptance of female sexuality, its connections to the social order, are shaped and modulated by its complex theatricality. It is a theatricality which brings ideas *into play* both in the sense of 'into operation' and 'into playfulness'. The serious ideas about sexuality and the state, the family and social stability which are central to Jacobean absolutism are also, in this scene, material for a series of twists and reversals which play along the delicate balance between comedy and horror.

The preamble to the scene, in which Evadne is undressed by her attendants, plays through opposing literary versions of the subject of wedding nights. Dula, one of the ladies in waiting, offers 'a dozen wanton words' to make Evadne 'livlier in her husband's bed' while Aspatia, whose beloved Evadne has married, presents a gloomy reminder of the dangers of thwarted passion. The sequence ends with each attendant singing a song, Aspatia's of unrequited love – 'Lay a garland on my hearse,/Of the dismal yew' – and Dula's a celebration of sexual adventuring:

I could never have the power
To love above an houre,
But my heart would prompt mine eie
On some other man to flie.

(II.i.83–6)

This opposition, crystallized in the songs, holds the movement of the rest of the scene in suspense, showing that its action will be concerned with a love affair, but not revealing if it will be tragic or comic, true or false.

The ensuing scene reverses not only all the expectations established by the songs but also the very range in which these expectations can function: it shifts to a different and totally unexpected narrative line.

The story initiated by Evadne's line is not one of true love betrayed as in Aspatia's song, or, as in Dula's song, of sexual pleasure enthusiastically enjoyed; it is a story in which sexual relations are simply the context in which other stories of honour and power are enacted. Evadne's defiant assertion of her sexual experience turns out to refer not to her autonomy as a sexually experienced woman, but to the prior claims on her favours held by the king. In spite of Amintor's passion, his threats of rape and murder, he finds in the very name king 'a word that wipes away all thoughts revengeful' and the scene ends in a quiet coda of resignation.

The story of honour and power, however, does not wipe out the story of sex and unrequited love. Evadne's two reversal lines, one about maidenhead and the other naming the king, are equal poles around which the scene is structured, creating the link between sex and politics which informs the remainder of the play. The situation offers scope for extended ironies: in the morning-after scene, both Melantius, Evadne's brother, and the king mistake the situation, assuming the marriage has been consummated. Both Melantius's teasing congratulation and the king's suppressed anger at their supposed disobedience are equally painful to the newlyweds and theatrically tense for the audience. The situation is, moreover, reworked throughout the action: Melantius is astonished into understanding his sister's situation and reacts to it as Amintor did. He interrogates Evadne as Amintor did and she, repentant, overcomes the scruples of their honour in order to kill the king herself.

Because of this initial situation, other issues are continually placed in sexual terms and the theatrical pleasure which many of the scenes offer is sexualized too. In the scene with Amintor, Evadne is undressed and ready for bed and the action constructs her (whether played by a boy or a woman) in the classic position of the tease. She refuses the sex which the occasion seems to demand, at the same time making quite clear that her refusal is no matter of

> A maidens strictness. Looke upon these cheekes,
> And thou shalt finde the hot and rising blood
> Unapt for such a vow; no, in this heart
> There dwels as much desire, and as much will
> To push that wish'd act in practise, as ever yet
> Was knowne to woman, and they have been showne both.
>
> (II.i.286–91)

The imagery of heart and will and blood are commonplaces of Jacobean writing about sexuality: the placing of the lines and the context of the action make possible a seductive delivery with considerable voyeuristic appeal. However, it is not sex but knowledge which is first withheld and then released. The narrative information that the king is Evadne's secret lover is banal enough but is made more exciting by the audience's knowledge that this kind of scene should culminate in sex but will always avoid it in view of what is possible on stage. The audience are thus entertained both by the image of the scantily dressed character on stage and by the narrative problem of how the consummation will be avoided.

A similar effect of sexualized suspense occurs in the scene where Evadne kills the king. The sexual tone is established from the beginning as Evadne approaches the king asleep in bed: on waking to find himself tied up, he enquires

> What prettie new device is this Evadne?
> What, doe you tie me to you? by my love
> This is a queint one: come my deare and kisse me.
> Ile be thy *Mars*, to bed my Queen of love,
> Let us be caught together, that the gods may see,
> And envie our embraces.
>
> (V.i.47–52)

The reference to Mars and Venus, caught in a net by Venus's husband, Vulcan, both ironizes the king's speeches and shows the playfully sexual world which he inhabits. Evadne's new role, however, comes from a different theatrical context. She begins the scene with a self-searching speech reminiscent of Hamlet's over Claudius at prayer. The teasing dialogue which ensues when the king wakes up (and he takes comically long to do so) is the result of the interplay between his comic sense of the scene and her insistence on its tragedy. But the teasing also plays with the audience's expectation of seeing a king killed on stage with all the resonances for that act which have been built up throughout the action.

Beaumont and Fletcher's play with narrative knowledge, with audience expectation, and with dramatic conventions is further developed in their treatment of the cross-dressed heroine. Aspatia, Amintor's former lover, rejected for the king's convenience, is presented through most of the action as an emblem of wronged virginity. Her mournful presence on stage places her in the long line of such victims from 'the nymph Oenone/When Paris brought home Helen' to Dido and Ariadne. However, she also has the dramatic potential to save the situation, presenting a tragicomic counter-action to the tragic plot with Evadne and the king. In Act V, she appears 'in man's apparell' presenting herself as her own brother, come to demand a reckoning from Amintor. To her frustration (and the audience's delight), Amintor will not quarrel with her and the hoped-for consummation of death has, literally, to be kicked out of him. Amintor does eventually fight and fatally wound her just as Evadne enters with a bloody knife to claim Amintor as her reward for killing the king.

As Amintor's summary to Evadne makes clear, this is the moment in which all possibility of a romantic happy ending is denied:

> Behold
> Here lies a youth whose wounds bleed in my breast,
> Sent by his violent Fate to fetch his death
> From my slow hand, and to augment my woe,
> You now are present, stain'd with a King's bloud,
> Violently shed: this keepes night here
> And throwes an unknowne Wildernesse about me.
>
> (V.iii.144–50)

The unknown wilderness of Amintor's imagination is the wilderness where love, marriage, and sexual obedience are not inextricably linked into a neat narrative pattern of challenge and restoration. Evadne kills herself and Amintor returns too late to stop her; Aspatia, who has been dying throughout the scene with Evadne, wishes to live when she realizes that Amintor still loves her but is too badly wounded to survive; Amintor kills himself in despair.

The play, of course, does not end on this note of chaos. Behind the lovers' action there has been a skeletal plot of Calianax, Melantius, and Lysippus and it is brought to the foreground in the final scene, ensuring the rightful succession of Lysippus, the king's son, who states a comfortable moral as the final lines of the play:

> May this a faire example be to me,
> To rule with temper, for on lustfull Kings
> Unlookt for suddaine deaths from God are sent,
> But curst is he that is their instrument.
>
> (V.iii.292–5)

Lysippus's closing moral sounds dully conclusive after the witty refusal of consummation elsewhere in the play. It closes off the play's world in the commonplacely political, which suits the conventions of drama set in the court but makes no contribution to the play with sex and knowledge, convention and form which has animated the principal action. It demonstrates the problematic relationship between reductive versions of ideology – sexual or political – and the dance of wit with which Beaumont and Fletcher transform its implications.

II

For the treatment of sex and power was not simply a matter of ideology. The dramatic forms which Fletcher and his collaborators had at their disposal permitted very different theatrical treatments of the same material. In *The Custom of the Country*, for example, the motif of the lustful ruler again provides the initial impulse of the plot but since the corrupt prince is now pitted against a witty heroine rather than a tragic hero, the action provides a different variety of discussions around the characters' dilemma and their attitudes to sex. Arnoldo, the heroine's lover and potential victim of the lustful ruler, takes a characteristically fatalistic view of the situation. But the potential for tragic action is comically cut off by his brother Rutilio's guying mockery. He responds to the news of the custom of *ius primae noctis*, which will thwart Arnoldo of his bride's virginity, with an enthusiastic comic envy of the duke's position:[3]

> How might a man achieve that place? a rare Custom! An admirable rare custom.
>
> (I.i)

The energy of Rutilio's enthusiastic endorsement of male promiscuity derives from a wit which acknowledges no allegiance to conventional morality or conventional power. He is equally witty at the expense of the duke's exploitative lust, denouncing him as

> A Cannibal, that feeds on the heads of Maids
> Then flings their bones and bodies to the Devil
>
> (I.i)

and the same spontaneous vitality informs his contempt for the heroine's father's craven plan to solve the problem of the duke's lust by marriage:

> Would any man of discretion venture such a gristle,
> To the rude claws of such a Cat-a mountain?
> You had better tear her between two Oaks; a Town Bull
> Is a meer Stoick to this fellow, a grave Philosopher,

And a Spanish Jennet, a most vertuous Gentleman.

(I.i)

The language of satire, whose frame of reference is most frequently misogynist, is here used to mock male lust. However, this treatment of lust is concerned less with moral opprobrium than with vulgarity. The duke's behaviour is less a decline from what is expected of princes than a ludicrous narrowing of what is expected from a man.

This witty reworking of the conventional language of sex and sexual relations, however, serves dramatic as much as ideological demands. As so often in Fletcher's work, a possible closure of the action in keeping with one version of a solution is teasingly proffered at the beginning of the play when the heroine's father suggests that she might marry the duke. By rejecting that offer, Zenocia, the heroine, saves the action of the play as well as endorsing the ideal of her own sexual autonomy. The dramatic function of these ideals is evident in the scene between Zenocia and the duke himself. Having rejected one version of a plot in which a duke marries a commoner, the text exploits the ideological language of that scenario. Zenocia rejects the duke's sexual advances, not by stressing her chastity but by disingenuously and comically insisting on her unworthiness:

I must not think to marry you,
I dare not, Sir, the step betwixt your honour
And my poor humble state. . .

(I.i)

She then pushes the point further by elaborating on the disadvantages of marriage, made familiar by the long tradition of misogynist diatribes against her sex.

The intense competition between men and women, the exploitation of lust by power, the tussle between desire and social control – all these issues are evident in the action. However, they are rendered wittily so that they amuse rather than threaten. The characters invite the audiences to share a knowing play with ideas; ideological struggles become grist to a theatrical mill. As in *The Maid's Tragedy* the subversive potential of this mockery of convention is held in check in the conclusion, though even there the rewards and punishments seem part of the game. Rutilio has his attitude to sex thoroughly chastened by an exhausting stint in a male brothel and after adventures with pirates, a nymphomaniac, and her vengeful son, the characters combine in conventional ways. The pleasure of the play lies less in the happy and conventional conclusion than in the wit with which Fletcher holds such potentially offensive material within the bounds of decorum while mocking decorum at every turn.

In part, Fletcher's success at achieving this witty play with dangerous questions of sex and power lay in his ability to disentangle dramatic convention from social convention. Marriage and sexual relations were as much dramaturgic elements which could be combined in different ways as they were social institutions. The ways in which they held both the narrative structures of the drama and the institutions of society together were analogous; but they were not the same. Early in his career, Fletcher indicated his interest in the dramatic and theatrical potential of sexuality and sexual relations. In *The Faithful Shepherdess* he presents, in a highly decorated poetic form, a round dance in which chastity is set off against lust, successful against unsuccessful love. Where earlier treatments of sexual relations had concerned the conflict over love thwarted or restored, the acquisition of sexual partners or the trials of wifely obedience, the new drama focused very squarely on chastity. There is no social context for the action: the sexual identities of the characters are given rather than dramatically constructed. Amoret and Perigot, the chaste lovers, are simply opposed to unchaste lovers such as Cloe whose comic enthusiasm for lust – 'It is impossible to ravish me, I am so willing' – is an equally static characterization.

The play demonstrates the differences between an ideological and a theatrical treatment for although chastity is discussed in familiar moral terms, it only has a narrative and theatrical interest when it is besieged. The sense that chastity is infinitely precarious is established from the beginning of the play. The Priest of Pan lists while exorcizing the 'wanton, quick desires/That do kindle by their fires' and, as soon as the couples who make up the cast find themselves in the wood where the action takes place, they are subject to just the torments and temptations which the priest has warned against. Given the static characterization, however, none of the chaste can become lustful or the lustful chaste and so the whole action turns on a magical plot in which no one is what they seem.

In this context, where action is controlled by situation and clearly established character types, ideas about lust and chastity can be given free play. The play's characteristic style is endless poetic scrutiny of the meaning of sexual behaviour in which the poetic effects have a certain autonomy from the moral direction of the play. Chaste love is described in the most sensual terms and the opposing horrors of lust are dramatized with all the power of the language of satiric misogyny; but the two can be combined in the same dramatic moment. When Perigot, for example, reassures Amoret that the assignation he proposes will be chaste, he vividly reminds her and the audience of the alternative to chastity:

> some dame
> Whose often prostitution hath begot,
> More foule diseases, then ever yet the hot
> Sun bred through his burnings, whilst the dog
> Pursues the raging Lyon, throwing fog
> And deadly vapour from his angry breath,
> Filling the lower world with plague and death.
>
> (I.ii.131–7)

The familiar divisions between coy women and lustful men are completely abandoned, not only in the action but in the language. Amaryllis, rejected by Perigot, for example, announces:

> I must enjoy thee boy,
> Though the great dangers twixt my hopes and that
> Be infinite
>
> (I.ii.191–3)

and Cloe, finding no outlet for her eager lust, enquires:

> Is it not strange, among so many a score
> Of lusty bloods, I should picke out these thinges
> Whose vaines like a dull river farre from springs,
> Is still the same, slowe, heavy, and unfit
> For streame or motion.
>
> (I.iii.146–50)

Fletcher's innovation here is not in presenting women who are not chaste; it is rather in simply transposing the discourses of male lust onto them, making the connections between gender, language, and action arbitrary and thus infinitely malleable to the dramatic action.

The same free play with character and sexual identity is evident in the plot device of the 'false Amoret', the lustful Amaryllis who transforms herself into Amoret's double, causing confusion about identity and dismay at the unpredictability of lovers' behaviour. The two parts could be played by the same boy actress and the confusion between the two characters allows for dramatic variation in the scenes with Perigot as well as suggesting the coexistence of chaste and lustful feelings in love. When 'false Amoret' makes the first pass at Perigot, he coyly replies:

> Forbeare deare soule to trye,
> Whether my hart be pure: Ile rather dye,
> Then nourish one thought to dishonour thee.
>
> (III.i.293–5)

Perigot's response comes from the plots of other comedies which underscores the comedy of his situation, but it is also usually a woman's line which makes it funnier still. It then proves the opportunity for misogynist generalization, 'thinkst thou such a thinge as Chastitie,/Is among women' (296–7) taken from a different theatrical context, usually by a man, to be made by the woman character. This play and reversal of theatrical convention, together with the disguise, neutralizes the scene's potential for engaging the audience emotionally. It always holds onto the possibility of resolution even when Perigot's horror at false Amoret's lust turns to violence. The more dangerously ironic sequence occurs when the true Amoret comes on stage and Perigot stabs her. However the rhyme and the pattern of the verse show that these events are another turn in the dance:

> AMORET: My *Perigot*
> PERIGOT: Here
> AMORET: Happye.
> PERIGOT: Haplesse first:
> It lights on thee, the next blow is the worst. [*Wounds her.*]
> AMORET: Stay *Perigot*, my love, thou art unjust.
> PERIGOT: Death is the best reward that's due to lust.
>
> (III.i.343–6)

The spectacle of the chaste victim falsely accused offers up its theatrical pleasures in cameo form and the sequence is actually repeated later in the play, after Amoret has been rescued and healed by the god of a magic spring. Other couples are similarly tried and tested and the problems of ocular proof of chastity, so difficult to achieve in the social world, are solved with the aid of a magic taper. In the end, of course, the lustful are humiliated, the chaste lovers restored, and the irredeemable held up as an example. However, the morals of closure are the predictable end which allows the pleasures of spectacle and songs and lush poetic protestations free play. The value of chastity is somehow taken for granted, held in abeyance, while the kinds of scenes which the siege of chastity can generate are explored to the full.

III

It is difficult to know how to read *The Faithful Shepherdess*'s treatment of sexuality. At one level the text acts out fantasies of women who are infinitely available and infinitely controllable. The play has no social context in which women are exchanged in culturally sanctioned ways, so their definition purely in sexual terms has no boundaries. Male sex can be withheld from the lustful or imposed on the chaste while any ensuing danger will be annulled by the arrival of the god of the river, or the priest of Pan, or the morning which heralds the end of the dream. The very ease of this reading, however, renders it suspect, for it says nothing of the poetic and theatrical pleasures of the text which are offered to the audience so as to complicate thematic or moralizing reading. The most severe censure of lust in a reading, for example, could not exceed the poetic denunciations of Perigot, or its most libertine proponents the enthusiasm of Cloe or the brutality of the Sullen Shepherd. In its thorough coverage of all the possible ways of talking about sexuality and sexual relations, the text is constantly one jump ahead of any account which is restricted to 'interpretation'. If, however, we go beyond 'interpretation' to the 'conditions for making' the text, we might ask about the circumstances of production in which these poetic and theatrical pleasures were made available.[4]

Our understanding of that historical context is made a little easier by the fact that the play failed at its first performance: the real reasons can never be fully known but the terms in which it was defended by Fletcher and his contemporaries reveal a number of pressures on the profession. Fletcher was clear that his audience was in the wrong. He wrote a prefatory epistle to the printed text of the play, distinguishing the kind of European-influenced aristocratic pastoral which he was writing from the popular dramatic tradition of 'country hired Shepheards, in gray cloakes, with curtaild dogs in strings . . . whitsun ales, creame, wassel and morris dances'.[5] Jonson and Chapman, too, in their commendatory verses, defended the play against the taste of the vulgar, Jonson pouring characteristic scorn on the whole audience and Chapman contrasting Fletcher's play with 'a thing/That every Cobler to his patch might sing'.[6] Their dismissal of the ignorant audience was, however, more than a venting of pique: it was contributing to the definition and construction of a new audience.

The new audience was constructed only partly in terms of social class: equally important was its sophisticated awareness of the role and use of theatre. In *Knight of the Burning Pestle*, for example, Beaumont presented a comic portrayal of the kind of audience he felt his plays to be up against. The citizen and his wife who interrupt and take over the play are a delightful couple but they are the antithesis of a sophisticated audience. The Citizen Grocer insists in spite of the prologue that the new drama intends to abuse the city:

> if you were not resolv'd to play the Jacks, what need you study for new subjects, purposely to abuse your betters? Why could not you be contented, as well as others, with the legend of *Whittington*, or the life and death of sir *Thomas Gresham*?
>
> (Induction, 16–20)

By her own admission, the Citizen's Wife 'was nere at one of these playes as they say, before' (Induction, 50–1), and the last time she was promised such an outing it was to see the old-fashioned *Jane Shore*.[7] As a result, her judgement is constantly out, not only in preferring the outdated heroic style of a Grocer errant to the city comedy of *The London Merchant* but more particularly in her moral assessment of the characters and their behaviour. One of the actions in the play involves Jasper, the apprentice, planning to elope with his master's daughter. Both the citizen and his wife ignore the narrative convention at work, and denounce the immorality of the characters.

> Fye upon am little infidels, what a matters here now? well I'le be hang'd for a halfe-penny, if there be not some abomination knavery in this Play, well, let 'em looke toot, *Rafe* must come, and if there be any tricks a brewing. . .
>
> (I.i.61–4)

Sophistication, for Beaumont and Fletcher, was not merely a matter of independence of judgement – 'In his owne censure an explicite faith' as Beaumont puts it in his commendatory epistle – but also a willingness to recognize the difference between the play with theatrical form and the moral and commercial calculations of everyday life. An old-fashioned perception of the drama was equated with an old-fashioned, instrumental sexual morality. *The Knight of the Burning Pestle*, like many of the other contemporary parodic plays, presented an image of its ideal audience.[8] It flattered the aspirations and taste of those who could appreciate the conventions and style of the drama by distinguishing them from 'the common prate of common people': it created a sense of a coterie, knowledgeable in both artistic and moral matters, indulging in a fashionable, because exclusive, exercise.

The definition of this audience was, in the early years of the century, rather unstable. *The Knight of the Buring Pestle*, like *The Faithful Shepherdess* was unsuccessful at its first appearance and the terms of the reception of the new drama had to be reiterated again and again in prefaces and epistles and prologues. By the 1630s, however, Fletcherian drama was the dominant mode of the fashionable theatre. *The Faithful Shepherdess* was successfully revived at court in 1634 and the terms of the new style's success explicitly laid out in the commendatory verses to the Folio of Beaumont and Fletcher's plays compiled by Humphrey Mosely after the closing of the theatres.

The intellectual functions of the drama continued to be insisted on but the familiar aesthetic formula of profit and pleasure was now presented with a different emphasis. James Shirley, who succeeded Fletcher as principal dramatist to the King's Men, described the

> Authentick witt that made Blackfriars an Academy, where the three howers spectacle while Beaumont and Fletcher were presented, were usually of more advantage to the hopefully young Heire, then a costly, dangerous, forraigne Travell . . . it cannot be denied but that the young spirits of the Time, whose Birth and Quality made them impatient of the sowrer wayes of education, have from the attentive hearing these pieces, got ground in point of wit and carriage of the most severely employed Students, while these Recreations were digested into Rules, and the very Pleasure did edifie.[9]

Shirley's suggestion that the plays could replace traditional modes of education was partly tongue in cheek, a joke which is compounded by its extension to 'passable discoursing dining wits' who 'stand yet in good credit upon the bare stock of two or three single scenes'. Nevertheless, his description suggests a more explicit recognition of the financial implications of profit together with the recognition that the education of a man about town had less to do with learning than with fashion and style: points of wit and carriage, recreations, pleasures.

Shirley's preface showed how the theatre had become commercially available leisure, addressing its audience as consumers and offering a commodity which would enhance their lives. Many comments on the conspicuous consumption of theatre were vaguely disapproving, distancing the desired audience from the fop, the groupie, and the unlettered parvenu. In Fletcher's work, however, the notion that a play was a commodity was treated quite matter of factly: as the epilogue to *Valentinian* unapologetically concludes, 'We have your money and you have our wares.'

The impact of this new relationship between the production and consumption of drama on the plays themselves is difficult to assess and is complicated by other aspects of the dramatic and theatrical tradition. The relationship with the audience constructed by the plays is, moreover, not the same as the actual social relationships in the audience for any given production. Nevertheless, the commendatory verses seem to suggest that, by the closing of the theatres, the plays were appreciated in terms of the theatrical pleasures of newness, wit, and value for money:

When thou wouldst Comick be, each smiling birth
In that kinde, came into the world all mirth,
All point, all edge, all sharpnesse; we did sit
Sometimes five Acts out in pure sprightful wit,
Which flowed in such true salt, that we did doubt
In which scene we laught most two shillings out.
Shakespeare to thee was dull, whose best jest lies
I'th' Ladies questions, and the Fooles replies;
Old fashioned wit, which walkt from town to town
In turn'd Hose which our fathers called the Clown.[10]

This shift in artistic taste seems to have involved, among other changes, a particular focus on the sexual dimension of the actions portrayed.

In Philaster, for example, the 'serious concerns' are to do with dynastic competition resolved by sexual exchange.[11] Philaster's kingdom has been taken over by Arethusa's father in a war. The king now seeks to consolidate his heir's right to the throne by marrying her to Pharamond the Prince of Spain who would thus usurp Philaster's right. The narrative problem is of course solved by Arethusa marrying Philaster, neatly endorsing both inheritance by right and inheritance by force of arms. The tone of the play, however, and the means by which it works out the action, are very different. Far from taking the exchange of women for dynastic purpose for granted, the action is accompanied by continuous commentary which suggests a series of very different views of the roles and functions of women at court. It is Arethusa who first presents Philaster with the conundrum of her desire for both kingdoms:

> *Philaster*, know
> I must enjoy these Kingdomes.
>
> (I.ii.53–4)

Her earlier conversation with a waiting lady had firmly set the context of love and creates a romantic if not a sexual resonance around her.

Philaster, for the moment, is unmoved and finds it unworthy of his future fame that he should give

> His right unto a Scepter, and a Crowne.
> To save a Ladies longing.
>
> (I.ii.60–1)

In the main action 'a Lady's longing' is seen as a trivial counterweight to the politics of men but it is nevertheless just those questions of longing which drive the action.

Set against Arethusa's role as a means of consolidating political deals is the figure of Megara who is described by Dion in terms which play on sexual and political meanings:

> Faith, I thinke she is one who the state keepes for the Agents of our confederate Princes: She'll cog, and lye with a whole Army, before the league shall breake: her name is common through the Kingdome, and the Trophies of her dishonour, advanc'd beyond *Hercules* pillars. She loves to try the severall constitutions of mens bodyes; and indeede, has destroyed the worth of her owne body, by making experiment upon it, for the good of the Commonwealth.
>
> (I.i.47–54)

In the commentary which accompanies the first encounter between Philaster, Pharamond, and the king, the relative political suitability of each of the princes, discussed by the men, is contrasted with the ladies' comments on their relative attractiveness. Dion had noted at the beginning that Arethusa does not seem to love Pharamond – a common enough way of indicating unsuitability, but this is made quite explicitly sexual in Megara's appreciation of Pharamond:

> but eye yon stranger, is he not a fine compleate Gentleman? O these strangers, I doe affect them strangely: they do the rarest home things, and please the fullest: as I live, I could love all the Nation over and over, for his sake.
>
> (I.i.284–8)

Megara and Pharamond are, of course, the villains and a good deal of the action concerns Megara's spiteful accusation of unchastity directed at Arethusa. Nevertheless, they have a lusty vitality like Cloe in *The Faithful Shepherdess* which is appreciated by the commentators on stage who guide the responses of the theatre audience.

The action of sexual revenge begins when Megara is caught in Pharamond's lodging, an action which is presented in a confusing mixture of tones. Dion at first informs the king in comic bawdy language that he has been unable to find Megara. The scene then shifts to one of suspense as the courtiers knock on Pharamond's door and he tries to forbid their entry. Finally, in a comic moment Megara appears on the upper level presenting herself with a mixture of pathos and anger to threaten revenge and foreshadow the next movement of the plot. What is most surprising in this scene, however, is the courtier's final comment. It offers no moral judgement or fear at the outcome but presents a frank enjoyment of the comic possibilities. The king has asked that the disgraced Pharamond be conducted 'to my lodging and to bed'. After his exit Cleremont jokes:

> Get him another wench, and you bring him to bed indeed

and Dion comments:

> 'Tis strange a man cannot ride a stage
> Or two, to breathe himselfe, without a warrant:
> If this geere hold, that lodgings be search'd thus,
> Pray God we may lie with our owne wives in safety,
> That they be not by some tricke of state mistaken.
>
> (II.iv.129–33)

Megara's appearance on the upper level was greeted, in her words, by 'your hootings and your clamours' and a similarly unrestrained comic reaction is possible to a number of other sequences in the play. For, in spite of Pharamond's villainy, he is also presented as a comic stud. After his first appearance and his speech of courtship to Arethusa, Cleremont notes:

> This speech calls him *Spaniard*, beeing nothing but a large inventory of his owne commendations.
>
> (I.i.152–3)

Pharamond's vanity is completely sexualized and his conflict with Philaster over the kingdom is presented as an unseemly display of male bravado before Arethusa, whose sexual response rather than political significance is at issue. Pharamond ends the scene by making a grosss pass at her which confirms his unsuitability as a hero. However, when he complains, in an aside, 'The constitution of my body will never hold out until the wedding', he confirms his comic role in the action.

Alongside this comic treatment of morally outrageous behaviour, the play offers other moments of blatant sexual display. A good deal of the action hinges on the young page, Bellario, whom Philaster uses as his go-between to the princess. The character would have been played by a boy since in the denouement he disproves all the accusations against Arethusa by proving he is a girl. As a result, although his/her sex is not revealed until the end of the play, there is an androgyne quality to his performance, reinforced by the way he is introduced in a poetic set piece as an emblem of pathos:

> sitting by a fountaines side,
> Of which he borrowed some to quench his thirst,
> And payd the Nymph againe as much in teares.
>
> (I.ii.114–16)

His passion for Philaster is expressed by skirting round the discourses of homosexuality and there is a similar tinge to the scene in which he and Arethusa talk of love. Arethusa is indeed accused by Megara of being unchaste with Bellario. This generates the central section of the action, but more important than the plot is the argument about sex and sexuality which this accusation provokes. When Philaster is told that Arethusa and Bellario have been caught together he responds at first with sophisticated argument that she could find no pleasure in an inexperienced boy. When Philaster accuses Bellario he proceeds by a voyeuristic interrogation about Arethusa's behaviour to him and his opinion of her:

> Tell me gentle boy,
> Is not she parrallesse? Is not her breath,
> Sweete as *Arabian* winds when fruits are ripe?
> Are not her breasts two liquid Ivory balls?
> Is she not all, a lasting mine of joy?
>
> (III.i.200–4)

The other side of these fantasies is of course the misogynist fantasy of women's perfidy indulged by the king against Megara and by Philaster against Arethusa. Megara's and Arethusa's behaviour is quite different but that is, anyway, irrelevant to these outbursts which conjure up myths of women's total availability, bypassing all constraining social forms.

This wished lack of constraint culminates in the violence of the famous hunting scene. The title-page of the 1620 quarto depicts Arethusa with her breasts exposed, the country fellow (here transmuted into a 'countrie gentleman') beside her and Philaster slinking off into the trees. The change of scene from court to country offers the possibility of a further range of sexualized fantasy. It opens with Philaster speaking a paraphrase from Juvenal's sixth satire, contrasting the evils of women with the pastoral joys of earlier ages which include 'some mountaine girle,/Beaten with winds, chaste as the hardned rocks' (IV.iii.7–8). What he actually finds in the woods is first Bellario, pursuing him with unwanted devotion and then Bellario with Arethusa in his arms. At this moment tragicomedy teeters between farce and disaster. Philaster is given an entrance in which he resolves to explain the situation calmly to Arethusa but this is followed by a potentially comic double take which launches a speech of melodramatic excess, followed by mutual deference about who is to die. The culmination is also knocked off balance by the arrival of the country fellow who interprets the ritual both with his vulgar desire to see the sights and his simple morality of

> Hold, dastard, strike a woman.
>
> (IV.v.85)

With such a variety of effects the scene can offer no single coherent point of view, for pleasure in classical tropes and passionate rhetoric vies with comic undercutting, a sense of aristocratic moral virtuosity with the country fellow's simple views, the simple excitement of a stage fight with the more drawn out sadomasochistic wounding of Arethusa.

The scene is similar in structure to the one in *The Faithful Shepherdess* in which Amaryllis is rescued by the Satyr, though the pleasures there were offered in a more abstract form. In *Philaster*, the narrative framework is tighter and the action can go through further complications and false endings until the final revelation, startling even the audience, that Bellario is a girl. The whole plot had been predicated on contrasting fantasies, drawing on a range of literary styles enacted through a sophisticated dramaturgy of obvious sexual display. Teasing innuendo is accompanied by comically undercutting the very fantasies which sustain the main action. The serious concerns of the play have to fight for attention against literary games and theatrical effects which can be turned in either comic or tragic direction.[12]

IV

This witty treatment of sex as commodity and pastime offers welcome relief from the more common Jacobean display of women as victims and necessarily complicates any monolithic account of 'ideology' concerning women and sexual relations in the period. The problem for a feminist reading, nevertheless, is how to connect the varied treatment of women as heroines with the construction of women as an audience for these displays. Women were addressed directly in both the commendatory verses to the Folio and in prologues and epilogues to the plays themselves. Together these texts address an audience of women who were felt to bring a particular sensibility to the theatre audience. Richard Lovelace, the cavalier poet, wittily attributed the invention of tragicomedy to Fletcher's concern for the ladies' feelings:

> But ah, when thou thy sorrow didst inspire
> With Passions, blacke as is her darke attire,
> Virgins as *Sufferers* have wept to see
> So white a Soule, so red a Crueltie;
> That thou hast griev'd, and with unthought redresse,
> Dri'd their wet eyes who now thy mercy blesse;
> Yet loth to lose thy watry jewell, when
> Joy wip'd it off, Laughter straight sprung't agen.[13]

The dramatists, too, presented themselves as the ladies' champions:

> Ladies to you, in whose defence and right,
> Fletcher's brave muse prepar'd herself to fight
> A battaile without blood, 'twas well fought too,
> The victory's yours, though got with much ado

The battle which was so easily won once again involved art as well as morality. It repudiated the old-fashioned misogyny of the quarrel over women as both clichéd and tedious but recognized that men and women quarrelling had significant theatrical potential. In *The Woman Hater*, Gondarino's misogyny is mocked as affectation but it does produce comic sequences in which the witty woman is more than a match for the railing man. Oriana teasingly pretends to love Gondarino and then Gondarino to love Oriana, with the comic contrast between true and false feeling opposing different ways of talking about sex made even funnier by the knowing way in which they are used by each character. Oriana gloats sarcastically over the way Gondarino was taken in by her pretence:

> by my troth good Lord, and as I am yet a maid, my thoght 'twas excellent sport to heare your Honour sweare out an Alphabet, chafe nobly like A Generall, kicke like a resty jade and make ill faces:
> Did your good Honor thinke I was in love?
> Where did I first begin to take that heat?
> From those two radiant eyes, that piercing sight?
> Oh they were lovely, if the balls stood right;
> And there's a legge made out of dainty stuffe,
> Where the gods be thanked, there is calfe ynough.
>
> (III.i.213–23)

Gondarino, for his part, can just as easily put aside the satiric prose of his usual attitude to women:

> Hee that shall marry thee, had better spend the poore remainder of his dayes in a Dung-barge. . .
>
> (III.i.231–2)

for the poetic courtship of

> Shall I find favour Ladie?
> Shall at length my true unfained penetence
> Get pardon for my harsh unseasoned follies?
>
> (III.i.235–7)

Gondarino's final punishment is to be tied to a chain and have all the ladies court him.[14] It was a scene which dramatized the theatrical triumph of witty women over misogynist men, an artistic preference for Beatrice over Griselda.

This artistic shift, however, does not necessarily affirm a feminist triumph on Fletcher's part. The witty play with dramatic style, the ability of each character to act the roles of love and hatred equally well, plays once again on anxiety about how far the truth of sexuality can be known. The plot still turns on a woman's chastity and Gondarino can worry even the urbane duke, Oriana's beloved, with the familiar problem of ocular proof:

> Doe's your Grace thinke, wee carry seconds with us, to search us, and see faire play: your Grace hath beene ill tutord in the

> businesse; but if you hope to trie her truly, and satisfie your selfe what frailtie is, give her the Test . . . put her too'it without hope or pittie, then yee shall see that goulden forme flie off, that all eyes wonder at for pure and fixt, and under it, base blushing copper.
>
> (V.ii.47–54)

The test consists of abducting Oriana and locking her in a brothel; a courtier is then sent to tell her that she has been condemned by the duke but could escape by lying with the courtier. She resolutely refuses, is threatened with rape, and rescued by the duke who has been watching the whole scene. The sequence encapsulates the basic plot of so many plays on women's chastity, demonstrating the constant and repetitious necessity for women to display their virtue to men. The witty, ingenious, virtuous, theatrically imaginative women must throughout this drama submit to the test of chastity. For the theatrical pleasures of Gondarino baited by women or Oriana threatened with rape are offered to those who can distinguish wit from tedium but who also control those definitions.

A similar reworking of theatrical misogyny is offered in *The Women's Prize*, which presents an updated sequel and contrasting response to *The Taming of the Shrew*. Petruchio has now remarried Maria who is determined not to follow in Katherine's footsteps. She distinguishes herself from the trained hawk of Shakespeare's play, claiming triumphantly that she is

> The free Haggard
> (Which is that woman that has wing, and knowes it,
> Spirit, and plume) will make a hundred checks,
> To shew her freedom, saile in ev'ry ayre,
> And look out ev'ry pleasure; not regarding
> Lure, nor quarry, till her pitch command
> What she desires.
>
> (I.ii.149–55)

The speech is a powerful assertion of independence. However, the play presents sexual relations less as a reversal of male supremacy than as a kind of bargaining, a negotiation of terms in the free market. The dramatic initiative is handed over to the women who withhold their sexual favours until better terms are agreed.

The precarious link between sexual relations and the ideology of marriage is exposed in the debate between Maria, Petruchio, and her father. Maria refuses to obey her father on the grounds that she, and her allegiances, have now been transferred to her husband. Petruchio then offers the apparently reasonable arguments of the new contractual mode of married relations in which the husband and wife are bound by mutual obligations:

> as I take it, sir, I owe no more
> Then you owe back again. . .
> You do confesse a duty or respect to me from you again
> That's very neere, or full the same with mine?
>
> (I.iii.198–234)

However, when Petruchio accepts the new terms, Maria throws it back with:

> Then by that duty, or respect, or what
> You please to have it, goe to bed and leave me,
> And trouble me no longer with your fooling.
>
> (I.iii.235–8)

This sophisticated discussion of contesting ideologies, however, is grist to a comic mill. It takes place in a parody of a parley scene as Maria and her friends, fortified on the upper acting level, threaten Petruchio and his forces with full chamber pots. Their relative positions dramatize the threat of male violence which underlines the argument and the measures the women take to defend themselves. If the women have, literally, the upper hand in these scenes, the men console themselves with the familiar solace of witty misogyny. Rowland and Tranio amuse the audience with a discussion of the 'great Schoole question', 'Whether that woman ever had a faith/After she had eaten' (II.iii.7–8), and Jacques produces a mock heroic set piece describing the advancing army of city wives who come to Maria's support (II.iv.42–84).

As the frustration mounts, so the rhetoric of misogyny becomes more violent, Petruchio's soliloquy (III.iii.146–71) addressed directly to the 'Gentlemen' of the audience vividly describes his past unquiet marriage, with explicit emphasis on the problem of sex, presented as rape, a matter for violent insistence and a source of humiliation for the unfortunate man:

> had I ever
> A pull at this same poor sport men run mad for,
> But like a cur I was faine to shew my teeth first,

And almost worry her.

(III.iii.163–5)

The issue here is less the struggle for power between men and women than a negative view of monogamy. Marriage is no longer presented as a sacred institution: rather it is seen as a limit on free sexual activity in the market to an arena where restrictions render it a matter either for constant miserable negotiation or violent rapine. Neither of these is an attractive prospect for an urbane audience. As Mike Bristol explains:

> Although every individual husband has a compelling interest in his wife's sexual fidelity . . . men collectively desire the subordination and sexual availability of all women . . . . The much more arduous and difficult choice is that between marriage on any terms at all, and the freedoms and privileges of the unattached male.[15]

Petruchio's soliloquy addresses the audience as a collection of unattached males for, whatever its actual composition, that is the point of view from which the jokes and the narrative makes sense. The play no longer imposes obedience by violence in the interests of 'an awful rule and right supremacy', but after the comic gags are over, Maria must recognize that she loves Petruchio and come to an agreeable understanding with him.[16]

The process by which these plays comically modify the excesses of both patriarchy and predatory sexuality reinforce the values and the self-image of the urbane young men who were their original audience. The highly polished glass in which this audience viewed itself reflected similarly urbane images of the witty woman and the wife who sought more civilized relations with men. The wittiest and most attractive women of these plays are those who accept the terms of sexual relations offered by the new consumerist ideology, for when sex becomes a matter of commodity relations women occupy the ambiguous position of sharers in this consumption and the commodity itself. Berkenhead's verses to the First Folio praise:

> Thy Sence (like well-drest ladies) cloath'd as skinn'd
> Not all unlac'd, nor City starch't and Pinn'd.

(xiii)

It was a common enough critical trope but the extension of the metaphor and the precision of its reference locate it as especially applicable to the taste of urbane gentlemen. This particularity of appeal is rendered even more precisely in the epilogue to *Valentinian* where the audience are urged to accept the play:

as yee would choose a Misse,
Only to please the eye a while and kisse,
Till a good wife to got.

(18–20)

The plays, like mistresses, were to be seen as the pastimes of a young, free, urbane male audience for whom pleasure and value for money lay behind their social as much as their commercial transactions.

The dangerous prospect for men in this world is that the free market was equally available to women. When Maria uses her sexuality as a bargaining counter, she accepts that her husband might find the commodity elsewhere. However, as a free agent on the open market, she too can find other purchasers:

PETRUCHIO: Well there are more Maides then Maudlin, that's my comfort.
MARIA: Yes, and more men then Michael.
PETRUCHIO: I must not to bed with this stomach, and no meat Lady.
MARIA: Feed where you will, so it be sound and wholesome,
Else live at livery, for i'le none with ye.

(I.iii.221–5)

The really desirable, upmarket version of sex is to be found among women who hold themselves chaste for wit or for virtue but it is available elsewhere. Maria's image of sex as horseflesh available either as the accoutrements of a gentleman or for more mundane purposes 'at livery' is then extended by her associate Byancha who advises Petruchio:

You had best back one of the dairy maids, they'l carry.
But take heed to your girthes, you'l get a bruise else.

(I.iii.226–7)

For the plays make a very clear distinction between the witty chaste women whose individualism and wit match those of the new men and women who, since they merely service their needs, are the butts of their wit, meeting the pleasure of sex and laughter at the same time. This distinction between the sexual behaviour of different classes is a further complication in the dramatization of misogyny. In *The Scornful Lady*, the eponymous heroine has plotted successfully to humiliate her lover Elder Loveless and he vents his rage in a misogynist soliloquy which reveals a number of the pressures which lie behind this witty and urbane presentation of sex:

> This senselesse woman vexes me to th'heart,
> She will not from my memory. . .
> Sure shee has
> Some Meeching raskall in her house, some hinde,
> That she hath seene beare (like another *Milo*)
> Quarters of Malte upon his backe, and sing with't,
> Thrash all day, and ith evening in his stockings,
> Strike up a hornepipe, and there stink two houres,
> And nere a whit the worse man; these are they,
> These steelechind rascalls that undoe us all.
> Would I had bin a carter, or a Coachman,
> I had done the deed ere this time.
>
> (V.i.1–2, 11–20)

Ferdinand has a similar fantasy about his sister in *The Duchess of Malfi* but where Ferdinand's vision is presented as that of a pathological villain, the Elder Loveless's dramatic status is in no way affected by this misogyny. His fault in the play is rather that he loves too well and his dramatic development consists of learning to trick and humiliate his mistress as she had tricked and humiliated him earlier in the action. For the Scornful Lady is a witty woman who, unlike Maria, is not controlled by being married to the object of her wit and the play has to negotiate both the value of her wit in making her a suitable partner for the hero but not witty enough to get the better of him.

Throughout the action this procedure is worked through by a play with literary convention and a rejection of the familiar fit between old-fashioned ideology about sex and old-fashioned dramatic expressions of it. The plot opens conventionally enough with the lady sending her lover away because he has revealed their love, but the language and style of the discussion reveals a social world in which matters of chastity and love, socially accepted behaviour and individual integrity, coexist uneasily with a constant potential for breakdown and disaster. The language, however, also displays an energetic lack of piety about the situations described. The Scornful Lady's language is not that of the morally righteous but that of the stylishly wilful; and the marriage described less one of sacrament than of the fulfilment of certain social rites:

Believe me; if my Wedding smock were one,
Were the gloves bought and given, the Licence come,
Were the Rosemary branches dipt, and all
The Hipocrists and cakes eate and drunke off,
Were these two arms incompast with the hands
Of Bachelers to lead me to the Church;
Were my feete in the dore, were *I John*, said,
If *John* should boast a favour done by me,
I would not wed that yeare.

(I.i.144–52)

A similar pragmatic air pervades the action where Elder Loveless returns to charge his lady with cruelty, she pretends to swoon and die at this treatment but when he repents his harshness revives to laugh at him. The conventions of misogynist denunciation, the references to face painting, or a taste for coaches which had become the stale commonplaces of complaint are revived in this exchange partly by the rhetorical *élan* with which they can be delivered but also by the sense that they arise out of the particularities of the relationships. The language of patronage and service, of the old-fashioned poetic notions of sexual allegiance, are turned into sarcastic rejection of a set of ideals which can no longer be lived up to:

You have us'd me, as I would use a jade,
Ride him off's legges, Then turn him into the Commons;
If you have many more such prettie Servants,
Pray build an Hospitall, and when they are old,
Keepe um for shame.

(IV.i.190–5)

This extension and combination of metaphors of older ideals of love and service is witty in itself and although the audience knows that Elder Loveless is only trying his mistress, they indicate a cynicism about love and service which says more for the characters' wit than their integrity. They also indicate that Loveless, in ridding himself of the old allegiances, is liberated into placing love where it belongs – as a luxury commodity to be enjoyed like art and music:

O 'tis brave
To be one's owne man. I can see you now
As I would see a Picture, sit all day
By you and never kisse your hand: heare you sing,
And never fall backward; but with as set a temper

> As I would heare a Fidler, rise and thanke you . . . I can eate mutton now, and feast my selfe
> with my two shillings, and can see a Play
> for eighteene pence againe.
>
> (IV.i.207–18)

In this scene the Elder Loveless is humiliated for his railing by the lady's trick of pretended horror which brings about his repentance. But the action of the play endorses his view that the Scornful Lady must be tamed, though by a wittier trick than denouncing her virtue.

In the hilarious denouement, the Elder Loveless pretends to be about to marry a country wench, in fact his friend Welford in disguise. The lady, in a fit of pique, insists on his earlier vows to her and marries him before she can find out the truth. Welford in disguise has all the comedy of a farcical cross-dressing scene but it is also the occasion for working through yet more of the questions of women and correct sexual relations. The lady is at first completely unfazed by the strange apparition. When Welford goes into his routine as the paradigm submissive wife seeking only to please her lover and proud that she uses 'no paint, not any drugs of art' to enhance her beauty, her behaviour is seen as prodigious rather than exemplary and the lady enquires disingenuously:

> Why what thing have you brought to shew us there?
> Doe you take money for it?
>
> (V.ii.101–2)

The Elder Loveless insists that his new love transcends the cash nexus as 'a Godlike thing not to be bought for mony' and praises her virtues in contrast with those of the lady who has rejected him:

> She cannot sound in jest, nor set her lover tasks, to shew her peevishnes, and his affection: nor crosse what he saies, though it bee Canonicoll. Shee's a good plaine wench, that will doe as I will have her, and bring mee lusty boyes to throw the Sledge, and lift at Pigs of lead: and for a wife, shee's farre beyond you: what can you doe in a household, to provide for your issue, but lye a bed and get um? your businesse is to dresse you, and at idel houres to eate; when she can doe a thousand profitable things: She can doe pretty well in the Pastry, and knows how pullen should be cram'd: she cuts Cambricke at a thrid: weaves bone-lace, and quilts balls: And what are you good for?
>
> (V.ii.176–86)

The impact of the speech is complex; Loveless's charge that the lady is but an idle ornament carries some weight. However, the parody of marriage handbooks shows that the alternative is not to be found in a virtuous country companion who could prove no match for a witty man about town. In the end the desirable attributes are those of a woman whose wit can match the man's but only enough to appreciate the merits of his superior trickery. The action, the language, and the imagery of this play show a writer who had a most acute understanding of the conflicting arguments over women and sexual relations and could assume an audience who did so too. The older ideals of chastity and service would clearly no longer do either as theatrical conventions. The wit which makes the plays more entertaining can also bring more tangible rewards. Elder Loveless's hopeless and humiliating passion for the lady is contrasted with the careless attitude of his friend, Welford. Welford gets the best of the action too. His part in Elder Loveless's plot results in him going to bed, still disguised as a country wench, with the Scornful Lady's sister. His wit thus brings him an heiress and they are bound together by a shared joke, not by bonds of service or patriarchy.

The style and ethos of *The Scornful Lady* were repeated with more or less good humour in numerous other comedies up to the closing of the theatres. They offered their urban audience an image of a world where sex was significantly more important than honour and where relations with women had to be renegotiated, unfettered by older conventions of chastity and service and the smooth passage of women from fathers to husbands. The humanized patriarchy of Shakespearian comedy is transferred to a world of competitive individualism which was liberating for those women with the wit and the resources to survive within it. However, the release from the familiar narrative and moral patterns of the *querelle des femmes*, the contest between misogyny and adulation, was only a release into patterns of wit and urbanity in which women could as often be the victims as the heroines of the action. Moreover, it is impossible to tell how far these shifts in the representation of women were a result merely of the play with theatrical conventions and how far they indicated that women as well as men were in a position to renegotiate the terms of their sexual relations. In an elegant play with the titles of some of Fletcher's comedies, G. Hill's commendatory verses claim that Fletcher

> taught (so subtly were their fancies seized)
> To Rule a wife, and yet the Women pleas'd.

He confirms that the terms by which sex acted as the narrative and social dynamic of these plays had shifted to include a more pleasing image of women but that the rule of the father, the tyranny of the lustful king was replaced by the rule of witty men and the women who consented to become their partners in wit.

NOTES

This essay first appeared as chapter 8 of the author's *Renaissance Dramatists*, Feminist Readings Series (Hemel Hempstead: Harvester, 1989), 193–223.

1 In order to avoid the minefield of the authorship of the Beaumont and Fletcher canon, I am using 'Fletcher' to refer to plays by Fletcher and his collaborators. Where possible I have used the editions prepared under the general editorship of Fredson Bowers, *The Dramatic Works in the Beaumont and Fletcher Canon* (Cambridge: Cambridge University Press, 1966–1991).

2 See, for example, Herbert Blau, 'The absolved riddle: sovereign pleasure and the baroque subject in the tragicomedies of John Fletcher', *New Literary History* 17 (3) (1986), 539–54. Suzanne Gosset, in ' "Best Men are Molded out of Faults": marrying the rapist in Jacobean drama', *English Literary Renaissance* 14 (3) (1984), 305–27, discusses some Fletcher plays in the context of dramatic treatments of rape in the period.

3 *The Works of Francis Beaumont and John Fletcher*, ed. Arnold Glover and A. R. Waller (Cambridge: Cambridge University Press, 1905–12), vol. I.

4 See the more general discussion of this problem at the beginning of chapter 3 of McLuskie, *Renaissance Dramatists*.

5 Bowers, *Dramatic Works*, vol. III, 497.

6 ibid., 493.

7 Jokes about the occasional, inexperienced visitor to the theatre abound. In *Playgoing in Shakespeare's London* (Cambridge: Cambridge University Press, 1987), Andrew Gurr quotes Peacham's paradigm example about a citizen's wife who mistook a pickpocket's advances as sexual. Its mockingly superior tone is very similar to that of Fletcherian comedy.

8 See R. A. Foakes's account of the importance of this moment in 'Tragedy of the children's theatres after 1600: a challenge to the adult stage', in D. Galloway (ed.), *Elizabethan Theatre* (London: Macmillan, 1970).

9 Glover and Waller (eds), vol. I, xi.

10 Glover and Waller (eds), vol. I, xxxix.

11 See Peter H. Davison, 'The serious concerns of *Philaster*', English Literary History, 30 (1963), 1–15.

12 For a fuller account of these plays, in particular the different comic and tragic treatment of the 'lustful tyrant' motif, see my section in Lois Potter, with G. E. Bentley, Philip Edwards, and Kathleen McLuskie, *The Revels History of Drama in English, 1613–1660* (London: Methuen, 1981), vol. IV, 188–94.

13 Glover and Waller (eds), vol. I, xxiv.

14 Compare the end of the anonymous *Swetnam the Woman Hater Arraigned by Women*, in *Swetnam the Woman Hater: The Controversy and the Play*, ed. C.

Cradall (Lafayette, Indiana: Purdue University Studies, 1969), in which the misogynist is tried and found guilty by a court of women who punish him with violent pinching. The play is discussed at length in Linda Woodbridge, *Women in the English Renaissance* (Urbana, Illinois: Illinois University Press, 1984), 300–22.

15 Michael Bristol, *Carnival and Theater: Plebeian Culture and the Structure of Authority in Renaissance England* (London: Methuen, 1985), 164.

16 See *The Taming of the Shrew*, Act V. See also my 'Feminist deconstruction: Shakespeare's *Taming of the Shrew*,' *Red Letters*, 12 (1982), 15–22.

6

PREREVOLUTIONARY DRAMA

Walter Cohen

To what extent might one argue that the English Revolution constitutes the crucial reception of the tragicomedies composed between 1610 and 1642, that the plays are prerevolutionary in more than the obvious chronological sense, that they are shaped by the forces that led to civil war and that they often anticipate many of the conflicts of the revolutionary era? Before turning to the evidence of the drama itself, it may be useful to suggest the rationale and method of such an approach.

I

Over the past decade often radical political criticism has come to occupy a leading place in the academic study of literature in England, the United States, and other parts of the English-language world. Given the prominence of Renaissance scholarship in this movement, one would expect early Stuart tragicomedy to respond well to a political critique. The usefulness of such a critique is another matter, however. With the exception of Shakespeare's romances, very few of the tragicomedies first performed between 1610 and 1642 are sufficiently well known to have been read even by specialists in Renaissance drama. Further, since consideration of these plays does not open up the canon to marginal or repressed voices, shift literary criticism in the direction of the politically more promising field of cultural studies, or address larger questions of literacy and the social function of education, apparently neither immediate pedagogical purposes nor significant ideological projects can loom large here. On the other hand, work on tragicomedy might help develop theoretical inferences of interest outside the field and modify previous political accounts of Renaissance drama. My own purpose is, first, to contribute to the ongoing discussion of the relationship between gender and class, particularly as part of the enterprise of forging a viable Marxist–

feminism, and, second, to argue for the prerevolutionary character – in the strong sense – of all early Stuart drama. The conclusion develops a more general argument about contemporary political criticism.

The real economic changes for women between late Tudor and early Hanoverian times – most obviously, declining participation in household production – may have been safeguarded, if that is the right word, by the Revolution. At the level of ideology, the analogy between patriarchal family and patriarchal monarchy is alien to modern distinctions between private and public: the position of women before 1660 was understood to be intimately connected to the nature of the state. Yet this period also witnessed a crisis of gender relations. The patriarchal model regularly ran into theoretical trouble. Puritan household manuals stressed the spiritual equality of husband and wife. In political treatises the hierarchies of father and child and of king and subject lined up rather nicely, but the (admittedly unequal) partnership of husband and wife more plausibly supported a Parliamentary perspective on the limits of royal power. The well-known, quite open controversy over the nature and status of women in early Stuart England also suggests the instability of traditional categories and perhaps of modes of behaviour as well. Legal records reveal that the years from 1560 to 1640 marked a high point in the disciplining of women – through trials for scolding or witchcraft. This repression formed part of a more general judicial offensive by the propertied against the poor. In light of the analogical thinking just noted, the attack on women may have partly involved a symbolic reassertion of social order through a displacement from the level of the village, where assaults on the class hierarchy were direct and hence difficult to crush, to the level of the family, where challenges to the gender hierarchy were only indirect and hence relatively easy to control. But though it would therefore be wrong to equate the conflicts over women with the conflicts that led to civil war, the connection between them – as mutually implicating struggles, as interacting causes and effects – is surely closer than all but the most recent historical studies indicate.[1]

The evidence from the revolutionary years themselves points to a related, if not quite identical, conclusion. The extent of women's public political participation increased remarkably. Occasionally soldiers or rioters, women also petitioned Parliament – on behalf of peace or of the Levellers – in large, organized groups. For example, 500 women presented a pro-Leveller petition that was signed by 10,000 women. In addition, women were the prime movers in the founding of several local separatist churches. And, perhaps most important, they were disproportionately represented on the left wing of the Revolution and especially among the radical sects, where they may have constituted an absolute majority. Primarily of lower-class origin, often prophets or preachers, and at times open opponents of sexual prohibition, their behaviour undermined many of the principles of gender hierarchy. Yet many of the limitations of the past remained. After 1643, one cannot discover any independent women's organizations, and at no time do there seem to have been groups dedicated predominantly to women's issues. Still, women occupied a less subordinate, if still subordinate, position on the left than was available to them elsewhere in England at the time.[2] If it is hyperbolic to call the radical wing of the Revolution a women's revolution, its defeat was a major defeat for women, and not just because most women, like most radicals and sectarians, or for that matter like most English*men*, were members of the lower classes. Finally, the various strains of political and social thought that developed on the revolutionary side during this period were important inspirations for the group of self-conscious feminist thinkers who emerged in the second half of the seventeenth century.[3]

A concern with prerevolutionary theatre also runs into quite a different difficulty from the problematic relationship between women and revolution. The conservative revisionist historiography of recent years has questioned the character, the significance, and at times even the existence of the Revolution. Much of this work challenges ostensibly Marxist beliefs in the teleological progress of early modern English history and in the correlation of the motives and actions of historical agents with their class positions. Yet neither position is central to a Marxist view of revolution, which instead focuses on the interaction of subject and structure in producing long-term causes and consequences. In particular, the argument that the English Revolution was a bourgeois revolution depends not on the claim that any men or women of the mid-century thought they were engineering a bourgeois revolution, but on the conclusion that this is in fact what they did.[4] Second, whereas a rejection of teleology on however dubious grounds responds to a pronounced, traditional, and arguably excessive historiographical emphasis on discovering causes of the English Revolution, there has been almost no interest before the present decade in viewing the theatre as one of those causes, except by erroneously positing it as a hated symbol of royal power. In this context the study of prerevolutionary theatre is new hat.

A final problem with this approach is that tragicomedy does not seem to provide the most fertile ground for identifying a prerevolutionary tradition. Generic criticism has itself often received sceptical treatment in contemporary theory, in Derrida's essay on 'The law of genre', for instance, or, to move closer to Renaissance tragicomedy, in Terry Eagleton's recent book on Shakespeare.[5] Eagleton's *explicit* disavowal at the outset of the standard generic divisions of Shakespeare's corpus, followed by his *implicit* adoption of those divisions in the body of his book, may suggest their continuing utility for political criticism, however. Still, Margot Heinemann has argued that the more radical early Stuart plays have been effectively invisible in part because 'nineteenth-century dramatic editors tended on the whole to be less interested in satire and chronicle than in the "purer", more timeless imaginative forms of tragedy, comedy and tragi-comedy.'[6]

This position, at least as it applies to tragicomedy, is consistent with the view of leftist critics who work along generic lines. Franco Moretti and Jonathan Dollimore, among others, have located the radical or subversive tradition of Renaissance drama primarily in tragedy.[7] The same is true of recent 'British' feminist critics such as Catherine Belsey, Dympna Callaghan, and Ania Loomba.[8] When they turn to Shakespearian tragicomedy and romance, some of these writers join a chorus of political denunciation.[9] Arguing at a higher level of abstraction, Fredric Jameson perhaps defines the assumptions underlying this stance when he suggests that in romance the antagonism between two distinct 'moments of socioeconomic development . . . is not yet articulated in terms of the struggle of social classes, so that its resolution can be projected in the form of a nostalgic (or less often, a Utopian) harmony'.[10] Even Martin Butler, who has been almost uniquely sensitive to the dissonant resonances in the primarily tragicomic drama of the Caroline court, locates an independent or oppositional thrust much more readily in city comedy, estates satire, and emblematic moral forms. For him, 'the more purely courtly tradition . . . is both the least interesting and least significant aspect of the period'.[11] Finally, Lois Potter has demonstrated the close connection between tragicomedy and royalist ideology in the 1640s and 1650s.[12] Hence tragicomedy provides a particularly hard test of a general claim for the prerevolutionary character of early Stuart theatre. Especially given its prominence in the period, one might reasonably assume that if it can be plausibly connected to the upheavals of the mid-century, the same conclusion holds for the entire spectrum of dramatic forms in the three decades before 1642.

It is difficult – indeed, for me, impossible – to break entirely with the tradition of assigning a conservative valence to romance and tragicomedy. But an effort to bring into focus the more contestatory dimensions of these forms can usefully rely on both historical and structural patterns. One might begin by noting recent American psychoanalytical and feminist treatments of Shakespeare. This work often seems like a photographic negative of Marxist studies: relatively speaking, the histories and tragedies are depreciated, while the romantic comedies, problem plays, and romances receive sympathetic commentary. Carol Thomas Neely, Peter Erickson, and others have charted a trajectory in Shakespeare's career from a more misogynistic, patriarchal representation to a less hierarchical, reasonably humane portrayal of gender relations especially characteristic of the romances.[13] The generalizability of this account of Shakespeare to drama after 1610 is a matter to which it will be necessary to return.

The historical trajectory of tragicomedy itself offers another way into counter-interpretation. Broadly speaking one can designate three successive phases of the form between 1576 and 1642: the romantic, non-classicist plays of the late sixteenth century, indebted to the medieval heritage and analogous to drama of the period in France, Spain, and elsewhere; the mixed tragicomedy of the opening years of the seventeenth century composed primarily by Marston and Shakespeare; and the more unified tragicomedy that emerges in 1608, indebted to Italian neo-classical dramatic theory and practice, and associated above all with Beaumont and Fletcher.[14] Three qualifications are relevant here, however. The self-consciously Italianate manner of unified tragicomedy is already present in the second and, to some extent, even in the first phase. More crucially, the relatively popular, Elizabethan romantic style survives after 1610, albeit in modified form.[15] The modification, however, seems to result in a narrowing of range as 1642 approaches.

One may nevertheless speak of two main strains of tragicomedy in the period, one classical and the other popular. It should be kept in mind, however, that this is a tendential rather than an absolute distinction; that neither strain is likely to appear in pure form; that given the almost total absence of extant plays written for the outdoor theatres after 1620, the distinction cannot be systematically correlated with the split between the public and private stage; and that a consideration of revivals and, hypothetically, of lost public theatre plays would certainly accord greater prominence to the popular tradition than would a scrutiny of new plays alone.[16] From this perspective the prerevolutionary charge of tragicomedy may be subjected to a further historical partition, based on the successive stages of the Revolution. Presumably, neo-classical forms could be aligned most closely with the crisis of 1640, while popular works would reveal affinities with the successively more radical movements of the subsequent years. As we will see, however, this is generally but not universally the case.

Such historical differentiations may also be understood in structural terms. This more synthetic perspective requires delineation of the ideology of the form, a matter touched on earlier in the survey of negative judgements by leftists of the prerevolutionary possibilities of tragicomedy and romance. A play may anticipate the Revolution in various ways, ranging from manifestly self-conscious representation of central social conflicts to apparently more inadvertent, and for that reason particularly revealing, deviations from an implicit generic or thematic logic. One must therefore read symptomatically but not only symptomatically: this injunction entails attention to presences as well as absences. If such considerations should guide critical response to any dramatic genre, they have an especially important bearing on tragicomedy, a form designed to effect reconciliation following a period of serious conflict. This impulse betrays an organicist, hegemonic aspiration that in the early seventeenth century aligns tragicomedy more clearly than tragedy or satiric comedy, for example, with aristocratic, absolutist ideology. In so far as reconciliation implies incorporation rather than exclusion, however, one may occasionally hear marginal or oppositional voices. But of course the preceding conflict also opens still more critical possibilities, especially since a central pleasure of the genre is to render the situation tragically hopeless before saving the day. Hence, the always vexed question of narrative closure, the relationship between process and outcome, becomes particularly problematic here. The more the conclusion feels like a desperate expedient designed to extricate the dramatist from an impossible situation, the greater the probability of radical or subversive tendencies. Unusually messy tragicomedies will thus prove especially revealing.

Things are a little different in romance, where the passage of often long stretches of time, the restoration of families across generations, and the tendency to relegate conflict and evil to the period before the opening of the action can combine to produce utopian effects. A prerevolutionary reading of this configuration is almost too easy. Of course many plays synthesize tragicomedy and romance. But those romances that minimize serious antagonism – such as Jonson's *New Inn*

(1629) or Brome's *Antipodes* (1638) and *A Jovial Crew* (1641) – will remain marginal to the following remarks.[17]

II

English tragicomedies between 1610 and 1642 presuppose the analogy between family and state, deploying the love-and-honour code to produce a series of homologies and articulations that make women integral, even central to the fate of the nation. The plays characteristically raise and resolve interdependent fears about women and monarchs. Anxiety about uncontrolled female sexuality, often manifested in fraternal incestuous desire, points in somewhat mystified fashion to the threat of women's independence from men. Doubts about the king's fitness to rule receive far more open expression, a difference perhaps due to the absence of explicit opposition at the time to gender hierarchy but not to class hierarchy. Especially in the earlier years, the more popular plays deepen the critique of the crown by moving partly or wholly outside the courtly milieu and by challenging the aristocratic, often absolutist representational assumptions of the form. Such works may also reveal a relatively tolerant and flexible view of female sexuality. At times, even, one senses somewhere beyond the theatrical horizon a world whose norms are neither patriarchal nor aristocratic.

In Shakespeare's late romances, a single young woman figures prominently in the redemptive pattern. But in the earlier tragicomedies, *All's Well* and *Measure for Measure*, and in the tragicomedies composed by other playwrights after 1610, the magic number is two. In works by Beaumont and Fletcher, Dekker, Middleton and Rowley, Webster, Massinger, Ford, Arthur Wilson, Shirley, Heywood, Davenant, and Brome, *two* young women stand at the centre of the action, one or both of them enduring various kinds of mistreatment, including verbal and physical attacks on their sexual honour.[18] Their matchless virtue is underscored not only by their resistance to both the bribes and the threats of predatory males, but often by their solidarity with each other as well, a solidarity made all the more remarkable by the objectively competitive sexual situation in which they find themselves. One might mention Panthea and Spaconia in Beaumont and Fletcher's *A King and No King* (1611), Tormiella and the queen in Dekker's *Match Me in London* (also 1611), Rosinda and Cassandra in Shirley's *The Young Admiral* (1633), and Eumena and the Queen in Davenant's *The Fair Favourite* (1638).[19] In the end the men who have plagued them are suitably chastened, while the women are rewarded, usually, with the men of their choice.

Apparently, then, these plays have little or nothing of the misogynistic hysteria often encountered in early seventeenth-century tragedy or satiric comedy, forms that in this respect as in others tragicomedy explicitly challenges. The American feminist valorization of Shakespeare's last plays would thus seem highly relevant here as well.

Yet the triumph of the virtuous women is double-edged in a way that merits closer scrutiny, beginning with some obvious considerations. Often the products of female assertiveness, the concluding marriages also circumscribe that assertiveness, consigning it to an unequal partnership. Moreover, the condition of even this ambiguous accomplishment is almost always the preservation of virginity, an internalized norm of virtuous characters, male and female, and virtuous dramatist alike. Although this norm has a rational component in the period, it functions mainly to guarantee the control by men – fathers, brothers, husbands, suitors, and sons – of the sexuality of women.

In tragicomedy it is mainly brothers who exhibit an emotional concern with such power, conceptualized as masculine honour. As this concern approaches an obsessive extreme, particularly in the absence of physical control of the female body, it becomes a kind of competitiveness or jealousy sometimes indistinguishable from incest. In *A King and No King*, one of the founding works of the tradition, King Arbaces chivalrically promises his sister Panthea to the vanquished King Tigranes, conceives an incestuous passion for her himself, resolves to satisfy his need, and is prevented from committing a series of horrible crimes only by the happy revelation that he and Panthea are not in fact brother and sister. In Webster's *Devil's Law-Case* (1617) Jolenta informs one of her suitors – falsely – that she has borne her brother's child. Four other plays – Massinger's *Bondman* (1623), Ford's *Lover's Melancholy* (1628), Heywood's *A Challenge for Beauty* (1635), and Davenant's *The Fair Favourite* – portray brothers who are far more upset by their sisters' apparent, though in the event non-existent, breaches of sexual honour than are the sisters' suitors. In Davenant's work this anxiety is simply and repeatedly called jealousy. And Brome's *Lovesick Court* (1639) deploys both a young couple in love – until they discover they are brother and sister and happily go their separate marital ways – and a woman horrified by her overwhelming sexual attraction to her brother, who happens to be the very man who proves the real brother of the first woman – until they discover they are unrelated and can be conveniently paired off.

These plays reveal Renaissance tragicomedy's characteristic adaptation of *Oedipus* but with a distinctive generational inflection. In

Shakespeare's romances the core family relationships are vertical; here they are horizontal. The intense fraternal feelings suggest that tragicomedy is the anti-misogynistic genre that proves the misogynistic rule. However wrong the brothers may be about who their sisters are or about how well those sisters defend their virginity, they are right about one thing: these beautiful, virtuous women are incredibly desirable, so much so that no man can resist their attractions. And this is true even if, perhaps especially if, the women do everything in their power to discourage male attention. Thus Tigranes falls for Panthea despite having promised to marry Spaconia in *A King and No King*, the king abandons his queen for Tormiella in *Match Me in London*, the physician attempts sexual blackmail of Jane in Middleton and Rowley's *A Fair Quarrel* (1617), Leosthenes drops Statilia to take up with Cleora in *The Bondman*, the king rapes Eurinia in Wilson's *The Swisser* (1631), the prince rejects Rosinda for Cassandra in *The Young Admiral*, the king forsakes his queen for Eumena in *The Fair Favourite*, and Stratocles tries to rape Eudinia in *The Lovesick Court*. Caliban's attack on Miranda may belong here as well. Female sexuality is threatening when women express sexual desire and also when they do not. If the threat is that they will cause otherwise good men to lose control, the final marriages serve to remove them from circulation, to prevent them from doing any further damage. Some such explanation helps account for one of the more standard irritating features of these tragicomedies – the fact that the virtuous young women are always also beautiful. Their beauty makes their virtue necessary as a protection against its inevitable destructive effects.

The plays provide additional grounds for fearing female sexuality. *A Fair Quarrel* offers a heroine who gives birth while betrothed but unmarried, a mother who (falsely) accuses herself of adultery, a son whose concern with his mother's honour borders on incestuous desire in the manner noted above, and, in a cheerful vein, a bawd and a whore. *The Devil's Law-Case* presents a heroine who (falsely, again) claims to be pregnant by each of her two suitors, a mother who competes with her for the affections of one of them, and another young woman who really is pregnant out of wedlock. *The Bondman* provides adultery, premarital sex, and a near quasi-adulterous liaison between stepmother and stepson. And *The Lover's Melancholy* contributes an offer of premarital sex and a lesbian attraction. Even if one generally prefers psychological to sociological explanations of sexual ideology, this pattern of representation is difficult to understand without some appreciation of its historical specificity, without reference to the prevalent (learned, male) belief at the time that women were sexually more voracious than men[20] or to the more general gender instability outlined earlier.

These tragicomedies seem to anticipate the explicit responses after 1640 to revolutionary or sectarian women, whose words and deeds provoked a large body of satirical and hostile commentary from horrified men.[21] We learn that Joan Bauford 'taught in *Feversham*, that husbands being such as crossed their wives might lawfully be forsaken', that 'a wife hath put up a Bill in a publick Congregation against her husband, and her self to bee prayed for, because shee loved another man better than her owne husband', and that among the Ranters 'women are all in common'.[22] Women are warned 'not to *usurpe Authority over their Husbands*, but to be subject to them'.[23] They are repeatedly ridiculed for establishing 'A Parliament of Ladies', the proceedings of which 'grew to a meere confusion' in the participants' fundamental demands for greater sexual licence and for the right to 'have superiority and domineere over their husbands'.[24] This superiority is dangerous because women 'have not been onely extreamly evil in themselves; but have also been the main instruments and immediate causes of Murther, Idolatry, and a multitude of other hainous sins, in many high and eminent men . . . they onely are the greatest and most powerfull temptations to evill of all other'. In this enterprise they serve the devil: nothing 'predominates more over his [man's] understanding and will, than they by their subtile falacies, and bewitching illusions'.[25] The 'weaker Sex . . . in all Kings, Princes, and Noblemens Courts, have been, and yet are his [the devil's] only Engins to effect all his exorbitant desires.'[26] In these passages, as in the tragicomedies, uncontrolled female sexuality disrupts family and state alike. Yet the analogy is imperfect. The anxieties of the plays tend to remain latent. The more free-wheeling atmosphere of the revolutionary period, when gender relations like everything else were up for grabs, offers retrospective insight into conflicts that in tragicomedy remain obscure.

III

Things stand differently with matters of class and state. These were openly contested long before the Revolution, though of course in less decisive form than occurred after 1640. It is accordingly easier here than with considerations of gender to move from a general model to historical differentiation. Most tragicomedies are concerned with kings and their courts, all such plays find the royal setting defective, and in every case the defects are remedied by the end of the action. Affairs of state are inseparable from affairs of the heart. The problem with the court and the crown is in every case a sexual one. The gender conflicts and anxieties already described generate a range of additional failings: murderous monarchs in *A King and No King*, *Match Me in London*, and *A Challenge for Beauty*; murderous aristocrats in *Match Me in London* and *The Lovesick Court*; weak or immoral rulers in *The Young Admiral* and *A Challenge for Beauty*; and variously unpleasant courtiers in *A King and No King*, *The Swisser*, *The Young Admiral*, *A Challenge for Beauty*, and *The Fair Favourite*. If this focus narrows monarchical concerns from the nation to the bedroom, as a wise counsellor complains in *A Lovesick Court*, it also indicates the irreducibly political character of gender relations perhaps in the period and certainly in tragicomedy. Successful resolution of the problem of women is integral to successful resolution of the problem of power. The latter concern is usually presented in dynastic terms as a question of succession, but one also finds a rather close connection with war in *A King and No King*, *The Bondman*, *The Swisser*, *The Young Admiral*, and *The Lovesick Court*.

This typical tragicomic treatment of monarchy looks toward 1640, when the court faced the uniform opposition of the articulate population of the country, a population that none the less would have been satisfied by compromise and reform rather than by civil war and revolution. A brief historical survey that attends to the specificity of individual plays will reveal in addition more radical possibilities associated sociologically with the presence of the world outside the court and formally with a symptomatic inability to achieve closure, to produce a persuasive concluding reassertion of male, aristocratic, and usually absolutist control.

In the second decade of the seventeenth century tragicomedy seeks interclass alliances. One thinks of the inclusion of the shepherds in *The Winter's Tale* or the mariners in *The Tempest* within an aristocratic hegemony. The recurrent enterprise, however, is some form of synthesis between nobility and urban bourgeoisie. Beaumont and Fletcher demonstrate their characteristic comic condescension in the sole citizens' scene of *A King and No King*. But in Middleton and Rowley's *A Fair Quarrel*, atypically set in London rather than the Mediterranean, neither plot has anything to do with the court, and both are designed to effect a fusion between nobility and bourgeoisie that extends the boundaries of the genre. In the main action, from which the title derives, the aristocratic honour code as manifested in the gentleman soldier's duel is moralized through the triumph of such notions as justice, repentance, forgiveness, self-sacrifice, and virtue. The secondary plot dramatizes the victory of love between a poor gentleman and a wealthy citizen's daughter over the mercenary values of the father: property marriage is repudiated, but property in marriage most certainly is not. Hence, aristocratic and bourgeois extremes are equally rejected, thereby opening the way to a resolution that is ideological in the main plot and ideological as well as sociological in the secondary action.

In both plots, active female virtue is the mechanism that effects the reconciliation. Jane resists the financial pressure of her father and the sexual blackmail of the physician in order to marry the man she loves, who also happens to be the father of her child. The spirit of forgiveness that informs the play includes a toleration for premarital intercourse by a betrothed couple. If this outcome still entails the sexual control of women, the main plot far more forcefully converts female autonomy into victimization. There, the colonel's sister sacrifices her own feelings to the higher good of male bonding between her brother and his duelling foe. Thus, despite the play's careful articulation of class and gender, no homology exists between them. In both plots the class settlement implies a society in which monarchy is either limited or irrelevant. The ideology of gender possesses no such coherence. In addition to handling the two women in very different fashion, the play leaves unresolved the strange sexual byplay between Captain Ager and his mother, and leaves unincorporated the bawd and whore who appear in a comic roaring scene. Gender relations remain difficult to bring to full consciousness and difficult to stabilize.

A more pervasive formal and ideological uncertainty informs two other tragicomedies of the decade, Dekker's *Match Me in London* and Webster's *The Devil's Law-Case*. In the main plot of Dekker's play the king abducts and tries to seduce Tormiella, a shopkeeper's wife; in the subplot, the king's brother attempts to kill the king and seize the throne. By casting the king as potential victim, this secondary action mitigates the harsh judgement of him in the central plot. But it may also parallel the sexual conflict in suggesting the moral disorder of the court. Partly for this reason the court looks bad compared to the city – Cordoba and Seville, despite the title. Dekker's citizen ideology is evident in the portrayal of the king and his brother, in the decision to make the bawd a court lady, in the sympathetic rendering of the married love and work of the shopkeeping couple, and especially in the king's concluding encomium to Tormiella:

well were that City blest,
That with but, Two such women should excell,
But there's so few good, th'ast no Paralell.[27]

Appropriately, the king defeats his brother through pragmatic skill, whereas Tormiella escapes dishonour or death through providential intervention. The resolution grants moral superiority to a middle-class woman, while subordinately reintegrating the middle class into a monarchical polity and the woman into a patriarchal family.

Yet considering what has gone before, it is hard to find this outcome either metaphysically or socially satisfying. In the course of the play seven people are in danger of being murdered by six people a total of eleven times. There are too many near-deaths, too many villains to make the final reformation and restoration persuasive. Instead one gets the impression that the expected tragicomic movement has not really occurred, that the only pattern is of one damn thing after another. This feeling is strengthened by the unexplained return of the supposedly virtuous heroine to the court she was previously eager to flee. *Match Me in London* thus provides symptomatic evidence of the difficulty of adapting tragicomedy to, loosely speaking, bourgeois ends. But this messiness may correspond to the explicit ideological stance of the play, in the sense that both imply a critique of the aristocratic assumptions of the form.

Webster's work merits a closer look partly because it resembles Middleton and Rowley's in its materials: lack of any reference to the court; a love match between an impoverished aristocrat and a woman from a wealthy merchant family; the overt approval and covert sabotage of the proposed marriage by the mercenary male member of that family; a duel between aristocrats in which the loser repents having fought in a bad cause and tries to help his erstwhile foe to a happy and lucrative marriage; a widow who falsely accuses herself of adultery for the purpose, thwarted in the event, of controlling her grown son; and a pregnant woman who is ultimately able to marry the father of her unborn child. In two plays that may have been performed in the same year in the same theatre – the Red Bull – these similarities are sufficient to raise the question of influence. If there was any borrowing, it was probably by Webster, since *The Devil's Law-Case* may well be the later piece and since, unlike *A Fair Quarrel*, its plot has no known source.[28]

Yet the two tragicomedies are so utterly different in feel that it is tempting to think of *The Devil's Law-Case* as a systematic dismantling of the representational assumptions that govern the already innovative *A Fair Quarrel.* Webster's procedure is to heighten or exaggerate the traditional motifs of tragicomedy to the point where they self-destruct. The playwright alludes to the form's well-known complexity of plot in his address to the reader: 'A great part of the grace of this (I confess) lay in action' (7, lines 14–15). Not surprisingly the characters engage in a wide variety of duplicitous schemes and don a range of disguises, very few of which, however, have the intended consequences and many of which seem to have no consequences at all. The repeated references to the devil and the contrasting invocation of the church, the clergy, repentance, and restitution do not have the effect of suggesting that a diabolical design explains the disorderliness of human action, or that a providential pattern makes more consoling sense of things, or even that the allegorical logic of the morality tradition imposes a kind of coherence. The ending of the play, in which the characters' various plots and counterplots come to light, hardly constitutes a conclusion: weirdly inconsequential, it raises questions rather than providing answers. Although it is conceivable that Webster simply lost control of his complicated material – a charge that may well be true in part of *Match Me in London* – the action seems until very late to be heading toward a standard tragicomic outcome complete with the romance return of an important figure from the distant past, the union of the suffering lovers, the chastening of the blocking figures, and the reconciliation of all – within and across generations. That Webster exploits none of these conventional opportunities suggests a different logic at work.

The critical commonplace that tragicomedy subordinates character to plot refers to the overarching shape of a play. In *The Devil's Law-Case*, however, the unit of sense is the individual scene, which may have little to do with preceding or succeeding events. Thus Abraham Wright noted in about 1650 that 'The plot is intricate enough, but if rightly scanned will be found faulty by reason many passages do either not hang together, or if they do it is so sillily that no man can perceive them likely to be ever done.'[29] Instead the noted theatricalism of tragicomedy, reinforced by passages of theatrical self-reference, is so played up that larger concerns with form are undermined. The episodic nature of the plot also puts considerable pressure on the characterization. The odd and apparently inconsistent behaviour of many characters inevitably raises questions of motivation, questions that are not answered; indeed the play betrays no awareness that such questions exist. This is a world of discontinuous subjectivity, a world where interiority is repeatedly invoked but reveals precious little stability.[30]

As comparisons to *A Fair Quarrel* will suggest, a similar combination of exaggeration and irrelevance marks the treatment of class and gender issues. The merchant is not simply rich but incredibly rich, and he is not simply avaricious but murderously so. The impoverished but loving aristocrat does not merely lack money; he compulsively gambles it away. The young woman pregnant out of wedlock is not betrothed to the father of her child; the older woman who falsely accuses herself of adultery does so not in the private space of her home in order to protect her son, but in the public domain of the legal court in order to destroy him. Although these economic and sexual concerns are delineated in detail and closely intertwined, one should not assign them any meaning, much less speak of an articulation or homology between them. For despite the frequency of moralizing rhetoric, *The Devil's Law-Case* possesses only the most pallid value-system. From a formalist perspective its opacity derives from the importation of a tragic and especially a satiric sensibility into tragicomedy. The resulting negativity informs the play. And it is this negativity that calls into question the rationale of tragicomedy more radically than does the class mutation of the form engineered by Middleton and Rowley. It is a radicalism, however, that does not even hint at an alternative construction of reality.

A Fair Quarrel and perhaps *The Devil's Law-Case* as well were written and performed for public theatre audiences. After 1620 one can rarely be certain that this is the case and can often be certain that it is not. Thus arguments for the popular character of the plays are necessarily more inferential than are similar claims for earlier tragicomedy. The increasing prominence of the learned tradition requires even greater reliance on symptomatic reading in order to discern critical or subversive tendencies. This point may be briefly illustrated by reference to Ford's *Lover's Melancholy*, a Shakespearian pastiche without villains or serious conflict and overwhelmingly devoted to tearful aristocratic reconciliation. Its sweeping denunciations of the court in the familiar terms of state, class, and sexuality ('commonwealths totter', 'Our commonwealth is sick', 'the unsteady multitude', 'The commons murmur and the nobles grieve,/The court is now turned antic and grows wild,' 'wanton gentry', 'vices which rot the land')[31] are all the more interesting given their utter irrelevance to the plot of the play.

Massinger's *Bondman* is apparently a different matter. Set in a city-state ruled by a republican aristocracy, it retains the full social range of the popular tradition despite being a private theatre work, and is primarily devoted to an attack on the failings of that aristocracy and the painful correction of its sins. Margot Heinemann's claim that the play reveals 'a burning anger at tyranny against nobility and gentry, coupled with an acute sense that the multitude must and should be kept down', combined with Annabel Patterson's argument that it also constitutes a sympathetic 'comment on the new anti-Spanish militancy of Charles and Buckingham' suggest Massinger's characteristic stance of qualified aristocratic opposition and render unnecessary all but a few remarks.[32] *The Bondman* differs from most tragicomedies in its elegant linkage of state and sexuality, of gender and class. The aristocracy has lapsed into military unpreparedness by devoting all its wealth to female luxury. The need to fight then opens the way for a slave rebellion, which has as one of its beneficial consequences the punishment of the lascivious behaviour of aristocratic women. Unruly female sexuality gives rise to unruly popular assertiveness, assertiveness that imposes the necessary control on women. But how will popular unrest be recontained? Here the play indulges in fantasy, allowing the aristocrats to overcome a rebellion noteworthy for fierce and courageous military action by means of purely symbolic theatrical effects. The slave rebellion is also indirectly the mechanism by which the hero wins the desirable woman from his rival. The gap between the personal and political in this instance is difficult for the protagonist to bridge in his concluding speech of self-justification. Furthermore, Massinger's typically misleading method of characterization allows for nice theatrical reversals while inadvertently calling into question the coherence and continuity of the behaviour of the two rivals. In such symptomatic slippages in an otherwise artfully constructed play, one catches glimpses of the anxieties and inadequacies of the circumscribing strategies of aristocratic opposition.

Attention to similar moments – elisions, deflections, unintended admissions – proves even more crucial with the tragicomedies of the 1630s. Shirley's *Young Admiral* deploys its unpleasant rulers in order to place the titular figure in impossible, emotionally affecting love-and-honour dilemmas before happily unraveling the plot. But since this is not the world of Corneille or even of Dryden, the hero's choices have no resonance. Given the option of fighting against his native land or of witnessing the murder of Cassandra, the woman he loves, Vittori exclaims that compared to treason, ''Tis a lesse sinne to kill my Father'.[33] The logic is that parricide, unlike treason, is merely a private crime. Since Vittori is here speaking to Cassandra, his remark seems obliquely intended to warn her that she must die.

This is not what he has in mind, however. Instead, he lengthily defends a different resolution: in the refusal to commit treason, 'I die my Countries Martyr' (III.i.228). Only Cassandra's dim recognition that his rhetoric has run away with him enables Vittori to recognize that it is not his life that is at stake but hers. She then delivers an extended, more appropriate, and less sincere martyrdom speech of her own that seems to parody his and that causes him finally to opt for treason, a decision antithetical to the initial public–private hierarchy and possessed of no other consequence than the immediate one of keeping Cassandra alive. Shortly thereafter, when his situation becomes crueller still – if he doesn't fight, his lover will die; if he does fight, his father will die – Vittori does nothing at all. Asking 'which blessing rather/I should now part with, a deere wife, or father' (III.ii.128–9), he is saved by the resourcefulness of the other heroine from a decision whose pseudosymmetry is achieved by the silent elision of the political act of treason. This sequence reveals more than the primacy of plot and the depoliticizing tendency of the form. The debating of ethical and political dilemmas is nothing other than irrelevant, sentimental posturing. Subjectivity is either discontinuous or, more likely, only intermittently existent at all. Decisions have no consequences and indeed do not really have to be made. At such moments the vacuity, the absurdity of the aristocratic norms of tragicomedy inadvertently come into view.

In Davenant's *Fair Favourite* the unintended effects are more explicitly political. The play seems designed to produce an unusually absolutist message. Complementing meditation on the divinity of monarchs, the king and his courtiers repeatedly reflect on the painful burdens of power, as in this characteristically self-pitying passage:

> How wearisome, and how unlucky is
> The essence of a King, gentle, yet by
> Constraint severe; just in our nature, yet
> We must dissemble; our very virtues are
> Taken from us, only t'augment our sway![34]

Similarly, the king's apparently adulterous love for Eumena, the fair favourite, is not what it seems. Before the action opens, some of his advisers abduct Eumena, whom the king already loves, convince him that she is dead, arrange a politically advantageous property marriage for him, and return her to the court the night the wedding is celebrated. Thus his apparently destructive passion is really the sign of virtuous fidelity distorted by evil courtiers. The queen remarks on the secrets and gossip of the court, three choral courtiers ridicule old courtiers and court ladies, and the king himself expresses contempt for his cowardly and unprincipled counsellors.

The people, who never appear on stage, fare no better. Despite the king's efforts to make Eumena popular with them, the 'vulgar' or 'popular' belief is that she is a slut (II, pp. 230, 231), and it is 'the people's secret scorn', the 'people's malice' that causes Eumena's brother to doubt her chastity (I, p. 216, and V, p. 270) and succumb to incestuous 'jealousy' (e.g. II, p. 223). It is 'the people', again, 'that dull crowd, whom Kings through cursed fate/Must please' who initially prevent the king from pardoning the brother when he apparently commits a murder. Partisans of the common law against the newer royal courts, they 'will have all laws observ'd . . ./. . . not 'cause th'are wise, but/'Cause th'are old.' They 'call for Justice', in the king's bitter and, in the context of the next decade, prophetic words, only 'When it is us'd to punish those above/Them, not themselves.' They are 'Rude and ill manner'd/ . . . /When they are pleased to see a tragic show' (IV, pp. 261–2). The king, however, knows better:

> in legal skill I should connive
> At those disorders which the furious in
> Their growing spirits oft commit; for else
> The body of a State, – effeminate
> With lasting peace, – when a strange war shall
> Come, like bodies natural, – confirm'd by strict
> And quiet temperance, – will want the benefit
> Which the use of small disorders bring, that
> Make each violent disease less new, and violent.
>
> (IV, p. 262)

And in the end rationality prevails, with the triumph of this superior principle of aristocratic, misogynistic justice.

Yet this extreme royalism depends oddly on removing all initiative from the crown. Action, as opposed to reaction, implies immorality and so must be consigned to defective courtiers and, to employ a pleonasm in the context of this play, to the defective people. Conflicts involving class and state generate the sexual problems of the play – adulterous love and fraternal 'jealousy' – and these problems in turn define the crisis of the monarchy. Despite the pairing off of couples at the conclusion that resolves this crisis, the resulting wedge between crown and court glorifies absolutism only at the price of depriving it of its immediate social base. This is one version of that contradictory

Caroline synthesis of loyalty to the king and hostility to his counsellors, a synthesis that came apart in the 1640s.[35] Similarly, the grumbling invocation of the people registers the lack of autonomy of the court, the existence of a multiclass society, the constraints on royal prerogative, and the political weight of the mass of the population. These too are the truths of the 1640s, rendered visible, ironically, by the strength of the dramatist's commitment to the monarch.

By contrast the more popular tragicomedies of the 1630s, though inevitably registering the weight of monarchical power in a way that is not true of public theatre tragicomedy before 1620, are explicitly critical of the crown and sympathetic to oppositional forces. Wilson's *Swisser* presents a hostile view of the court and of the king, who is actually a rapist; locates virtue in the retired or banished lords, who constitute something like a country party; and briefly but approvingly registers the power of the common soldiers, who repudiate their general – and force the king to accept that repudiation – in favour of one of the country lords. This political configuration implicitly goes well beyond 1640, perhaps even to the days of the New Model Army. The radical thrust is contained in the ordinary way, however – through the traffic in women. The king consents to marry the woman he raped, though only after learning that she is of noble rather than humble birth and is indeed the woman he has long loved. But the feeling is not mutual, and his future bride must renounce all claims on the man *she* loves in order to restore both her honour and the king's. The effect of this outcome is to render pointless the elaborate disguises she has adopted to be near the object of her affections, an effect of which the play is oblivious, however.

In Heywood's far narrower *A Challenge for Beauty*, the extravagant adherence to the honour code by two sea captains may perhaps be viewed as a downward and rather dubious appropriation of courtly ideology. The object in relation to which they competitively demonstrate their nobility and who accordingly functions as the mechanism of male bonding is of course the woman they love, who is forced to put up with a series of elaborate testing rituals. In the other, and ideologically compatible plot, an Englishwoman of 'birth, not high degree'd,/Nor every way ignoble'[36] contracts an interclass marriage with a Spanish lord, in the process scoring a victory over the proud and brutal Queen of Spain. The international resolution combines amity with a recognition of English superiority. The unsatisfying quality of the various compromises, which may be contrasted with those of *A Fair Quarrel*, results from the desire to have everything both ways.

Brome's *Lovesick Court* also focuses on extravagant bouts of honour between two men, the prize of which is not only the woman they both love but also succession to the throne. The play has been seen as 'a full-scale parody of the absurdities of courtier drama'[37] – a somewhat misleading view. Far more than such tragicomedies as *The Devil's Law-Case* and *The Lover's Melancholy*, where the indebtedness to Shakespeare takes the form of pastiche, *The Lovesick Court* is Shakespearian in its structure as well, in its multiple, mutually interrogating plots and social levels. The aristocrats' intrigue is self-consciously parodied by the servants – a barber, a tailor, a waiting-woman, and a tutor. The effect of highlighting the excessiveness of courtly conduct is to render it both limited and admirable, however. Moreover, the initiative of the servants in unravelling their own love intrigue produces the romance resolution of the aristocratic dilemma, a resolution that requires the sorting out of parentage and, as noted earlier, the apparently unproblematic adjustment of subjectivity entailed by the conversion of incestuous desire into either married love or the love between brother and sister. Similarly, the four rustics, who were thought to favour the candidacy of the unscrupulous military hero for the crown, save the lives of the heroes and the virginity of the heroine by their timely intervention against that hero. The autonomy and effectiveness of non-aristocratic figures are thus not the inadvertently revealing by-products of an absolutist stance as in Davenant's play, but signs of a capacious social vision. The activity of shepherds and servants solves the problem of sexual desire, on which the fate of the nation in turn depends. The precise character of the circumscription of the lower classes and of women may be indicated by noting that the crisis resolved by the romance ending originates twenty years before as a result of civil war. Apparently intending a non-absolutist monarchical model of national unity prior to social breakdown, *The Lovesick Court* atually produces a benevolently hierarchical utopian vision of reconciliation in the wake of revolutionary upheaval.[38]

IV

Two recurrent problems have shaped this account – the relationship between gender and class, and the relationship between tragicomedy and the Revolution. The first of these connections may be understood either as articulation or as homology, and often as both in the same play. In most of the tragicomedies, where the ultimate aim is royal restoration, resolution of gender difficulties is equivalent to or quickly leads to resolution of the political crisis. If the court is not the focus, women serve as the means of class reconciliation. Finally, in plays concerned with both the state and the interaction of various social classes, class tensions influence gender issues, which then shape the disposition of political power. The homology between gender and class depends most generally on the patriarchal model of both family and state. In tragicomedy this mode of thinking results not only in the equation of the crisis of sexuality with the crisis of monarchical rule, but also in the parallel treatment of women and the lower classes, in the implicit or explicit dramatization of an often oppositional autonomy followed by the celebratory reconciliation that integrates and thereby circumscribes that autonomy. But the parallel also extends to the inadequacies of that resolution, to the failure of closure.

In pursuing this last matter, symptomatic reading has proved an essential method. The tragicomedies quite openly adopt a stance compatible with the widespread hostility to the court in 1640, a stance that the form's emphasis on love relationships, with their implicit challenge to a strong patriarchal model, may reinforce. But it is primarily through symptomatic analysis, particularly of the relatively elite plays, that one can discern more radical or revolutionary alternatives anticipatory of the positions developed in the next ten to twelve years. First, tragicomedies that register the independent efficacy of the lower classes, such as *The Swisser*, *The Lovesick Court*, *The Bondman* (ambiguously), and *The Fair Favourite* (inadvertently), seem to point to the revolutionary period itself. Second, a number of relatively orthodox plays, including *A King and No King* and *The Lover's Melancholy*, covertly reveal anxieties about female sexuality that came out into the open in the reactions to revolutionary and sectarian women. Third, the discontinuous subjectivity and rejection of coherent narrative that characterize *The Devil's Law-Case* in particular, but also in various ways such works as *Match Me in London*, *A Fair Quarrel*, *The Young Admiral*, and *The Lovesick Court* were theoretically espoused among the sects, pre-eminently by the Ranters.[39] And, finally, *The Lovesick Court* projects a postrevolutionary interclass reconciliation that, however hierarchical, was quite emphatically rejected by men of property in 1660, in 1688, and later still. Thus relatively radical options are entertained primarily though not exclusively in the popular plays, especially from before 1620. In the years approaching 1642 tragicomedy seems to have become increasingly unable to resist a focus, however critical, on the court, a pattern that strikingly enough does not hold for comic as opposed to tragicomic romance.

The approach employed here interprets history backwards, using the mid-century as a vantage point from which to discover the multiple forces in the tragicomedies of the preceding decades that may have contributed to the collapse of royal power and to some extent of the social order it upheld. The more general historical thesis behind the particular argument is that the Revolution should serve as the conceptual organizing principle for all work on seventeenth-century theatre. The comparable political thesis is that recovery of a partly concealed radical tradition in the drama may prove useful today.

Yet at least two problems remain, with which it may be appropriate to conclude. The first is that the method of symptomatic reading, whatever its intellectual rigour, may be a form of wishful thinking, a procedure designed to discover a radicalism unavailable to seventeenth-century audiences and most modern readers alike. The doubts here arise first from the speculative character of the argument, from the absence of either seventeeth-century evidence of the posited subversive effects or, to return to a point noted at the outset, of any critical vitality of the plays today.[40] A second concern about symptomatic reading is the wildly contradictory results that have emerged in recent years from the analysis of Renaissance drama in the light of contemporary theory. To take a central example: totalizing arguments now exist for both the coherence and the dispersal of subjectivity in the plays, and for both the progressive and the reactionary character of either alternative. One cannot easily avoid the conclusion that political commitment predetermines critical position.[41] A satisfactory general theory would surely have to recognize the absence of an inherent political charge to different theories of subjectivity, as well as the varying degrees of heterogeneity of different subjects and subject-positions. Such a view is admittedly more accessible to a critic willing to entertain the possibility of fragmented subjects than to one committed to fixed human essences, however.

The value of this approach depends in part on how one understands the relationship between past and present, or for that matter between text and interpretation. Even though everyone would presumably agree that all writing about the past has political consequences in the present, there is some tension today between those critics who emphasize the political function of Renaissance drama in the Renaissance and those who focus on its contemporary political appropriation.[42] As this polarization as well as some of my introductory comments will suggest, I have been assuming a non-identical, dialectical relation between then and now, a relation of similarity and difference among authorial intention, textual form, initial impact, and modern effect. It might be useful to think in terms of a series of interlocking structures: the structure of seventeenth-century reception interacts with aesthetic structure in one way, while the structure of contemporary reception interacts with aesthetic structure in a different way. This formulation is aimed against both the desirability and the possibility of either a purely subjective or a purely objective appropriation. Though it does not explicitly provide criteria for evaluating the respective claims of competing interpretations, it is not an argument for relativism.

From this perspective a work that was contestatory in its own time is more likely to have subversive potential today than one that was not. A politically motivated concern with decentred subjectivity in Renaissance drama stands or falls on its critical power in contemporary culture, but it has a better chance of standing if one can also show that it had a subversive thrust in the Renaissance. This dual oppositional effect is precisely what a number of critics have sought to demonstrate. My own argument has emphasized discontinuous subjectivity at various points as a wedge against putatively unitary dominant discourses of class, gender, and morality. Although the period does offer abundant evidence of essentializing rhetoric, this is hardly the whole story, at least as far as Renaissance theatre is concerned. Even if one forgoes inferences about performance, the dramatic texts do not reveal the existence of a powerful norm of coherent subjectivity. What is now commonly designated the humanist subject seems to have been little more than one option among many: the nature of subjectivity was in dispute. Thus evidence of decentred subjectivity does not in itself indicate subversive effect. More particularly, a review of early Stuart tragicomedy reveals the equally discontinuous subjectivity of male and female characters. These plays also highlight by way of contrast the relatively more homogeneous subjectivity of Shakespearian drama and perhaps even of early Stuart tragedy. The two observations may be combined to produce a third: the case for the greater instability of women's subject-positions is strongest where there seems to be an effort to construct coherent male characters. But one might well hesitate before arguing that as a result tragicomedy had greater subversive potential than tragedy or than Shakespearian drama in the early seventeenth century.

Because tragicomic subjectivity can thus serve legitimately as only a limited index of prerevolutionary crisis, I have not made claims for its disruptive force except where it intertwines, or at least coexists, with other potentially oppositional gestures. Yet in so far as these gestures come into focus through symptomatic reading, one may well wonder whether seventeenth-century audiences could have felt, should have felt, or actually felt the subversive force of this drama. As indicated earlier, the answer depends on the relation between the structure of tragicomedy (or of individual tragicomedies) and the structure of reception, on the extent to which social and cultural life produced a mode of appropriation sensitive to the more troubling features of the plays. Hence this essay has aimed to demonstrate neither the inherent nor the empirical subversiveness of tragicomedy but the continuity of its concerns with those of the Revolution. Ultimately, an appeal to coherence rather than to proof also informs even the most empirically minded essays in this volume.

Since an assessment of tragicomedy's contemporary critical potential calls for a similar line of reasoning, it can be quite brief. To the extent that Shakespeare's influence is related to his relative modernity and that modernity is in turn related to a powerful aspiration toward complexly coherent subjectivity in a number of his plays, the relatively dispersed subjectivity of the tragicomedies may help explain their marginal position today in theatre, education, and scholarship. There seems little point in bemoaning this marginality or in lobbying against it. As I acknowledged at the start of this essay, discussions of Stuart tragicomedy can have only the most highly mediated impact on the present, primarily through their reconstruction of larger fields such as Renaissance drama of which they are part and which continue to exert some influence. The radicalism of even a successful intervention is not beyond dispute, however. Although recent writers have had no trouble in demonstrating the essentialist view of character that has long dominated Shakespearian criticism, one may ask whether emphasis on decentred subjectivity will retain much oppositional force in post-modern culture. There are at least two very different replies, both of them suggested earlier. One is that the political interest of these plays depends not on matters of subjectivity alone but on their cumulative subversive force. And the other is that recognition of internally contradictory subjectivity is in itself neither left wing nor right wing. It is simply accurate and as such provides a necessary basis for any plausible account of political agency.

Attention to relatively marginal aesthetic artifacts may also provide an opportunity for theoretical reflection, however. The second major problem raised but not resolved by this essay falls into this category. It is the danger that gender may in the end be subordinated to class –

owing to the more open resistance to class inequality than to gender inequality in the seventeenth century, or to the primacy of class in a Marxist theory of revolution. The difficulty lies not so much in the interpretation of the tragicomedies as in the larger historical thesis which that interpretation serves. Perhaps class *was* more important than gender in the English Revolution, but one would not want to assume in any case either that the relative weight of gender and class at this particular moment authorizes broad historical generalization or, more importantly, that all gender issues of the century are adequately approached through a revolutionary prism. Emphasis on the centrality of political opposition and hence, ultimately, of the Revolution places the focus on a pivotal event, dominated by political and religious conflicts. Such a choice seems inevitably to belittle the experiences of women, whose struggles, however much influenced by decisive confrontations of this sort, have been played out over longer periods of time. A traditional Marxist stress on the bourgeois, and hence more broadly social, character of the Revolution addresses this concern only to a limited extent.

But an even more profound obstacle to a plausible Marxist–feminism is implicit in the immediately preceding account of subjectivity. An awareness of the unevenness in the representation of subjectivity in Renaissance drama virtually presupposes a recognition of the multiple forces that shape subject-positions. If subjectivity results from the intersection of an indefinitely large number of determinations, the turn from a monistic model to a binary one will purchase increased empirical plausibility at the expense of conceptual clarity. There is nothing distinctive to either Marxism or feminism in this difficulty. The addition of race, sexuality, subjectivity, the body, or all of these issues to the list would only highlight the dilemma – the need for an account that overcomes both monistic reduction and pluralistic vacuity.[43] This essay is at best a halting step in that direction. More generally, the methodological and theoretical problems that have occupied its last few pages obviously resonate well beyond an immediate interest in the persuasiveness of the preceding account of prerevolutionary theatre.

NOTES

1 Most of this information on English women before 1660 comes from Susan Dwyer Amussen, *An Ordered Society: Gender and Class in Early Modern England* (Oxford: Blackwell, 1988).

2 The information in this paragraph comes from Keith Thomas, 'Women and the Civil War sects', *Past and Present* 13 (1958), 42–62, and 'The Puritans and adultery: the Act of 1650 reconsidered', in Donald Pennington and Keith Thomas (eds), *Puritans and Revolutionaries: Essays in Seventeenth-Century History Presented to Christopher Hill* (Oxford: Clarendon Press, 1978), 277–8; Claire Cross, ' "He-goats before the flocks": a note on the part played by women in the founding of some Civil War churches', in G. J. Cuming and Derek Baker (eds), *Popular Belief and Practice*, Studies in Church History, 8 (Cambridge: Cambridge University Press, 1972), 195–202; Christopher Hill, *The World Turned Upside Down: Radical Ideas during the English Revolution* (1972; Harmondsworth, Middlesex: Penguin, 1975), 306–23; Patricia Higgins, 'The reactions of women, with special reference to women petitioners', in Brian Manning (ed.), *Politics, Religion and the English Civil War* (New York: St Martin's Press, 1973), 177–222; Christine Berg and Philippa Berry, 'Spiritual whoredom: an essay on female prophets in the seventeenth century', in Francis Barker *et al.*, (eds), *1642: Literature and Power in the Seventeenth Century*, Proceedings of the Essex Conference on the Sociology of Literature, July 1980 (Colchester: University of Essex, 1981), 37–54.

3 Hilda L. Smith, *Reason's Disciples: Seventeenth-Century English Feminists* (Urbana: Illinois University Press, 1982), x–xi, 9–10, and 53–6. Some of the claims in this study are to be treated with caution.

4 For recent corroborating arguments see Mary Fulbrook, 'The English Revolution and the revisionist revolt', *Social History* 7 (1982), 249–64, and Lawrence Stone, 'The bourgeois revolution of seventeenth-century England revisited', *Past and Present*, 109 (November 1985), 53.

5 Jacques Derrida, 'The law of genre', *Glyph* 7 (1980), 202–29, and Terry Eagleton, *William Shakespeare* (Oxford: Blackwell, 1986).

6 Margot Heinemann, *Puritanism and Theatre: Thomas Middleton and Opposition Drama under the Early Stuarts* (Cambridge: Cambridge University Press, 1980), 201.

7 Franco Moretti, ' "A Huge Eclipse": tragic form and the deconsecration of sovereignty', *Genre* 15 (1–2) (Spring–Summer 1982), 7–40, and Jonathan Dollimore, *Radical Tragedy: Religion, Ideology, and Power in the Drama of Shakespeare and His Contemporaries* (Brighton: Harvester, 1984). For a slightly different approach, but one that still finds subversive possibilities primarily in tragedy, see Francis Barker, *The Tremulous Private Body: Essays on Subjection* (London: Methuen, 1984), 14–41.

8 Catherine Belsey, *The Subject of Tragedy: Identity and Difference in Renaissance Drama* (London: Methuen, 1985); Dympna Callaghan, *Woman and Gender in Renaissance Tragedy: A Study of* King Lear, Othello, The Duchess of Malfi *and* The White Devil (Atlantic Highlands, N.J.: Humanities Press, 1989); and Ania Loomba, *Gender, Race, Renaissance Drama* (Manchester: Manchester University Press, 1989). A striking exception is Kathleen McLuskie, *Renaissance Dramatists* (Atlantic Highlands, N.J.: Humanities Press, 1989), where sustained attention to the formal and conventional dimensions of the plays precludes the attribution of a distinctive thematic or ideological tendency to any genre. Belsey teaches in Wales, Callaghan is Irish and teaches in the United States, and Loomba is Indian and teaches in India – hence the quotation marks around 'British'.

9 See Peter Hulme, ' "Hurricanes in the Caribbees": the constitution of the discourse of English colonialism', in Barker *et al.*, *1642: Literature and Power in the Seventeenth Century*, 55–83; Moretti 21–4; Barker and Hulme, 'Nymphs and Reapers Heavily Vanish: the discursive con-texts of *The Tempest*', in John Drakakis (ed.), *Alternative Shakespeares* (London: Methuen, 1985), 191–205; Paul Brown, ' "This thing of darkness I acknowledge mine": *The Tempest* and the discourse of colonialism', in Jonathan Dollimore and Alan Sinfield (eds), *Political Shakespeare: New Essays on Cultural Materialism* (Manchester: Manchester University Press, 1985), 48–71; and Dollimore, 'Transgression and surveillance in *Measure for Measure*', ibid., 72–87.

10 Fredric Jameson, *The Political Unconscious: Narrative as a Socially Symbolic Act* (Ithaca, N.Y.: Cornell University Press, 1981), 148.

11 Martin Butler, *Theatre and Crisis, 1632–1642* (Cambridge: Cambridge University Press, 1984), 4.

12 Lois Potter, ' "True Tragicomedies" of the Civil War and Commonwealth', in Nancy Klein Maguire (ed.), *Renaissance Tragicomedy: Explorations in Genre and Politics* (New York: AMS Press, 1987), 196–217.

13 Richard Wheeler, *Shakespeare's Development and the Problem Comedies: Turn and Counter-Turn* (Berkeley and Los Angeles: California University Press, 1981), 12–19; David Sundelson, *Shakespeare's Restorations of the Father* (New Brunswick, N.J.: Rutgers University Press, 1983), 6–7; Peter Erickson, *Patriarchal Structures in Shakespeare's Drama* (Berkeley and Los Angeles: California University Press, 1985), 9–13 and 170–3; and Carol Thomas Neely, *Broken Nuptials in Shakespeare's Plays* (New Haven: Yale University Press, 1985), 21–2 and 209.

14 This history is surveyed in Marvin T. Herrick's standard study, *Tragicomedy: Its Origin and Development in Italy, France, and England* (Urbana: Illinois University Press, 1962), 215–312. Herrick, however, identifies only two phases – before and after Beaumont and Fletcher.

15 See Heinemann's essay on popular tragicomedy, chapter 7 in this volume.

16 On this last point, see Butler, *Theatre and Crisis*, 181–250.

17 But see Butler's essay on late Jonson, chapter 8 in this volume. Butler revises the revisionist interpretation, arguing for the orthodoxy of the final plays.

18 In Ford's *Lover's Melancholy* and Wilson's *Swisser* there are actually three women, but the functional group when it comes to sorting out love relationships is usually two.

19 Unless otherwise noted, all dates are from Alfred Harbage and S. Schoenbaum, *Annals of English Drama, 975–1700* (London: Methuen, 1964).

20 Thomas, *Religion and the Decline of Magic* (New York: Scribner's, 1971), 568.

21 For general misogynistic attacks see, among others, G. Thorowgood, *Pray Be Not Angry: or, the Womens New Law* (London, 1656), and W. B., *The Trial of the Ladies* (London, 1656), reprinted as *A New Trial of the Ladies* (London, 1658).

22 [Thomas Edwards?], *A Discoverie of Six women preachers* (London, 1641), 4; Richard Carter, *The Schismatick Stigmatized* (London, 1641), sig. A3r (see also sig. B1r); and Samuel Sheppard, *The Joviall Crew, or, The Devill turn'd Ranter* (London, 1651), sig. B4v. See also John Holland, *The Smoke of the Bottomlesse Pit* (London, 1646), sig. A3v.

23 John Brinsley, *A Looking-Glasse for Good Women* (London, 1645), sig. E2v (see also sig. A3v); *The Joviall Crew*, sig. A4v; and *A Spirit Moving in the Women-Preachers* (London, 1646), sig. A2r.

24 For the quoted passages, see *The Parliament of Women* (London, 1646), subsequently reissued as *A Parliament of Ladies* (London, 1647), sigs B2v and B4v. On sexual licence, see sig. B4v and two works by Henry Nevile, *The Ladies Parliament* (London, 1647), and *The Ladies, A Second Time Assembled in Parliament* (London, 1647). For a feminist attack on 'that Tyrannical Government, which men have over us', see *Now or Never: or, a New Parliament of Women* (London, 1656), sig. A2r.

25 *A Brief Anatomie of Women* (London, 1653), sigs A2r and A3r.

26 *A Spirit Moving in the Women-Preachers*, sig. A1v.

27 *Match Me in London*, in *The Dramatic Works of Thomas Dekker*, ed. Fredson Bowers (Cambridge: Cambridge University Press, 1958), vol. III, V.v.86–8.

28 Elizabeth M. Brennan, introduction to *The Devil's Law-Case*, by John Webster, ed. Elizabeth M. Brennan (London: Ernest Benn, 1975), x. References to the play are noted in the text.

29 Quoted in Brennan, x.

30 My discussion of subjectivity is indebted, within Renaissance drama studies, to Barker, *Tremulous Private Body*, and to Belsey and the other feminist critics cited in note 8, above, though some of my conclusions differ. A more general debt, most evident in the conclusion of this essay, is to Ernesto Laclau and Chantal Mouffe, *Hegemony and Socialist Strategy: Towards a Radical Democratic Politics*, trans. Winston Moore and Paul Cammack (London: Verso, 1985), and Paul Smith, *Discerning the Subject* (Minneapolis: Minnesota University Press, 1988).

31 These phrases are taken from John Ford, *The Lover's Melancholy*, ed. R. F. Hill (Manchester: Manchester University Press, 1985), I.ii.1–21 and II.i.1–16.

32 Heinemann, 217, and Annabel Patterson, *Censorship and Interpretation: The Conditions of Writing and Reading in Early Modern England* (Madison: Wisconsin University Press, 1984), 85.

33 *A Critical Old-Spelling Edition of* The Young Admiral *by James Shirley*, ed. Kenneth J. Ericksen (New York: Garland, 1979), III.i.188. Subsequent references are in the text.

34 *The Fair Favourite,* in *The Dramatic Works of Sir William D'Avenant* (1872–4; reprinted New York: Russell & Russell, 1964), vol. IV, 211. Subsequent references are in the text.

35 Butler, 20–4, 89, and 209–10.

36 *A Challenge for Beauty*, in *The Dramatic Works of Thomas Heywood* (1874; reprinted New York: Russell & Russell, 1964), vol. V, V.69.

37 Butler, p. 267, agreeing with R. J. Kaufmann, *Richard Brome: Caroline Playwright* (New York: Columbia University Press, 1961), 109–30.

38 For a more detailed argument about the utopian dimensions of tragicomedy, see David Norbrook's discussion of *The Tempest*, chapter 2 in this volume.

39 James Holstun, 'Ranting at the New Historicism', *English Literary Renaissance* 19 (1989), 189–226.

40 Potter's discussion of *The Two Noble Kinsmen*, chapter 4 in this volume, raises some of the same issues. The evidence of performance and publication

in the early seventeenth century suggests the conservative function of the play, whereas contemporary interpretation suggests other, more critical possibilities. In this instance, however, Potter's reading receives some support from a recent production of the play.

41 For more along these lines see my 'Political criticism of Shakespeare', in Jean E. Howard and Marion F. O'Connor (eds), *Shakespeare Reproduced: The Text in History and Ideology* (New York: Methuen, 1987), 18–46.

42 Most of the essays in this collection fall into the first category.

43 This is not meant to minimize the importance of a study like Loomba's, which is virtually unique in providing an extended account of the relationships among gender, race, imperialism, and to a lesser extent class in Renaissance drama.

7

'GOD HELP THE POOR: THE RICH CAN SHIFT': THE WORLD UPSIDE-DOWN AND THE POPULAR TRADITION IN THE THEATRE

Margot Heinemann

I

To focus solely on the drama of the court and the more expensive and socially exclusive indoor theatres would make it difficult to understand the connections between early Stuart tragicomedy and the 'real material history' of the times.[1] In what we now recognize as a troubled, unstable, and divided society, the deeper changes taking place (very roughly, from a social order based on rank and status to one based on wealth and money) affected every social grouping and its 'mentalities' in one way or another, so that dissent and conflict over political policy and social and moral codes can be discerned even within court masques or plays intended for a privileged and fashionable audience. In this sense the Earl of Newcastle, the Earl of Arundel, or Sir William Davenant can be seen at times and in some aspects as 'oppositional' figures within the courtly and gentry world. Outside that circle, in the popular open air theatres, the tensions appear in different and often simpler forms in the work of city dramatists like Thomas Heywood, Samuel Rowley, and Thomas Dekker. Most Renaissance playwrights, according to Stephen Greenblatt, 'honour the institutions that enable them to earn their keep and give voice to the ideology that holds together both their "mystery" and the society at large'.[2] In a prerevolutionary situation, however, no single ideology is capable of holding the society at large effectively together: that is one reason why it is a prerevolutionary situation.

The pressure of censorship (tightened up over the early Stuart period as a whole), and the dependence of all companies on court patronage and protection to be able to act at all, made it difficult for unease and disaffection on religious or social matters to be articulated in the popular theatres. Staging of any kind of mass plebeian protest against the social abuses and poverty which we know preoccupied writers like Dekker and Deloney would immediately have been associated by the censor with Anabaptism and Munster-style Communism, with which the playwrights and their companies probably had little sympathy anyway. Popular discontent and protest at this period is usually traditionalist and backward-looking in form (though it may be simplistic to call it 'conservative'); it presses the existing authorities, crown and gentry to uphold Elizabethan religious values and to enforce the economic rights of small craftsmen and peasants against arbitrary exactions by merchants, land engrossers, corrupt officials, or royal patentees. True, the consensus of deference and 'conservatism' must itself be in part a product of censorship and self-censorship; but, in any case, democratic ideas and 'levelling' aspirations developed more strongly in the years after 1640. Their beginnings can, however, be sensed in the plays of some city playwrights, as well as in pieces like the anonymous *The Whore New-Vamped, The Cardinal's Conspiracy* or Brome's *The Court Beggar*, which collided with the Laudian censorship of the late 1630s.

A distinctive contribution to political feelings and mentalities, then, was made by the tragicomedies of the popular theatres (and especially of open air playhouses like the Red Bull and the Fortune), not only by the original performances, some of them given before 1610, but also by the many revivals, perhaps aimed at political as well as commercial effect, which continued into the 1620s and 1630s.

These plays contributed to the growing cult of Elizabethan values and nostalgia for her reign as a golden age for citizens. In particular, the series of plays on Reformation history first performed during James I's early years, which were based mainly on John Foxe's historical narrative in *Acts and Monuments* rather than solely on Holinshed or Halle, appealed directly to strong feelings of anti-Popery and anti-clericalism in the popular London audience, rousing sympathy for further reformation in the church, assistance to the Protestant cause in Europe and the Netherlands, and reliance on the English common people (as distinct from the gentry and aristocracy) as the strongest supporters of the reformed religion. Several of the playwrights concerned (Heywood, Dekker, Munday, Webster) were also employed to devise city shows and entertainments, and episodes from past mayoral pageants are sometimes introduced in the plays. I shall concentrate here on Samuel Rowley's *When You See Me You Know Me* (1605), a particularly lively and subversive example from this group, based freely on Foxe's account of Henry VIII with imaginative alterations.

Some of the plays also appealed, if fleetingly and cautiously, to grievances about economic distress among craftsmen, the burdens of taxation, the exactions and extortions of courtiers, and the city rich. The key dramatist here is Dekker, especially in *If It Be Not a Good Play the Devil Is In It* (1612) and *The Wonder of a Kingdom* (printed 1636). Heywood's *Fortune by Land and Sea* (1609) and the anonymous *The Costly Whore* (1614?) are other examples which similarly treat such themes in terms of tragicomedy rather than satire.

In both groups the tragicomic effect depends on an element of popular utopianism, quite unlike the consistent satirical comic tone of Jonson or early Middleton. The improbably happy resolutions enacted for tragic problems have the quality of myth or fairytale. Totally just and godly monarchs hand down excellent laws and defeat foreign foes, working in idealized harmony with godly people, godly clergy, godly merchants, and godly nobility (as Queen Elizabeth is seen to do in Heywood and Dekker). On the other side, erring kings like the one in *If It Be Not Good* are miraculously restored to goodness and clemency.

Pervasive also is the popular culture theme of the world turned upside-down to right injustices and resolve social conflict. The common man assumes the role of prophet. The wisdom of clowns and yokels makes fools of noblemen and bishops; great princes of the church are humiliated and exposed by their jesters. The poor ragged ex-soldier is rewarded with high office while corrupt courtiers and officemongers are seen frying in hell; and the English Bible in the hands of heroic godly women becomes a magic talisman protecting their life and honour against assassins sent by the Roman Church. In imagination the powerless are empowered and the mighty cast down – a visionary element which can be traced back to the 'prophecy' plays of Robert Wilson and Tarleton in the 1580s[3] and to gospelling poets such as Crowley before that, or forward to the visions of Abiezer Coppe and his like in the 1650s. *Dekker's Dream* (1620), a powerfully fantastic apocalyptic pamphlet written from prison, is in the same 'poor man's heaven' tradition.

II

What have sometimes been called the 'Elect Nation plays' – dramatizing the recent Tudor and Reformation history which had been impossible to stage freely while Elizabeth lived, and based largely on Foxe's *Book of Martyrs* – provided one of the most successful kinds of tragicomic theatre in the popular playhouses. I want to consider here not the precise ways in which the dramatists adapted the Foxeian narrative and modified the history (already admirably studied in a seminal article by Judith Doolin Spikes), but rather the methods of theatrical and dramatic presentation, which are directly linked to their political effect.[4]

The general tone of these histories is tragicomic, first in the Fletcherian sense that many of them 'want deaths, which is enough to make it no tragedy, yet bring some near it, which is enough to make it no comedy'.[5] Excitement and suspense are engendered by the risks of martyrdom in the historical careers of Princess Elizabeth, Queen Katherine Parr, or Catherine Bertie, Duchess of Suffolk, as well as the actual executions of Lady Jane Grey, Sir Thomas Wyatt, and Thomas Cromwell, though the victory of the true Protestant religion is assured. But the plays are also 'mongrel tragicomedy' in the tradition maintained by Tarleton and Wilson and criticized by Sidney, 'mingling kings and clowns, not because the matter so carries it, but thrust[ing] in clowns by head and shoulders to play a part in majestical matters, with neither decency nor discretion'.[6] Sidney was writing in the early 1580s, but he could equally well have been describing Samuel Rowley's *When You See Me You Know Me* (1604) or Heywood's *If You Know Not Me You Know Nobody* (1605), staged a full generation later, and many times revived and reprinted, which not merely *mingle* kings and clowns, but often present their clowns as braver and indeed cleverer than the great people. Plays like *When You See Me* or *Sir John Oldcastle* (1599) helped to influence political mentalities through their form, their use in a historical-religious context of these well-tried stage contrasts of tragedy and carnival-style folk comedy.

Throughout the Foxeian plays (as indeed in the *Book of Martyrs* itself) the stage emphasis falls on the Protestant Reformation as a popular rather than an aristocratic movement. The common people are insistently shown as the principal supporters of 'the religion' – convincingly enough for London and Kent where most of the plays are set, and where the Lollard and anti-clerical traditions had always been strongest.[7] Historically the Marian martyrs were indeed mostly drawn, as Foxe shows, from the working people (especially clothworkers and printers) of London and south-east England. The reformed religion has its aristocratic and gentry heroes in the drama – Lady Jane Grey, Sir Thomas Wyatt – but it is the images of plebeian support that are most striking, based on nationalism and patriotism as much as religious doctrine.

> Anti-Catholicism . . . was a major ingredient in the religio-political ideology of ordinary people in sixteenth and seventeenth century England . . . Sometimes anti-Catholic feeling was stimulated from the top, whipped up by politicians and propagandists . . . but always the elite had plenty of raw material to work with.[8]

In Heywood's *If You Know Not Me*, for example, the Princess Elizabeth on her way from the Tower to house arrest at Hatfield is greeted by public demonstrations of townspeople bearing flowers, much to the fury of her harsh jailer Beningfield, who rages:

> Traders and knaves ring bells
> When the Queen's enemy passes through the town.

And Elizabeth herself underlines the political moral:

> The poor are loving, but the rich despise.

In prison, the princess is loyally supported against her Popish persecutors not only by her own servants (including a formidable cook who refuses to allow the constable's spies into his kitchen), but by the unwilling common soldiers ordered to guard her. When she is accused of treasonable conversation, the clown obligingly promises to arrest her fellow-conspirator, and leads a goat in from the garden to confront the comic-villain jailer:

> CLOWN: Here he is in a string my lord.
> BENINGFIELD: Why knave, this is a beast.
> CLOWN: So may your worship be for anything I know . . . But if you have anything to say to this honest fellow, who for his grey hair and reverend beard is so like he may be kin to you –
> BENINGFIELD: Akin to me! Knave, I'll have thee whipped.

The jailer's name is historical, but the treatment is pure popular slapstick.

The point at issue in Rowley's *When You See Me You Know Me*, dealing with the reign of Henry VIII, is not simply the fate of any individual but rather the fate of England. On the one side are the evil bishops Wolsey, Gardiner, and Bonner, using their power to press the king for a Catholic alliance and the persecution of Protestants; on the other the godly bishop Cranmer, the Protestant Queen Katherine Parr, and Prince Edward, seen here as a firmer opponent of the power of Rome than his father (as was the heir to the throne, Prince Henry, at the time of the play's first performance). The queen is shown as a strong-minded, argumentative, Bible-reading woman, openly challenging the bishops as greedy and unpatriotic, yet without attacking the king's supreme power in matters of religion. To their accusation that she is a traitor like Wycliffe she counters:

> You that are sworn servants unto Rome,
> How are ye faithful subjects to the King,
> When first ye serve the Pope, then after him?

At the climax of the tragicomic action, the bishops succeed in convincing Henry that Katherine is a heretic and a traitor, and get him to sign a warrant for her arrest, while blocking her access to him. They march on to the stage, as suits their power politics, carrying bills and halberds over their shoulders:

> BONNER: Who dare contradict
> His highness' hand? Even from his side we'll hale her,
> And bear her quickly to her longest home,
> Lest we and ours by her to ruin come.

The queen, knowing how dangerously capricious Henry is, is terrified:

> Oh, I shall never come to speak with him.
> The lion in his rage is not so stern
> As royal Henry in his wrathful spleen. . .
> This giddy flattering world I hate and scoff,
> Ere long I know Queen Katherine's head must off.

Katherine and England are saved, however, by an eleventh-hour interview (which young Prince Edward secures for her) with the angry, confused old king, who is still irrationally and self-pityingly convinced of her treachery:

> KING: God's holy mother, you'll remove me quickly
> and turn me out, old Harry must away,
> Now in mine age, lame and half bed-rid,
> Or else you'll keep me fast enough in prison.
> Haw, mistress, these are no hateful treasons these?

The dialogue here is colloquial, the tension painful, finally exploding in Henry's violent, pathetic, randy outburst of forgiveness, which alternates pardon, cuddling, and threats:

KING: Body a me, what everlasting knaves are these that wrong thee thus, alas poor Kate, come stand up, stand up, wipe thine eyes, foregod 'twas told me thou wert a traitor; I could hardly think it, but that it was applied so hard to me, Godsmother Kate I fear my life I tell ye, King Harry would be loath to die by treason now, that has bid so many brunts unblemished, yet I confess that now I grow stiff, my legs fail me first, but they stand furthest from my heart, and that's still sound, I thank my God, give me thy hand, come kiss me Kate, so now I'm friends again, whoreson knaves, crafty varlets, make thee a traitor to old Harry's life, well, well, I'll meet with some on them, Sfoot come sit on my knee Kate, Mother a God he that says th'art false to me by England's crown I'll hang him presently.

The speech and the whole scene are wholly orthodox in contemporary religious and political terms, in the sense that no one questions the king's right to decide on life and death in matters of religion (there is no hint that rebellion in the name of doctrine would be possible). Yet it is hard to see how the actors could have performed it without raising questions in the minds of some of the popular audience about the absolute control of the church by an ageing, irresponsible monarch; and this at a time when King James and Archbishop Bancroft had set themselves against any toleration for non-conforming ministers in the Church of England. The indecorum of presenting the king in naturalistic style as a gullible, rash-tempered old man is too easily dismissed as mere clumsiness or naivety in the popular dramatist. It is itself the political point, embodying the clash between the sacred and necessary power of monarchy and the fallible, imperfect individual who wields it. We tend to expect such life-and-death confrontations in the drama to take a highly charged poetic and rhetorical form, as they do in *Richard II* or Shakespeare's *Henry VIII*, or in earlier popular plays like *Edmund Ironside* or *Edward III*. To move the climax of the action into the comic-colloquial idiom gives a different and disturbing effect, which a little later forms one element of the king's torment in *King Lear*.

Alongside this central clash, the popular exposure of the Catholic Church and the patriotic resistance to its domination of England is rendered in clowning parody episodes, where the star role is that of Will Summers, Henry VIII's legendary plain-spoken fool, who is presented as a master of theological wit-combat as well as slapstick. Thus he boldly exposes the politics of Cardinal Campeius's Papal embassy:

KING: Come hither, Will, what sayst thou to this new title given us by the Pope, speak, is it not rare?

WILL: I know not how rare it is, but I know how dear it is, for I perceive 'twill cost thee twelve thousand pounds at least, besides the Cardinal's cost in coming.

KING: All that's nothing, the title of defender of the faith is worth yea, twice as much, say, is it not?

WILL: No, by my troth, dost hear, old Harry; I am sure, the true faith is able to defend itself without thee, and as for the Pope's faith (good faith's) not worth a farthing, and therefore give him not a penny.

In the popular tradition to which Lear's fool is also related, Will stands up for the poor, and denounces the greed of Wolsey and the expense and luxury of the Papal Church. Like Lear's fool, he is allied with the godly serious characters around the court (in his case Prince Edward and Queen Katherine); fearlessly tells the king of his faults; and is threatened with the whip by the villains and cadgers:

> WILL: I had rather [Henry] should have the poor's prayers than the Pope's.
>
> QUEEN: Faith I am of thy mind, Will, I think so too.
>
> KING: Take heed what you say, Kate, what, a Lutheran?
>
> WOLSEY: 'Tis heresy, fair Queen, to think such thoughts.
>
> QUEEN: And much uncharity to wrong the poor.
>
> WILL: Well, when the Pope is at best, he is but Saint Peter's deputy, but the poor present Christ, and so should be something better regarded.
>
> WOLSEY: Sirrah, you'll be whipped for this.

In the most memorable of these episodes of knockabout politics, the professional clowns Will and Patch (Wolsey's jester) get hold of the key to the wine cellar, where, staggering drunk, they find the treasure which Wolsey has extorted from the people and stored up to buy himself the Papacy. They confront him and the king with this discovery, and thus bring about his fall:

> WILL: If I would be a blab of my tongue, I could tell the King how many barrels full of gold and silver there was six times filled with plate and jewels, twenty great trunks with crosses, croziers, copes, mitres, maces, golden crucifixes, beside the four hundred and twelve thousand pound that poor chimneys paid for Peter pence. But this is nothing, for

when you are Pope, you may pardon yourself for more knavery than this comes to.

In terms of popular culture, what is characteristic is not just the mingling of kings and clowns, but that the clowns – privileged to speak what the common man dares only murmur – can expose and bring down lofty hypocrites. Tragicomedy wins against threatened tragedy. Since the audience knew that the fall of Wolsey was a fact, the point that fools may be wiser than kings is well taken, and does not work merely as a safety valve.

When You See Me is no doubt an extreme case. But the defence of monarchy, morality, and true religion by comic low-life characters is a common theme throughout the Jacobean popular drama, in sharp contrast to the court masques, where such low types appear in the anti-masques as ridiculous, threatening, or both at once. Intentionally or not, these figures in the popular plays seem to express and reinforce a kind of plebeian class awareness and confidence that is not without political effect.

III

Although Dekker's later plays are designed for an audience of the 'middling sort' and the lower orders – the craftsmen and apprentices, applewomen and labourers who went to open air theatres like the Red Bull and the Fortune – to call them 'middle-class culture' may be misleading. For to our ears the term 'middle-class' connotes stability, prosperity, even a certain smugness, whereas what these plays dramatize is the terrifying *instability* of life for small people, in a world where merchants are gaining power at the expense of craftsmen and petty traders, and poor husbandmen are being squeezed and evicted by landlords. Their context is the increasing division of the middling sort into prosperous yeomen and businessmen on the one hand and the poor, landless, and wage-dependent on the other. Writers, as insecure as anyone (unless, like Shakespeare, they managed to become company shareholders), were well placed to appreciate this process while they moved, as did Dekker, Day, and Daborne, between court and city favour and pageantry when they were in luck, and the abominable Hole in the Counter, the debtors' prison, when the luck ran out.

More than any other playwright of the time, Dekker dramatizes this insecurity. His own sufferings directly inspire his vision of a better world. Underlying the bitterness of the hell-scene in *If It Be Not Good*, and the cruelty of the spendthrift lord caricatured in *Wonder of a*

Kingdom, is the experience of imprisonment, the hopelessness of securing justice in this life, the yearning for true justice beyond the grave. The prologue to the pamphlet-poem *Dekker's Dream* (1620) images directly this fantasy of a poor man's heaven:[9]

> Out of a long sleep, which for almost seven years together seized all my senses . . . meeting in that drowsy voyage with nothing but frightful apparitions, by reason (as now I guess) of the place in which I lay . . . I did at last fall into a dream, which presented to my waking soul infinite pleasures, commixed with inutterable horrors . . . I climbed to the top of all the trees in Paradise, and ate sweeter apples than Adam ever tasted . . . I went into the Star-Chamber of Heaven, where Kings and Princes were set to the Bar . . . Jerusalem was the palace I lived in, and Mount Sion the hill, from whose top I was dazzled with glories brighter than sunbeams. This was my banquet: the course-meat was able to kill me. For I was thrown (after all this happiness) into a sea infernal, and forced to swim through torrents of unquenchable fire. All the jails of hell were set open.
>
> (III.16)

And in hell it is especially the torments of the rich that the dreamer sees:

> cursing that they sat
> At proud voluptuous tables, yet forgat
> Numb'd charity, when at their gaudy gates
> She begged but scraps of their worst delicates,
> Yet starved for want . . .
>
> (III.44)

The depth of Dekker's anger against poverty is felt most intensely in the bitter satirical pamphlet *Work for Armourers* (1609), whose title-page bears the epigraph 'God Help the Poor: the Rich Can Shift'. This tract images the conflict of rich and poor allegorically as an archetypal war between the armies of Poverty (the 'Hungarians' or hungries) and those of the Princess of Money. It opens, significantly, with Dekker's famous description of the whipping of a blind bear to entertain the crowd – a compassionate report which infers that a society which enjoys tormenting animals will be equally callous in enforcing the poor laws against human beings:

> At length a blind bear was tied to the stake, and instead of baiting him with dogs a company of creatures that had the shape of men,

> and faces of Christians, took the office of beadles upon them, and whipt Monsieur Hunks till the blood ran down his old shoulders . . . Yet methought the whipping of the blind bear moved as much pity in my breast towards him, as the leading of the poor starved wretches to the whipping posts in London (when they had more need to be relieved with food) ought to move the hearts of citizens, though it be fashion now to laugh at that punishment.
>
> (IV.99)

The rich, led by the Princess of Money, are shown as not merely uncharitable but violently aggressive towards the poor, enforcing new draconian laws against them:

> Constables were chosen of purpose that had marble in their hearts, thorns in their tongues, and flint-stones (like pearls) in their eyes, and none could be admitted into the office of a beadle, unless he brought a certificate from Paris Garden, that he had been a Bear-ward, and could play the bandog bravely in baiting poor Christians at a stake.
>
> (108)

Meanwhile the young landlords are expressly commanded to rack rents, call in old tenants' leases, change their copyholds, evict them, and then fix rents so high that no farmer can make a decent living. Then they will be able to 'pity your dead gaffers . . . for not having so much wit to raise profit as you their sons have'.

The power with which Dekker here represents the barbarities of the poor law, the whipping and stocking, the suffering of husbandmen and craftsmen, the neglect of disabled ex-soldiers, and the complacent luxury of the rich, lends a terrifying energy to his account of the troops mobilized by Poverty. A few may have been idle or prodigal; most are simply the victims of cruelty and indifference:

> But rather they grew desperate, and sticking closely (like prentices upon Shrove Tuesday one to another) they vowed (come death, come devils) to stand against whole bands of brown rusty billmen, though for their labours they were like to be knocked down like Oxen for the slaughter; but a number of Jack-Straws being amongst them, and opening whole Cades of counsel in a cause so dangerous, they were all turned to dry powder, took fire of resolution, and so went off with this thundering noise, 'that they would die like men, though they were but poor knaves, and counted the stinkards and scum of the world'.

Although the war is allegorical and metaphorical, Dekker deliberately names the leaders of actual past peasant risings as a warning of real dangers, and ends the conflict not with a reign of justice but with an uneasy truce. In the theatre no such open war-cry can be sounded, but the driving force of the fable is still the demand of the dispossessed for justice, a poor man's heaven, revenge on the rich.

In *If It Be Not a Good Play the Devil Is In It* (1611–12) this is given a utopian, millenarian form. A good young king, succeeding to the throne of Naples, sets out so to order and administer things that law shall be just, soldiers and scholars protected, and charitable funds properly directed to relieve the poor. But a team of active devils sent by Pluto, Prince of Hell, soon pervert this ideal monarch into a greedy luxury-loving monster, farming out the taxes to grasping monopolists. His wise counsellors are overruled and replaced by a corrupt devil-favourite who 'hugs' him with pretended love. Another devil, with royal approval, attacks the charity of the church, grabbing the Abbey's gold for rich men's use, and stopping the relief of poor travellers, who are now stigmatized as rogues and vagrants (a hit at the cruelties of the current poor law). A third becomes a 'city-devil', operating at the Bourse, helping merchants to bankrupt craftsmen and courtiers and seize their lands. 'The spirit of gold instruct thee,' says his master, Pluto. As for the poor, they are now to be 'cured with a halter'. Only a successful war and rising (led by the wise counsellors) restores the king to goodness and understanding, breaks the power of money, and establishes true order – in his words:

Here we begin
Our reign anew, which golden threads shall spin,
Justice shall henceforth sit upon our throne,
And virtue be your King's companion.

If It Be Not Good has sometimes been unfavourably contrasted with Jonson's later re-use of the idea in *The Devil is an Ass*, where he shows that people are so bad there is no need for devils: hell is a grammar-school compared to London. But in one respect, at least, Dekker's play is bolder and sharper than Jonson's, in blaming not only the monopolists and their agents, but the king by whose favour they exist. Bartervile, Dekker's wicked usurer and patent-holder, flourishes by the king's tax-farming, collecting impositions on weddings, lawsuits, brothels, food, and salt. When he is struck down by heaven for his perjury, however, his 'office' is instantly bestowed by the king on a courtier who resells it to the highest bidder. Bartervile is indeed the type of an unscrupulous city oligarch growing rich through royal favour, and boasting: 'Nature sent man into the world alone/Without all company, but to care for one,/And that I'll do.' His attendant devil comments: 'True City doctrine, Sir.' But it is equally shown as the doctrine of a corrupt crown and court.

Monopolies and projectors are satirized in some masques (*Triumph of Peace*) and upmarket theatres too, but without Dekker's concern for their effects on ordinary people. Bartervile's defence of his part in the system stresses this burden:

> Methinks 'tis fit a subject should not eat
> But that his prince from every dish of meat
> Should receive nourishment. . .
> Besides, it makes us more to awe a king
> When at each bit we are forced to think on him.

In *Devil is an Ass*, on the other hand, the most visible victim of the predatory monopoly-monger Meercraft is the bird-brained gentleman Fitzdottrel, who loses only money he can well afford, and is so stupid that he deserves to be duped anyway. The crown's responsibility never arises. No emotional anger against the patent system is aroused in Jonson's play, as it is in Dekker's, nor any sympathy for its casualties.

The final act of *If It Be Not Good* – a postscript to the happy ending on earth – shows the wicked burning in hell, where Bartervile joins the political villains Guy Fawkes and Ravaillac. Their torments are prolonged in grotesque detail for the satisfaction and edification of the audience; the next world is to right the wrongs of this one. Utopia and dystopia alike partake of a visionary element. The world upside-down satisfies in imagination the wrongs and fears of the deprived and powerless, appealing above all to those for whom the fall into poverty means truly 'a hell in this life'.

In the fable-play *The Wonder of a Kingdom*, probably his last play (licensed 1631), Dekker returns to dramatizing the cruel treatment of the poor. This is personified in the prodigal Lord Torrenti, who orders his servants to

> invent odd engines
> To manacle base beggars, hands and feet. . .
> And whip them soundly if they approach my gates.
> The poor are but the earth's dung fit to lie
> Covered on muck-heaps not to offend the eye.

Torrenti refuses charity even to his own brother, a ragged ex-serviceman returned from imprisonment in the Turkish galleys, who finally fires his pistols into the air and helps himself to the food he needs. Another wounded veteran denounces the rich broker who has forced him to pawn even his wooden leg, thus providing a powerful stage image:

> To this hell-hound
> I pawned my weapons to buy brown bread
> To feed my brats and me: they forfeited,
> Twice as much as his money I him gave
> To have my arms redeemed; the griping slave
> Swore 'Not to save my soul', unless that I
> Laid down my stump here for the interest,
> And so hop home.

The utopian ending necessary to turn this harsh social indictment into tragicomedy is provided by the good Lord Gentili, a contrasting model of old-fashioned noble hospitality and generosity, who punishes the villainous broker and appoints the gallant veteran as his steward, while Torrenti ends in poverty and disgrace. This conventional non-subversive happy ending was no doubt satisfying to the spectators as well as the censor (much like the endings brought about by philanthropists such as the Cheerybles in Dickens's novels). Whether it indicates an ideological consensus, a general confidence that the existing aristocratic and royal order can be relied upon to right the wrongs of the people is, however, more questionable.

NOTES

1 The phrase is Raymond Williams's, and implies that there is such a thing as material history – political events and social and economic changes – as distinct from the ideological perceptions of the age. Images are not the only realities. Albert Tricomi puts a similar point: 'I do not wish to privilege history over literature by rendering the former as a static, linear "truth" that theatrical representation merely "reflects" . . . Nevertheless, history is for me event-centered as well as language-centered' (*Anti-Court Drama in England 1603–1642* (Charlottesville: Virginia University Press, 1988)).

2 Stephen Greenblatt, *Renaissance Self-Fashioning: From More to Shakespeare* (Chicago: Chicago University Press, 1980), 253.

3 *The Cobbler's Prophecy* (printed 1594); *The Pedlar's Prophecy* (printed 1595); *Three Ladies of London* (printed 1584); and others.

4 Judith Doolin Spikes, 'The Jacobean history play and the myth of the elect nation', in *Renaissance Drama*, ed. Leonard Barkan (Evanston, Illinois: Illinois University Press, 1977), 117–48.

5 John Fletcher, 'To the reader', introducing *The Faithful Shepherdess* (published before 1610).

6 Sir Philip Sidney, *An Apology for Poetry*, ed. Geoffrey Shepherd (1598; Manchester: Manchester University Press, 1973), 135.

7 Plays with a Kentish connection include *Sir John Oldcastle, Sir Thomas Wyatt*, and a much later example, Middleton's *Hengist, King of Kent*.

8 Barry Reay, 'Popular religion', in Barry Reay (ed.), *Popular Culture in Seventeenth Century England* (London: Croom Helm, 1985), 107. See also Peter Lake, 'Anti-popery: the structure of a prejudice', in *Conflict in Early Stuart England*, ed. Richard Cust and Ann Hughes (London: Longmans, 1989), 72–106.

9 References to Dekker's pamphlets are taken from *The Non-Dramatic Works of Thomas Dekker*, ed. Alexander B. Grosart, 4 vols (London: The Huth Library, 1884–6; reprinted 1963), vols III and IV.

8

LATE JONSON

Martin Butler

Whatever they were, they certainly were not 'dotages'. Jonson's late plays have been long overshadowed by Dryden's uncomprehending label, but now that they are at last being addressed on their own terms their problems are coming to be seen as arising not from the incompetence of their author but from the unfamiliarity of the issues he was attempting to confront and from the changes in technique which this entailed. In the two remarkable ground-breaking books which have done so much to transform understanding of late Jonson, Anne Barton's *Ben Jonson, Dramatist* and David Norbrook's *Poetry and Politics in the English Renaissance*, Jonson is seen not as a major author declining into senility but as a beleaguered intellectual courageously rethinking his priorities and making the painful accommodations necessary for him to survive in the uncongenial Caroline environment. Though Professor Barton and Dr Norbrook differ on matters of detail, there is a broad similarity between their perceptions of Jonson in the late 1620s and 1630s. In both studies, Jonson figures as a writer who in later life was increasingly alienated from Whitehall, ill at ease with those royal masters who had previously been the objects of his panegyric, yet whose political investment in the Stuart court was too substantial to permit a full-scale revision of earlier assumptions and allegiances. Consequently (runs this argument) he cultivated an artistic ambivalence that echoed his discomfort with a court that no longer commanded his whole-hearted respect. Within this perspective, the problem of his late plays, with their experimentation with new and previously despised forms, their ironic self-defensiveness, and their changed attitude towards such matters as love and the past, seems less a matter of private artistic failure – of dotage – than of a complex negotiation between competing and changing pressures, both personal and political.

The two principal fronts on which this Jonsonian negotiation is seen as going forward are politics and romance. In Professor Barton's thesis, political ambivalence is registered as a revaluation of earlier artistic preferences, in particular a realignment towards romantic forms from which Jonson had once deliberately turned away, but which he came to find were indispensable. Professor Barton suggestively explicates the late plays, with their country settings, festive plots, and motifs of disguise and discovery, separation and reconciliation, as a kind of Jonsonian equivalent to Shakespeare's romances, but romances problematized by their similarity to political forms of nostalgia under King Charles, a harking-back to earlier and better days. Dr Norbrook argues more specifically from Jonson's presumed discomfort with the glamorous and irresponsible court favourite Buckingham, under whom he is likely to have felt alienated. His late plays, with their sour attacks on the superficiality of court masquing and their veneration of aristocratic honour bring to mind the ideological stance adopted by aristocratic opponents of Buckingham whose distaste for the upstart favourite effectively pushed them out into the cold. More than one study has linked Jonson's sentiments in these plays with the cult of honour promoted in the Caroline period by the Earl of Arundel, a conservative and old-style nobleman whose hostility towards Buckingham left him in the 1620s effectively one of the leaders of an aristocratic 'opposition'.[1] Dr Norbrook also notes in Jonson's neo-Elizabethanism and nostalgia for the past a tentative appropriation of the political rhetoric associated with Spenserian poets such as Drayton and Wither who similarly cast back to the days of Elizabeth as a means of reflecting adversely on the age of the Stuarts. In both accounts, Jonson is characterized as a playwright whose relationship with the court came to be distinguished by anxiety, detachment, and disillusion.

There is much to be said for this view of late Jonson: it responds to those things in the plays which seem to be eccentric, and other information about Jonson in these years supports it, for example the artistic quarrel with Inigo Jones, the drying-up of masque commissions, the famous poems mendicant, and all the other evidence of poverty and apparent neglect. And yet illuminating as this idea of a tentative double-edged late Jonsonian radicalism is, I find myself wanting, on the whole, to resist it. It seems to me that however far Jonson went in his rapprochement towards romance, his use of romantic motifs remained even in this period deeply circumscribed and circumspect, and he continued to be wary of the form's structural openness and moral indeterminacy. In the *Ode to Himself*, Pericles is still reckoned to be only a 'mouldy tale', and in *The Magnetic Lady* it is the idiotic spectator

Damplay whose idea of a plot with business in it consists of a hero who grows from a child into a knight, does wonders in the Holy Land, kills monsters, marries the emperor's daughter, and returns home lame and laden with miracles, all his travelling to be done between the acts. If this is a reconciliation with romance, the terms on which Jonson appropriated such motifs perhaps need defining more precisely. Similarly, I find it hard to believe that Jonson would have associated himself unreservedly with either the rather pompous and self-regarding aristocratic hauteur of the Earl of Arundel or with the more assertively populist rhetoric of the Spenserian poets. Indeed, Jonson had in the past been bitterly at odds with the Spenserians, of whose ideological assumptions – patriotic Protestantism and anti-Spanish militancy – he was profoundly distrustful. If he is to be cast as a poet of 'opposition', plainly it is unlikely to have been opposition of this type.[2]

But, more fundamentally, I do not find that this view can be consistently maintained in relation to the larger formal dimensions of the late plays themselves. For all that we now recognize in these plays a kind of dissatisfaction with things as they are, it is still possible for the amount of disjunction at this point of Jonson's career to be overstated. Much that has been interpreted as a circumscribed late Jonsonian radicalism can be understood just as appropriately as an adaptation by Jonson of old strategies to serve the needs of the Stuart monarchy in new social and political circumstances.[3]

I

The question can be conveniently approached from outside the plays by dwelling briefly on what is known about the patrons and friends to whom Jonson attached himself in these last years. It is interesting that for all the correspondence which commentators have felt they perceived between Jonson and the aristocratic disaffection represented by the Earl of Arundel, Jonson chose not to address himself to Arundel, who had been in open enmity with Buckingham and had attempted to thwart him in Parliament, but to the Earl of Newcastle who was politically much more cautious.[4] Certainly Newcastle was out of step with Caroline Whitehall, and he fully shared Arundel's distrust of the upstart nobility whose influence threatened to displace the older aristocratic families. In another context I have described Newcastle's two amateur comedies which, in a sub-Jonsonian mode, voice reservations about the court's willingness to promote 'meane People' who sneered at the old nobility for their lack of modishness and dancing skills, and its betrayal of the good old ways of Queen Elizabeth who had kept up order and ceremony and title.[5] In his political testament, a treatise of advice to the future Charles II written some time before the Restoration, Newcastle used the age of Elizabeth as a stick with which to beat the shortcomings of the age of Charles I.

But though Newcastle may have felt isolated at court and marginalized by his attachment to traditional ways, his disaffection was not of the kind to push him into postures of confrontation. Rather, it would be truer to think of him before the Civil War less as alienated from the court than as seeking to bridge court and country. He had begun his political career as a client of Buckingham, sitting in the 1621 Parliament in a Villiers-controlled seat, and subsequently he was named as guardian of Buckingham's heir. In the 1620s he had been an assiduous governor of his shire, who commanded the loyalty of the bench and whose hospitality and constant residence in the country earned him the praise even of Lucy Hutchinson. Richard Cust describes him as an 'honest broker', trusted by both the court and the court's critics,[6] and the conservatism that made him distrustful of the counsellors with whom Charles was surrounded in the 1630s turned him equally readily into a devoted royal general in the 1640s; his subsequent advice to Charles II is all concerned with ways of establishing a strong, centralized monarchy. Newcastle commissioned three entertainments from Jonson and was the patron to whom he turned in the late 1620s when the commissions for court masques ceased to come. Two poems from the *Underwood*, of around 1628, praise Newcastle for his horsemanship, 'the ancient art of Thrace', and his skill in fencing and knowledge of the requirements of 'true/Valour'.[7] Both poems contain close verbal resemblances to language used by or of Lovel, the nostalgically aristocratic hero of *The New Inn*.

Equally interesting is Jonson's other principal patron in this period, Richard Weston, Earl of Portland and Lord Treasurer from 1628. Weston had been no friend of Buckingham in the 1620s, but after the duke's death he inherited the mantle of hatred (in the last moments of the 1629 Parliament, Sir John Eliot shouted that all the court's evils were contracted in him), and in the early 1630s he was perhaps the most powerful Privy Councillor. An Essex gentleman who rose to high place through a modicum of success with the royal finances, he was not personally close to the king, but he was a leading advocate of the royal policies of prerogative finance and peace with Spain, and (not surprisingly) he was firmly opposed to the recall of Parliament, from which he could not expect fair treatment. In religion he was without strong commitments, though his wife and daughters were recusants and he himself probably died in the old faith.[8] The *Underwood* includes a series of epigrams, epistles, and epithalamia for members of the Weston family written between 1631 and 1635, and an epigram to Venetia Digby imagining the scene when her husband Sir Kenelm Digby reads Jonson's lines 'at the Treasurer's board/(The knowing Weston) and that learned lord/Allows them' (*Underwood*, 78.27). These poems include a rebuke to the 'seed of envy' who are hostile to Weston, that statesman 'whom bad men only hate' (*Underwood*, 73); a description of Weston as 'great say-master of state, who cannot err', and who uses all 'legal ways/Of trials, to work down/Men's love unto the laws, and laws to love the crown' (*Underwood*, 75.99); and a panegyric praising him as a counsellor:

> To compose men and manners, stint the strife
> Of murmuring subjects, make the nations know
> What worlds of blessings to good kings they owe,
> And mightiest monarchs feel what large increase
> Of sweets and safeties they possess by peace.
>
> (*Underwood*, 77.18)

It seems clear from these poems that Jonson found Weston's views on peace, economy, and firm royal government congenial, and it is particularly noteworthy that he should have paused to praise his skill in making the law serve the crown, given that Weston had been personally forward in using the courts and Star Chamber to prosecute merchants who had been refusing to pay tunnage and poundage. In addressing himself as a client to Weston, Jonson was attaching himself to a statesman second in unpopularity only to William Laud.

And if we turn from Jonson's patrons to his friends, a very similar story can be told. Clarendon's autobiography – with its account of his convivial London life around 1630 and his friendships with philosophers, poets, and wits – and Jonson's own poems to the Earl of Falkland and other acquaintances of Clarendon's, tell us that Jonson's closest friendships at this time were among those men who were eventually to become the Great Tew circle, the crucible of English Socinianism. Intellectually, Clarendon, Falkland, and their friends were rationalist, humanist, and liberal. In religion, they were favourers of the light of reason, advocates of toleration in matters indifferent, and opponents of bigotry and sectarian polemic. In politics, they were moderate, constitutional, and peace-loving: Falkland and Clarendon were to be enthusiastic champions of reform in the early months of the Long

Parliament, though their aims were for a balanced, conservative settlement, and once royal power seemed to be under threat they became the nucleus of the moderate royalists. Of this group, Jonson seems to have been closest to Sir Kenelm Digby who, interestingly, had leanings in the direction of Rome.[9]

On the other hand, events may have been conspiring to push Jonson apart from those older friends whose politics were leading them into confrontation with the king in the late 1620s. The most significant examples were John Selden and Robert Cotton, scholars and antiquaries who were longstanding friends of Jonson and both clients of the Earl of Arundel, but whose authority on matters constitutional and historical sucked them into the controversial politics of the 1628 and 1629 Parliaments. As politics came to sensitize questions of precedent, ancient liberties, and the interpretation of statute, antiquarianism ceased to be an innocent pursuit, and Cotton found himself useful as a constitutional expert working closely with Arundel, while Selden emerged as an opponent of the crown's emergency financial measures whose collaboration in 1629 with the parliamentary radical Sir John Eliot left him in prison and his papers under seal. Cotton's library too was closed in 1629, following the circulation of a scandalous pamphlet emanating from it, but by this time it had already become established as a focus for opinion hostile to Buckingham. Cotton's librarian, Richard James, was the author of a panegyric on Buckingham's assassin called *Felton Commended*, and Jonson himself was questioned about verses *To His Confined Friend Mr Felton* which he admitted having seen at Cotton's but denied the charge of authorship. It is sometimes supposed that these lines do indeed voice Jonson's views on Buckingham's death, but it seems very unlikely that Jonson would have applauded a popular assassin for removing even an upstart aristocrat. Even allowing for the extreme language customary in contemporary affidavits, Jonson's 'deep protestations' at his examination 'vppon his christianity & hope of Salvation' that such opinions were to be 'condemned' and regarded 'with detestation' sound as though they meant what they said.[10] Nor will the sentiments of this poem square with those expressed in Jonson's lampoon on Alexander Gill, in which Gill, who had been sentenced to be mutilated for disrespectful remarks about James, Charles, and Buckingham, is said to deserve being 'whipped,/Cropped, slit [and] neck-stocked' (*Ungathered Verse*, 39.15). The bizarre Irish nurse in *The New Inn*, with her foolish chatter about heraldry, lineage, and records, may perhaps be taken as exemplifying Jonson's thoughts about antiquarianism in 1629.

In the light of Jonson's poverty, begging letters, and lack of masque commissions, it is tempting to represent him towards the end of his life as both alienated from the court and neglected by it. The epilogue to *The New Inn* ('had he lived the care of king and queen,/His art in something more yet had been seen' (line 21)) certainly sounds like a rebuke to a slack patron.[11] Yet on the basis of the evidence cited so far, there is some reason to suppose that the polarizations of political life may have been working to drive a wedge between Jonson's loyalties to his former friends and his loyalties to the king, and to reinforce rather than call into question his earlier views on government. I shall be arguing for the rest of this essay that much the same is true for the late plays. Despite the apparent technical disjunction between Jonson's early and late plays, the ideological assumptions on which they rest – their social priorities and political commitments – remain the same.

II

The political interest of *The New Inn* derives from its composition immediately prior to the recall of the last of Charles's early Parliaments, in March 1629. I would like to suggest that the play may be read as partly a response to the expectations of a moment in which rapprochement or accommodation, rather than confrontation, might at last have been achieved between the court and the court's critics – expectations brought about, needless to say, by the assassination of Buckingham six months earlier. With Buckingham removed, the possibilities of a new relationship between King and Parliament became suddenly available, and it is barely conceivable that a play licensed ten days in advance of the new assembly, and which revolves around a gamesome mock-parliament debating matters of love and honour and foregrounding a running commentary on the decline of the nobility can have been thought of as devoid of political content. The play seems on one level to be offering a fable about the loss and recovery of a traditional aristocracy. By the end of the play, the complaints of Lovel and the Host that titles have been vented at the drum and that academies of honour have departed quite from the institution have been answered not only by the fantastic resurrection of the Frampul dynasty but more seriously by Lovel's sustained apology for an ideology of honour and by Lord Latimer's remarkable decision to marry the significantly-named chambermaid Prudence. If this fable may be understood as promoting an image of an aristocracy re-educated in its moral and social responsibilities and revivified by the recovery of old blood and the promotion of new merit, it is difficult not to think of Buckingham's removal as being both the occasion and the necessary precondition for its invention. Certainly Jonson is unlikely to have thought it worth writing before August 1628, and the prospect of a Parliament makes it seem only more timely.

Of course strictly speaking it is not a parliament but a court of love which we see, in which the participants plead as advocates before a bar presided over by the mock-sovereign Pru, but they have a way of creating situations or using language which resonate with the political discourse of 1628–9. The Host's complaints against Lovel's penuriousness, that his mean living is against the freehold, inheritance, and Magna Carta of an inn (I.ii.23–4) gain their edge of aggression from his appropriation of the language of parliamentary complaint, and Lovel's reply that he has no wish 'to defraud you of your rights, or trench/Upo' your privileges, or great charter,/(For those are every host'lers language now)' (I.ii.34) sadly acknowledges that every innkeeper with a grudge against the great has started to pick up such loose constitutional terms. As these two characters come to understand one another, the Host quickly forgoes such language, only for it to be reappropriated by the idiotic Colonel Glorious Tiptoe who is upset by the mock-sovereign's refusal to patronize his bizarre acquaintance Fly, whom he wishes to recommend for a place in her court. As he blusters 'I ask my rights and privileges', 'My petition is of right' (II.vi.48,58) no one could have missed the disparaging echo of the most important legislative enactment of the 1628 Parliament.

Prudence, on the other hand, demonstrates herself to be a sovereign who is just, conciliatory, and surprisingly authoritative in her command of her subjects' desires. When Lady Frampul attempts to resist Prudence's command that she should kiss Lovel, Prudence turns it into a constitutional issue concerning authority and obedience. She warns Lady Frampul not to dispute 'my prerogative' (II.vi.105), and when Lady Frampul accuses her of tyranny she responds by warning her about rebellion:

LADY FRAMPUL: Prince Power will never want her parasites.
PRUDENCE: Nor Murmur her pretences.

(II.vi.138)

Lady Frampul's fault is that she gave her suffrage to Prudence, then attempted to withhold it when Prudence issued commands with which she disagreed. 'Would you make laws,' asks Prudence, 'and be the first that break 'em?' (II.vi.129). Prudence will not even allow her the dignity of offering her consent to the game that she proposes: 'Sovereigns use not/To ask their subjects suffrage where 'tis due;/But where conditional' (II.vi.249). The Host is so taken with Prudence's regal decisiveness that he hails her as a new Queen Elizabeth:

> First minute of her reign! what will she do
> Forty year hence?
>
> (II.vi.10)

So as Pru presides benevolently over the bringing together of two mistrustful lovers, the drift of these scenes is playfully to enact an image of a wise and benign royal justice, and to discredit those who oppose it (Lady Frampul and Tiptoe) as selfish or lacking in merit. Though the sovereign acts sternly, she also acts justly, and obedience brings its rewards. And in a similar way, Lovel's long, deeply felt speeches about love and valour are also supportive of the ideology, if not the political tendencies of Caroline Whitehall. His two discourses propound an aristocratic ethos in which Christian and classical traditions are fused into a cavalier code of self-control, self-reliance, and moral superiority, opposed to the merely brute passions of ordinary men:

> A wise man never goes the people's way,
> But as the planets still move contrary
> To the world's motion, so doth he, to opinion.
>
> (IV.iv.213)

His discourse on love is restrained, reasonable, and decorous. He treats love in terms of rational virtue and elegantly spiritualized sentiment, a matter not of passion but of 'weighing,/And well examining, what is fair, and good;/Then, what is like in reason, fit in manners' (III.ii.161). It is an equilibrium of reason and passion, in which strong feeling is present but kept under control. Its opposite, 'mere degenerous appetite' (III.ii.168), he censures but without horror or loathing; the senses may be subordinated to the mind, but there is no puritanical hatred of the body. Similarly, valour Lovel defines as a disciplined, morally directed energy, a matter of magnanimity, constancy, and quiet, 'a certain mean 'twixt fear and confidence', 'a true science of distinguishing/What's good or evil' (IV.iv.40, 42). Its opposite is passion or enthusiasm, of which the man who fights for virtue has no need; he will preserve his calm of mind even in the midst of common tumults. This Lovel himself exemplifies by intervening serenely to disperse the brawlers in the yard, and his listeners concur by dismissing the tawdry Colonel

Glorious from their company. Lovel's views on love are also publicly validated by the exposure of Pinnacia Stuff, the tailor's wife, who violates social and moral norms by dressing up as a lady and fornicating under an assumed name with her miserable husband. Tiptoe and Pinnacia are thus the antitypes who prove the validity of Lovel's ethical treatises, and it is difficult not to find in them some sort of reflection on the world according to Buckingham – one a flashy, hispanophile courtier, the other a nonentity who plays at being a duchess (IV.i.19).

From this perspective, *The New Inn* could be said to be engaged in the act of reconstructing an aristocratic ideology after the removal of Buckingham, but that it is doing so by conciliation, not confrontation: the reform proposed involves a reconstruction of the courtly ethos from within, not a destruction from without.[12] Indeed, despite being a sensational flop at the Blackfriars, the play reads like a seminal text for the court culture of the next generation. Lovel – melancholy, withdrawn, a man of honour and deep but hidden feeling, with a smattering of scientific interests and wearing his learning with effortless but commanding grace – is effectively the prototype for all those Van Dyckian courtiers whose portraits exhibit that distinctive combination of poised inwardness and relaxed, thoughtful self-assurance.[13] This play is strikingly prescient in the way that it defines what was to be the territory of romantic drama, and court drama in particular, down to the Civil War. In asking Lovel to speak on love and honour, Prudence's companions define precisely what were to be the leading preoccupations of all those interminable cavalier romances of platonic relationships and heroic, self-denying virtue, of which Davenant's tragicomedy *Love and Honour* is perhaps the archetypical example. Rather than being an oppositional play, *The New Inn* seems singularly constitutive of the court culture of the 1630s, though Jonson has also carefully used the fable to advertise the character of the royal government which he respects. The debates over love and honour chart out the cavalier codes of the coming generation, but the political authority of sovereign Pru, within whose court the debates take place, is legitimated less by hierarchy and descent than by the quality of responsible, benign, and conciliatory justice with which it seeks to act.

It is in this perspective that I would interpret the strange romance ending of *The New Inn.* Anne Barton has eloquently explicated it as a kind of Jonsonian *Winter's Tale*, a poignant moment of wish-fulfilment in which an unhappy past is boldly cancelled and rewritten,[14] but it seems to me to be rather more provisional. Plainly it is not parody, as once was thought, but neither is it quite a reassuringly Shakespearian transformation. Jonson has already warned us to hold romantic expectations in suspicion, for Lovel insisted admiringly that his former master, the old Lord Beaufort, modelled his life on the Homeric and Virgilian heroes, not on 'Arthurs, nor no Rosicleers,/No Knights o' the Sun, nor Amadis de Gauls' (I.vi.124): after this it is difficult to accept the arrival of a modern wandering knight without some disbelief. Moreover, unlike Shakespearian romance, the final transformations come out of the blue, entirely without preparation, and large sections of the play's society remain stubbornly untransformed, not only Tiptoe and the servants but even Lovel himself who, astonishingly, is offstage in bed until the last page and who, not surprisingly, ends the play almost speechless with amazement. This seems not so much a moment of transcendental illumination as an uneasy combination of celebration and scepticism, as though what is being affirmed is less an achieved resolution than a possibility that resolutions might yet be achieved. It is perhaps a measure of the difficulty in 1629 of imagining a post-Buckingham accommodation that Jonson drew back from allowing the Lovel plot to proceed to what, at the end of Act IV, seems to be developing as its natural conclusion.

III

Jonson's decisive personal break with Whitehall came early in 1631, when he quarrelled with Jones concerning artistic responsibility for his last masques. However, we do not have to assume that this disaster for Jonson's career meant a change in his political priorities. On the contrary, when *The New Inn* had flopped so disastrously at the Blackfriars, Jonson's response in the *Ode to Himself* had been to turn away loftily from his public audience and resolve to 'sing/The glories of thy King', 'tuning forth the acts of his sweet reign'.[15] Charles would be a better audience than the ignorant public spectators, and the two masques which Jonson produced for Whitehall in 1631, *Love's Triumph through Callipolis* and *Chloridia*, are possibly the most unproblematically celebratory of all his court entertainments. When Jonson was worsted in the quarrel with Jones, he reacted by publishing the text of *The New Inn*, together with the *Ode to Himself* with its statement about the poet's role as royal laureate, and in *The Magnetic Lady* (1632) he defiantly reiterated his governing assumption that the authorities of king and poet were reciprocally supportive.

In the choruses that punctuate *The Magnetic Lady*, guiding interpretation and blocking criticism, Jonson carefully establishes that the literary misinterpretation against which he struggles is the same voice of licentiously free censure that dogs his royal master. Says the overbearing spectator Damplay:

> I care not for marking the Play: Ile damn it, talk, and do that I come for. I will not have Gentlemen lose their privilege, nor I myself my prerogative, for ne'er an overgrown, or super-annuated poet of 'em all. He shall not give me the law; I will censure, and be witty, and take my tobacco, and enjoy my Magna Carta of reprehension, as my predecessors have done before me.
> (Chorus 4.19)

Damplay's jealousy for his privilege, his Magna Carta of reprehension, aligns his disrespect for Jonson's authority with criticisms of the poet's royal master made by the parliamentary gentry. Jonson is careful to flatter his audience as 'judicious spectators', but the play-boy who speaks for the author in the choruses is severely disparaging about spectators who have velvet outsides but who within share the 'popular ignorance' (Chorus 3.72). Though Jonson uses the choruses progressively to crush gentlemanly criticism and popular ignorance, it is the king to whom his epilogue turns for definitive judgement, conspicuously disregarding whatever might be the judgement of the playhouse:

> Well, Gentlemen, I now must under seal,
> And th'author's charge, waive you, and make my appeal
> To the supremest power, my Lord, the King;
> Who best can judge of what we humbly bring. . .
> To which voice he [the poet] stands,
> And prefers that, 'fore all the people's hands.

So too within the play, Jonson continues to take his artistic and political bearings from Whitehall as he constructs a fable of social and moral legislation. The plot is a dance of social types, all in need of some kind of reform: the ignorant doctor and self-seeking common lawyer, the frivolous gallant and the obstructive court official, the avaricious usurer and the zealously puritanical citizen's wife. All of these characters undergo discomfiture, though it is easily the citizens and the minor court official who come off worse. The city gossip Polish who has swapped her daughter at birth with the true heiress to Lady Loadstone is the play's villain; the grasping usurer Sir Moth Interest is punished for his avarice with a spectacular drenching; and the courtier Mr Bias, who uses his place to delay business or to cross the fortunes of his clients, ends the play affianced to a whore. Broadly speaking, this plot makes the play resemble Jonson's 'humours' comedies (and its subtitle harks back to those early plays), but unlike those plays *The Magnetic Lady* ends emphasizing reconciliation and rapprochement, and such punishments as are distributed are lenient; even Mr Bias escapes his marriage with the whore. One may wish to read this as a galloping case of late Jonsonian geniality, but it is also well in keeping with the consensual emphases of Charles's personal government, at least in its early years. Though Charles was governing without parliamentary finance, he could not afford to do so in a spirit of confrontation, but had to cultivate the goodwill of his social and political elites since without their active support his government could be neither financed nor administered. Jonson's conclusion, with its mixture of justice and appeasement, and his subtitle, 'Humours Reconciled', resonate with that Caroline need to foster a spirit of accommodation and consensus. The reconciling of humours, says the spectator Probee, is a greater undertaking than 'the reconciliation of both churches', the quarrel between the humours being 'the root of all schism and faction, both in church and commonwealth' (Chorus 1.112).

Like *The New Inn*, *The Magnetic Lady* draws at the end on romance motifs: two children have been exchanged at birth and the plot is resolved by the resumption of lost identities. Here, though, romance has been carefully prepared for in advance, and is unambiguously in the service of a political moral. All commentators emphasize that the characters who are the beneficiaries of these discoveries, the sociable scholar Compass and the blunt soldier Ironside, contain some kind of Jonsonian personal investment: brothers who maintain a competitive but symbiotic relationship, the soldier and scholar figure Jonson's own contradictory selves, and embody values which command authorial respect. In the conclusion, Ironside weds Lady Loadstone and Compass weds her niece, so spiriting the niece's fortune out of the hands of city usurer and court politician alike. The rediscovered identities and redirected inheritances which this involves diminish the financial power of the city on the one hand and the self-seeking of the court on the other, in the interests of promoting two deserving outsiders, one a man of blunt valour, the other a vigorous, sociable intellectual. Even more than *The New Inn* this conclusion seems a piece of social engineering, in which society's moral legislation is diverted into the hands of characters who deserve the responsibility, and who figure something of the poet's own character and circumstances – that poet who is also validated outside the play by the applause of the king.

Jonson completes his Caroline panorama by his inclusion of the clergyman, Parson Palate. Palate is a cleric in a position of social power and wearing all the elaborate Laudian vestments, 'prelate of the parish', a 'fine/Well-furnished and apparelled divine' who 'governs all the dames', and 'makes all the matches and the marriage feasts/Within the ward' (I.ii.15). However, he is neither terribly conscientious nor learned: he participates heartily in the meal that is eaten between Acts II and III and he is more interested in parish wakes and ales than he is in 'the Levitic law' (I.ii.29). He makes sure he obtains his 'blacks', his parish dues, from marriages and funerals (I.ii.29), and he is even prepared to conduct Compass's wedding outside the canonical hours of marriage in case it might lead to 'the loss/Of both my livings' (IV.vi.49). Archbishop Laud was keen to improve both the educational and the social standing of the clergy, and to free them economically from dependence on the gentlemen who controlled their livings: Margot Heinemann calls Palate 'exactly the kind of easy subservient priest, obediently carrying out the orders of his lay patron, whom Laud was anxious to extirpate from the Church'.[16] Jonson is still careful to be respectful towards the clergy: he has none of the humiliations in store for Palate that he reserves for his puritans, and Palate ends the play presiding genially over its various marriages. There may be a critical dig at the clergy here, but it is satire of a kind of which Laud could have approved, and the prominence Jonson affords Palate (he is, after all, almost completely irrelevant to the plot) is a measure of his desire to justify the Caroline dispensation, church as well as state.

IV

Though a less demanding play than *The New Inn, The Magnetic Lady* seems, then, to occupy much the same ideological space. In turning to *A Tale of A Tub* (with the late dating of which I am in full agreement), we have a play which appears to be situated much more ambiguously towards the court than either of its predecessors. It was 'not likte' at Whitehall,[17] and its openly-conducted satire on Inigo Jones and the minimalist masque with which it concludes seem particularly tactless inclusions. Anne Barton's reading of the play as a poignant celebration of rustic community and the golden age of Elizabeth casts it in a contestatory mode implicitly opposed to the ideology of the court: Jonson's nostalgia for a past characterized by trust, neighbourliness, and dependence becomes in her account a belated tribute to a lost golden age and an implied rebuke to the England of Charles I.[18] And yet there was more than one kind of nostalgia for the days of the Tudors current in Caroline England. The nostalgia of this play has been linked to the retrospective lauding of Elizabeth that generated such popular hagiographies as Thomas Heywood's *England's Eliza* (1631) and to the politically engaged neo-Elizabethan pastorals associated with the Spenserian poets.[19] But Jonson had not in the past been sympathetic to the veneration of Elizabeth that inspired the bells, bonfires, and sermons on her Accession Day and the demand for engravings, ballads, and biographies. The cult of Elizabeth as a sainted Protestant Amazon, however false to historical fact, was profoundly opposed to the priorities of a dynasty that had preferred conformity at home and lukewarmness abroad, and it fuelled sentiments of confessional militancy that were eventually to undermine trust in the Stuarts altogether. Jonson may have come to use some of the backward-looking rhetoric of England's godly, but he was less likely to have taken over their ideological assumptions wholesale or to have approved of their confessional perspective on English and European politics.

Jonson's evocation of mid-Tudor rural life in *A Tale of a Tub* has much less in common with this cult of Elizabeth than it has with the attitude to her reign voiced by the Earl of Newcastle in his advice to Charles II. Newcastle's remembrance was of a monarch who had been popular, but who had kept up her authority by selling herself dear, cherishing her nobility, maintaining ceremonies, encouraging respect and duty, mystifying the workings of state, and preventing the people talking politics. In particular, he advised Charles II to follow her example by encouraging May games, ales and revels, morris dancing, Christmas customs, innocent country games and sports: 'these things', he wrote, 'will much Diverte & please the People . . . amuse the peoples thoughts, & keepe them In harmles action which will free your Matie frome faction & Rebellion'.[20] As social historians have recently been arguing, Charles II's father and grandfather had indeed promoted innocent country revelry for the sake of upholding traditional ways and the systems of deference and obligation which they proclaimed.[21] Revelry could contain sedition and moderate disruptive individualism by dissolving social antagonisms in a common commitment to the life of the community, happily united under a benevolent king: on festival days, old ties were reaffirmed, strife allayed, and mutual amity promoted, the local community proclaiming its prosperity and mirroring the submissive contentment of the nation at large. Much to the horror of puritanical sentiment, James's *Book of Sports* (1617) licensed games on Sundays after church, and Charles was to reissue his father's proclamation in 1633, barely six months after the first record of *A Tale of a Tub*. The nostalgia of that play for a golden past may resemble a harking-back to a lost leader offensive to the court but it can be just as well understood as a cultivation of traditional ways and unchanging customary practices which the court was concerned to sponsor.

The plot of *A Tale of a Tub* promotes attitudes that serve the needs of the court by defusing threats to the ideology of deference: in particular, it shows potential collisions of interest between the court and provinces being resolved and dispelled. This play involves an astonishingly detailed depiction of the administrative workings of the early modern village community. At the centre of the farce is the High Constable Toby Turf, who stands at the apex of authority in Finsbury Hundred; he is one of the village notables appointed tri-annually to this onerous post, a prosperous yeoman farmer some notches below gentility. Below him Jonson carefully distinguishes all the lesser officers: the head-borough, petty constable, and thirdborough, supported by the parish clerk and High Constable's man. These are the parish officers, chosen by rotation from house to house, and they are men whose horizons are bounded by local affairs. Set over the constable is the local magistrate, Justice Preamble. He is a gentleman, and his role is to act as a channel of royal power overseeing the life of the parish. His authority does not come from the community, and his loyalties run upwards, to the monarch. An even higher authority is pretended by his clerk, Miles Metaphor, when in a plot to carry off the constable's daughter Audrey he disguises himself as a pursuivant, a royal messenger who pretends to arrive with a command from the Privy Council. With his appearance, the arm of princely government seems to extend directly into the life of Kentish Town. Finally, Squire Tub as lord of the manor is socially the leader of this community but administratively his power is much diminished. During the early modern period the parish authorities gradually assumed local responsibilities which had formerly been held by the manor, and the uneasy relationships between the Turfs and the Tubs derive partly from this shift in local politics.[22]

This is an unusually dense and precise representation of village power, and the action which it serves involves a collision between the community and the centre, the demands of neighbourliness and the demands of office. During the early modern period, parish officialdom had gradually acquired increasing responsibilities for the social and economic regulation of its locality. This process accelerated under the early Stuarts, and Charles I in particular sought to command his gentry back to the provinces and to tighten up the administration of discipline, bombarding his local officers with directives about policing the locality and reporting its affairs back to the council table. This way the provinces would be regulated in the absence of Parliament, peace maintained and channels of communication kept open between the centre and the localities.[23] Much of the burden of this royal interference in local life fell onto the constable. He stood at the pressure point where the demands of locality and centre met, and throughout the early modern period, but increasingly under Charles, he experienced dual loyalties. Constables were elected by their neighbours and had to live in their communities, but they were expected to function as agents of the central power, and the antagonisms from which many seem to have suffered arose from this conflict between their upward function as royal officers and their downward respect for their neighbours.[24] It is precisely this tension which the action of *A Tale of a Tub* is designed to exploit.

The villagers in *A Tale of a Tub* are attempting to perform a local celebration, the wedding of Audrey Turf, but first the wedding feast is interrupted by a false report about a robbery and the neighbours are forced to go charging around the countryside in search of a non-existent gang of thieves, then Squire Tub is himself arrested by a fake pursuivant who pretends to be bearing commands direct from the council-table. In each case the celebration of neighbourliness in the community runs up against the imperatives of office. In particular, the dynamic of the action involving Toby Turf is a hilarious collision between his duty to his place and his loyalty to his friends. Not only is his willingness to mount a hue and cry undermined by his consciousness that the wedding dinner is cooling, the accusation of robbery has been laid against the bridegroom and he is not over-eager to arrest his prospective son-in-law. Moreover, the members of the hue and cry are reluctant to search too closely in case they find too many criminals:

> Masters, take heed, let's not vind too many;
> One's enough to stay the hangman's stomach.
>
> (III.i.24)

The result is farce, but a farce which turns on the collision of local solidarity with interference from an external authority.

It might, of course, be possible to argue that there is a subversive point here. Leah Marcus, for example, suggests that in inviting the audience to observe 'what different things/The cotes of clowns are, from the courts of kings' (prologue), Jonson was exposing a gap between the courtly pastoralism of Whitehall and the riotous earthiness of Kentish Town.[25] Similarly, there might be a current of irony present in the constable's continual insistence on the dignity of his office, in spite of the self-evident limitations of his own competence:

> Does any wight parzent her Majesty's person,
> This hundred, 'bove the High Constable?
>
> (I.iv.53)

Given the local failures of authority which this farce repeatedly discloses, the acknowledgement that the glory of kingship is manifested among the people by clowns like Toby Turf carries potential for reflection on a court which was seeking to use local officers to enforce the dissemination of kingly power throughout the country. Yet, in the action Jonson has designed, such ironies work not on the whole to disparage but to affirm royal power. The farce creates situations in which potentially damaging tensions between central power and local solidarity continually threaten, but ultimately they turn out to be only the consequence of tricks and knaveries, and are dissolved in laughter without compromise either to neighbourliness or to authority. The constable may be foolish and his service inadequate, but if he labours loyally in his office everything falls out well and no serious damage is done. His insistence on the dignity of his office is amusing but harmless: it entitles him to be in the right even when he is in the wrong in trivial affairs such as the bizarre debate over who St Valentine actually was, but important matters have a way of sorting themselves out irrespective of the constable's wishes. The cotes of clowns can afford to be foolish because the courts of kings have an authority that does not depend on the dignity of their officers.

It appears, then, that this country play does not so much call the authority of kingship into question as enhance it, and it addresses itself to the sources of conflict between centre and locality in pre-Civil War England in order to show those conflicts being marginalized, defused, or transcended. A source of comedy rather than disaster, the perception of the distance between king and subject in Jonson's handling reinforces an ideology which puts power in the hands of the few rather than the many. But why set the play in the mid-sixteenth century rather than in the present if no disparagement is on offer? Here the point is not so much the contrast between Charles and Elizabeth as the casting back which it allows to traditional ideas of community, ideas which even in 1633 were coming under threat. The early Stuart period was witnessing a process of gradual polarization within provincial communities, between the village notables and the ordinary villagers. During the economic crises of the late sixteenth and early seventeenth centuries, the ordinary villagers were increasingly menaced with unemployment and poverty, and the response of the village notables, particularly those infiltrated by puritanical sentiment, was to attempt to contain economic crisis by imposing controls over social and moral behaviour within the parish – to restrict drunkenness, bastardy, Sabbath breaking, oaths, and all the disruptiveness that threatened the good order of the locality. From having been communities bound by hierarchies of rank and status, village societies became increasingly dominated by a divisive order which emphasized the distance between the better sort of villagers, who thought in terms of social and moral respectability and a culture of discipline, and the rest who still thought in terms of community, amity, and neighbourliness. It was this disturbing social development against which the Stuart promotion of a culture of traditional revelry was in part directed.[26]

Puritanical sentiments are voiced in *A Tale of a Tub* – Lady Tub thinks that on St Valentine's Day one ought not to 'look for lovers/Or handsome images to please the senses' (I.vii.14) while Toby Turf has doubts about the propriety of encouraging 'rondels' in the queen's paths (II.i.53) – but they do not last long in the face of the village's commitment to amity. Moreover, while the play works to reaffirm traditional ideas of community it is significant that Jonson reaches back *beyond* the myth of the godly Elizabeth to give the play a religious colouring that seems to be Catholic rather than Protestant. If this play is set in the reign of Queen Elizabeth – which is by no means certain[27] – it must be the very early days indeed of her reign, before it was clear whether the English church would join the cause of reform or remain within the Roman fold, for Chanon Hugh conducts marriage services in Latin and has a 'shaven pate' like a friar (II.iii.38) while Toby Turf swears 'by Our Lady o' Walsingham' (III.i.3). This may well be nostalgia for the golden days of Elizabeth, but what makes them golden is that Elizabeth had not yet taken the steps which would lead to the decisive break with Rome. Not only is the heroic rule of Elizabeth in the future, but so too are the religious controversies and social fragmentation which were part of the legacy of Protestantism. If this community and the loyalty and neighbourliness which it exhibits is an object of nostalgia for Jonson, that is because it is one which has yet to hear the odious name *Puritan*.

V

It seems to me, then, that for all that these three plays are a kind of Jonsonian experiment, in which Jonson explores new forms, conventions, and motifs, the ideological assumptions which the plays serve and underwrite have not undergone substantial revision, and that Jonson was still concerned to construct fables which reaffirmed rather than called into question the social and political hegemony of the court. Clearly, these plays do exhibit features which suggest a measure of distance from the court or criticism of it, and which project Jonson's hesitation about simply underwriting submission and deference. The plays educate as well as legitimate: they promote images of how responsible authority should act and of what the good society should be. But in the context of the loss of consensus which was the political legacy of the 1620s, that criticism was circumscribed by the political needs of an increasingly embattled court, and had to be contained within actions which were serviceable to the ideological outlook of Whitehall. Ultimately the plays had to work towards the dispelling of reservations about Caroline government and to operate within an attitude that remained at root deferential and respectful towards royal power.

Of course, Jonson did pass his last years in money difficulties, but he was not by any means the only courtier left hanging around for money at the financially straitened Caroline court; and although *A Tale of a Tub* was 'not likte' at Whitehall this may well have been as a result of its persistent sniping at Inigo Jones rather than its political implications which, I have been arguing, were responsive to the ideological and political priorities of Caroline Whitehall. Jonson may have been demoted as masque-writer for the court, but the products of his old age do not waver in their loyal support for the crown. The myth of the neglected Jonson writing dotages has a long history, but as the aesthetic achievement of these plays becomes more highly valued, so our understanding of their politics may have to be revised accordingly.

NOTES

1 This connection is made by Kevin Sharpe in 'The Earl of Arundel, his circle, and the opposition to the Duke of Buckingham' in his *Faction and Parliament* (Oxford: Clarendon Press, 1978), 209–44. He is followed by Anne Barton in *Ben Jonson, Dramatist* (Cambridge: Cambridge University Press, 1984), 303–4. But although Jonson clearly knew members of Arundel's circle (such as Robert Cotton and John Selden), there is no evidence of

direct contact with Arundel other than the verses addressed to him in *The Gypsies Metamorphosed* (1621), as Arundel happened to be one of the dignitaries in the audience at the Windsor performance. As I argue below, it does not seem to me that Jonson's nostalgia for lost values of aristocratic honour occupies the same ground as Arundel's cult of aristocratic dignity. Arundel's cult of birth was not the same as Jonson's respect for merit.

2 Jonson's relationship with the Spenserian poets had been fraught and volatile. He had bitterly lampooned George Wither in the court masque *Time Vindicated* (1623), and he told Drummond that he 'esteemed not' Drayton (C. H. Herford, P. and E. Simpson (eds), *Ben Jonson*, 11 vols (Oxford: Clarendon Press, 1925–53), vol. I, 136). David Norbrook is careful to emphasize that any rapprochement between Jonson and the Spenserian poets could only be an uneasy affair; see *Poetry and Politics in the English Renaissance* (London: Routledge & Kegan Paul, 1984), 246–8.

3 I should perhaps add that I have allowed the view against which I am arguing to colour the introductions to my own editions of *The New Inn* and *A Tale of a Tub* in *The Selected Plays of Ben Jonson* (Cambridge: Cambridge University Press, 1989), vol. II, and that this essay represents an attempt to revise my treatment of the subject.

4 On Newcastle, see my *Theatre and Crisis 1632–1642* (Cambridge: Cambridge University Press, 1984), 195–8 and the references cited therein; and my essay 'Stuart Politics in Jonson's *Tale of a Tub*', *Modern Language Review* 85 (1990), 12–28.

5 Butler, *Theatre and Crisis*, 195.

6 Richard Cust, *The Forced Loan and English Politics* (Oxford: Clarendon Press, 1987), 197–8.

7 Herford and Simpson (eds), *Ben Jonson*, vol. VIII, 228, 232–3. All references to Jonson are to this edition. (I have modernized the spelling of quotations.)

8 See Michael Alexander, *Charles I's Lord Treasurer* (London: Macmillan, 1975), *passim*; Martin J. Havran, *Caroline Courtier: The Life of Lord Cottington* (London: Macmillan, 1973), 111–23; and *Calendar of State Papers*, Venetian series, 1629–32, 204.

9 The most recent important treatments are by Hugh Trevor-Roper, 'The Great Tew circle' in *Catholics, Anglicans and Puritans* (London: Secker & Warburg, 1987), 166–230; and J. C. Hayward, 'New directions in the study of the Falkland circle', *The Seventeenth Century* 2 (1987) 19–48. Jonson's particularly close links to Kenelm and Venetia Digby are attested by the important poems addressed to them (*Underwood* 78, 84) and by the fact that Kenelm acted as editor for the posthumous second Folio (Jonson's *Works*, 1640).

10 Herford and Simpson (eds), *Ben Jonson*, vol. I, 242–4. On the Cotton–Selden circle and their activities, see especially Kevin Sharpe, *Sir Robert Cotton 1586–1631* (Oxford: Oxford University Press, 1979) – though Sharpe is inclined to underestimate the differences between Jonson and other members of the Cotton circle in this period.

11 Against this should be set the famous begging letter to Newcastle in which Jonson describes the earl as 'next the King, my best Patron' (Herford and Simpson (eds), *Ben Jonson*, vol. I, 214); and Jonson's allusion to the king as 'his Master . . . to whom hee acknowledgeth all' in *The Magnetic Lady*

(Chorus 2.52) – both without any hint of reflection on Charles's apparent neglect of him.

12 Jonson's continuing hostility to puritanism is implied in Lovel's speeches by his contrast between the serene trust of the valiant man in his ideals and the sacrilege of those who try but fail to destroy metaphysical absolutes: 'They that do pull down churches, and deface/The holiest altars, cannot hurt the Godhead' (IV.iv.207).

13 For which see R. Malcolm Smuts, *Court Culture and the Origins of a Royalist Tradition in Early Stuart England* (Philadelphia: Pennsylvania University Press, 1986), 203–6.

14 Barton, *Ben Jonson, Dramatist*, 281–2.

15 Herford and Simpson (eds), *Ben Jonson*, vol. VI, 494.

16 In a private communication. I am very grateful to Margot Heinemann for an extensive discussion of Palate on which my account here draws. For further comment, see my essay 'Why was Jonson's *Magnetic Lady* censored?', *Modern Language Review* (forthcoming).

17 G. E. Bentley, *The Jacobean and Caroline Stage* (Oxford: Clarendon Press, 1956), vol. IV, 633. This discussion of *A Tale of a Tub* condenses a case I have argued at length in 'Stuart politics in Jonson's *Tale of a Tub*'.

18 Barton, *Ben Jonson, Dramatist*, 335–7.

19 Norbrook, *Poetry and Politics in the English Renaissance*, 246.

20 S. Arthur Strong, *A Catalogue of Letters and Other Historical Documents Exhibited in the Library at Welbeck* (London: John Murray, 1903), 227.

21 See especially David Underdown, *Revel, Riot, and Rebellion* (Oxford: Clarendon Press, 1985); Leah Marcus, *The Politics of Mirth* (Chicago: Chicago University Press, 1986); and Peter Stallybrass, ' "Wee feaste in our defense": patrician carnival in early modern England and Robert Herrick's *Hesperides*', *English Literary Renaissance* 16 (1986), 234–52.

22 On Stuart provincial government see Joan R. Kent, *The English Village Constable* (Oxford: Clarendon Press, 1986); Anthony Fletcher, *A County Community in Peace and War: Sussex 1600–1660* (London: Longmans, 1975); William B. Willcox, *Gloucestershire: A Study in Local Government 1590–1640* (New Haven: Yale University Press, 1940); and Joel Hurstfield, 'County government *c*.1530–*c*.1660', in Ralph B. Pugh and Elizabeth Crittal (eds), *A History of Wiltshire, Victoria County History* (Oxford: Oxford University Press, 1957), vol. V, 80–110.

23 See L. M. Hill, 'County government in Caroline England', in Conrad Russell (ed.), *The Origins of the English Civil War* (London: Macmillan, 1973), 66–90; Anthony Fletcher, *Reform in the Provinces: The Government of Stuart England* (New Haven: Yale University Press, 1986); and Barnes, *Somerset 1625–1640*, chapter 7.

24 See Keith Wrightson, 'Two concepts of order: justices, constables and jurymen in early modern England', in John Brewer and John Styles (eds), *An Ungovernable People* (London: Hutchinson, 1980), 21–47; Keith Wrightson, *English Society 1580–1680* (London: Hutchinson, 1982), 155–9; Kent, *The English Village Constable,* chapter 7; and Fletcher, *Reform in the Provinces*, 62–83.

25 Marcus, *The Politics of Mirth*, 135–7.

26 This paragraph draws on Fletcher, *Reform in the Provinces*, 262–81; Under-

down, *Revel, Riot, and Rebellion*, 9–43; Wrightson, 'Two concepts of order'; Wrightson, *English Society 1580–1680*, 166–73; Keith Wrightson and David Levine, *Poverty and Piety in an English Village* (New York: Academic Press, 1979), 176–8; and William Hunt, *The Puritan Moment* (Cambridge, Mass.: Harvard University Press, 1983), 130–55.

27 A Marian rather than an Elizabethan setting is accepted by W. W. Greg in 'Some notes on Ben Jonson's works', *Review of English Studies* 2 (1926), 133–6; and L. A. Beaurline, *Jonson and Elizabethan Comedy* (San Marino: Huntington Library, 1978), 274–86.

9

SHE THAT PLAYS THE KING: HENRIETTA MARIA AND THE THREAT OF THE ACTRESS IN CAROLINE CULTURE

Sophie Tomlinson

On Shrove Tuesday 1626, Henrietta Maria took the stage at the English court, acting a French pastoral with the company of her 'demoiselles'.[1] The gesture was arresting, at once cultural intervention – an assertion of a different heritage – and theatrical innovation, for until this moment formal acting by women had not been witnessed, either on the English public stage, or in court entertainments.[2] Foreign ambassadors commented on the queen's 'youthful grace' and 'remarkable acting', noting at the same time the select nature of the invited audience, in spite of which precaution the performance 'did not give complete satisfaction, because the English objected to the first part being declaimed by the queen'.[3] The breach of the English taboo against members of royalty speaking on stage was exceeded, however, by the shock of sexual transgression, indeed usurpation, in Henrietta Maria's parley of women. For, as John Chamberlain reported, some of the participants 'were disguised like men with beards'. The impression thus conveyed by this female presentation was that of a theatrical overturning of Salic law, the arrogation of masculine role just brinking upon, or brushing up against male rule: 'I hear not much honour of the Quene's maske', remarked one ruffled English observer, 'for, *if they were not all*, soome were in men's apparel.'[4]

This theatrical coup by England's new Queen Consort marks the beginning of an alteration of language taking place in the Caroline period. Amidst the news which circulated about the performance Sir Benjamin Rudyerd blithely refers to the queen as 'a principal actress'.[5] As far as I am aware this was the first occasion that the term 'actress' had been used with the sense of 'a female player on the stage', supplementary to the general sense of a woman who does things or is active: a usage which thus predates that given in the *OED* by exactly three-quarters of a century.[6] Established theatrical history fails to register the changes which occurred in England between 1625 and 1643, during which time the concept of the woman-actor in *both* senses gained considerable currency, and indeed, a token acceptance in Caroline culture. If the introduction of women to the professional stage in 1660 was something of a non-event, as Katharine Maus has argued, this is precisely because the cultural event provoked by women's acting had already taken place.[7] With a new empirical basis in women acting at court and in some private houses,[8] female acting changed in status from a trope to a topic of discourse in the Caroline period, and was contested, both rowdily and discreetly, across a remarkably wide range of texts. William Prynne's attack on women-actors as 'notorious whores' in his clamorous *Histrio-Mastix* (1633) is a crucial juncture in this contestation.[9] Construed as a swipe at the queen's performance of Walter Montagu's *The Shepheard's Paradise* in 1633, his epithet, and the political scandal accruing to it, quickly turned female acting into a livewire issue. A number of plays from the 1630s dramatize or allude to the topic, seemingly in an attitude of defence, while satiric discourse of the period evinces a diffusion of the type of the uppity woman, or would-be woman-actor throughout the female audience.

Surprisingly, no attempt has been made at a synchronic study of the period which would chart the cultural event set in motion by the staging of women at the Caroline court, examining the ways that female performance is perceived and constructed in discourse. This term 'staging of women' implies something larger than female performance. The emphasis of court culture was broadly feminocentric. Together with female acting Henrietta Maria introduced a cult of platonic love, mediated through French romance and pastoral drama, which projected women centre-stage as the embodiments of ideal beauty.[10] Her penchant for pastoral itself linked into an English tradition of pastoral forms articulated both by and to the queen.[11] There is little doubt that Henrietta Maria's initiatives set in motion a cult of woman, or focus on the feminine in Caroline culture. The increasingly romantic and rarefied tenor of much of the drama, the proliferation of 'lady' play-titles in the 1630s, and the training of the gaze on the 'ladies' in the audience of the elite theatres, can all be traced to her influence.[12] Recent studies of Caroline culture have recognized the importance of Henrietta Maria, both as a theatrical patron and as a key participant in the direction of court masque and theatre.[13] Martin Butler's ground-breaking book *Theatre and Crisis* reads the drama which was an outgrowth of the platonic love-cult at court in terms of a 'politicization of love', the movement producing a platonic poetics in which romantic and political motifs coalesced.[14] Butler focuses in particular on the queen's alignment, before 1637, with an anti-Spanish, pro-Palatinate group of Protestants peers at court, and on a number of court entertainments and plays which he reads as participating in or responding to these 'oppositional' views.[15] Aside from these persuasively contextualized readings, however, the political ramifications of the feminocentric court culture *per se*, most especially the politics of female performance, have received no attention in revisionist accounts.[16]

I would locate this dimension first in the wider visibility accorded women as cultural consumers across the social spectrum after the advent of Henrietta Maria. The deferential publicity granted women in the elite theatre in the form of a chivalric address to the 'ladies' has been generally noted by literary historians.[17] What has not been sufficiently recognized is the corollary satiric perspective which depicts the female spectator of middling social rank (most often a female citizen or gentlewoman) passionately aspiring to courtly or fashionable status. This satiric construction of the female spectator, or seeker after culture, indicates an anxiety over female cultural consumption; attesting at once to the social dispersion of what Malcolm Smuts has characterized as an 'urban high culture',[18] and to the seductiveness of such culture for women further down the social scale. Of course, the courteous spotlighting of the 'ladies' in the elite audience was precisely designed to flatter the generality of women. The reverse side of this idealizing discourse discloses a fear of the social and sexual subversion to which women's identification with a feminocentric culture may lead.

An even stronger unease is conveyed by the new dramatic type of the courtly woman with a passion for theatre. This type commonly merges the perceived pretensions of the woman-actor with those of the platonic lady, whose role was essentially one of 'set[ting her]self at gaze',[19] playing prima donna to a multitudinous audience of servants. The satiric intensity of much of this dramatic material indicates that the interpolation of women as actors, and as such *agents* in cultural production, was perceived as a fundamental form of role transgression – what Natalie Zemon Davis has classically termed 'symbolic sexual inversion'.[20] There are obvious historical reasons why this was so. Prynne's equation 'women-actors, notorious whores' was a product of the contemporary ideology which worked to keep women out of the public view, discouraging them from speaking, taking the floor, or in any way making a show of themselves. Richard Braithwait's injunction to English gentlewomen to 'Make your Chamber your private Theatre, wherein you may act some devout Scene to God's honour',[21] is an apposite illustration of this code of confinement in its Caroline form. The presence on stage, however, of the female body and voice exactly reversed the order of things which placed 'woman' on the side of absence and silence. (It is important, in this respect, to register the distinction between the silent and emblematic participation of women in the Jacobean masque, and the far more dynamic potential for projecting female personality allowed by the declamation, action, singing, and dancing which made up the queen's theatrical diversions.) The threat of the actress in performance lay in the potential for presenting femininity as a vivid and mobile force: the spectacle of the woman-actor summoning up a spectre of the female subject. Henrietta Maria herself posed this threat in particularly acute form: both in terms of her theatrical flair, and her active engagement in Caroline politics – behaviour which was perceived as at once upstaging her husband and as constituting a political 'Popish' threat.

In this essay I shall attempt to sketch the cultural event set in motion by Henrietta Maria's initiatives at the Caroline court. I will argue that the performative aspect of the feminocentric court culture disrupted the symbolic ordering of gender, and that this disruption provided a model for female insubordination in the cultural sphere. I will suggest that the threat of the actress was compounded by Henrietta Maria's political engagement and I will end by speculating on whether these combined styles of performance might have spurred on the greater social, cultural, and political activity of women during the revolutionary period. In hazarding the idea of there being a more than symbolic relation between what I've termed the 'staging of women' at the Caroline court and women's participation in the activities of writing, preaching, prophecy, and political protest, I am drawing at once on Davis's thesis that symbolic images of sexual inversion can 'operate to widen behavioural options for women . . . and to sanction riot and political disobedience', and on the suggestive remark made by Margaret Cavendish in her *Poems and Fancies* (1653) that 'this Age hath produced many effeminate Writers as well as Preachers, and many effeminate Rulers, as well as Actors.'[22] I begin by briefly scanning the satiric construction of the female spectator and proceed to examine three of the plays which dramatize women acting.

UPPITY WOMEN

On Shrove Tuesday in the year following the queen's acting debut at court, 'the schollars of the free-schoole of Hadleigh in Suffolke' presented a play called *Apollo Shroving*, written as a carnival exercise by their teacher William Hawkins.[23] At the beginning of the play the latin Prologus, 'a young Schollar', is interrupted by Lala, 'a woman spectator', who insists on the right of the unlearned audience to hear a play in 'honest English', it being not merely 'every shee,/Whom here you see', but also 'many a good man that never/Was infected with this raving latin-fever.'[24] Once assured that the play is in English, she exits with the lines:

> It shall goe hard but I'le get a part amongst them. I'le into the tyreing house and scamble and rangle for a mans part. Why should not women act men, as well as boyes act women? I will weare the breeches, so I will.[25]

Hawkins's cameo of the upstart female spectator draws on all the conventional satiric indices of the protesting woman. Lala is a wasp, a tomboy, a shrew, and a lecherous maid, whose name derives from the Greek for 'babble'.[26] Nevertheless, this prologue functions as a graphic articulation of assertiveness on the part of the female audience, both as auditors and would-be actors.

This discourse depicting the female spectator in search of the theatrical spotlight should, I have suggested, be seen as the satiric obverse to the prominence politely accorded women in the elite audience following the advent of Henrietta Maria. In her sophisticated form the female spectator is characterized by her self-advertisement and ostentatious upward mobility. These features are summarily displayed in the initiating moment of Jonson's *The Staple of News* (1626) in which a crew of gentlewomen gossips actually usurp the stage bench, putting themselves on public show 'ladylike attired'. When Mirth leads the other gossips onto the stage (all four boy-actors presumably 'pranked up' like prime ladies) she declares to the Prologue 'we are persons of quality . . . and women of fashion; and come to see and to be seen'.[27]

The preening of the self-fashioned woman manifests one form of insubordination. This social desertion caused by an immersion in fashionable culture is paralleled in satiric discourse by the threat of sexual desertion. One of the anti-masque figures in Shirley's *The Triumph of Peace* (1634) is a country gentlewoman come up to town, whose name, Lady Novelty, illustrates the tendency of satiric discourse to naturalize in women an avidity for everything exotic and new. Catching a whiff of platonic innovation Lady Novelty discards the term 'wife', answering her husband, 'Your Wife! you might have fram'd a newer word; They can but call/Us so i'th'country.'[28] The two motifs of gentry desertion from country to town,[29] and the imitation of courtly trends are overlaid here with the threat of insubordination in marriage, a threat which Shirley fully elaborated in his play *The Lady of Pleasure* (1635). The fact that women's 'wandring abroad to Playes, to Playhouses, Dancing-matches, Masques, and publike shews'[30] separated them from the home, and their role as housewives, was highly unsettling to moralists of the period. Prynne ends his massive polemic with an hysterical appeal to 'the many wanton females of all sorts resorting daily *by troopes* unto our Playes'.[31] His image of women's mass mobilization in the pursuit of culture appears again, in a satiric frame, in Carew's masque *Coelum Brittannicum* (1634). Momus's speech satirizing the reforms of Charles's court shows women as a sex in rebellion against the kind of proclamation to the gentry to leave town which Charles had issued in 1632:

> Edicts are made for the restoring of decayed house-keeping, prohibiting the repayr of Families to the Metropolis, but this did endanger an Amazonian mutiny, till the females put on a more masculine resolution of solliciting businesses in their own persons, and leaving their husbands at home for stallions of hospitality.[32]

Crucially, *this* physical desertion is figured in terms of an inversion of gender: the threat of an Amazonian mutiny is offset, or rather, translated, into the women's acting in masculine fashion – 'putting on a more masculine resolution' – throwing off not simply the name, but the gendered role of wife. Carew's satiric sketch of masculine women banding to town forms the symbolic counterpart to Hawkins's cameo of the uppity female spectator who literally aspired to wear the breeches, to act the man's part. Satiric discourse thus produces an approximation between the active female consumer and the woman-actor, both of whom are seen to be engaged in a usurpation of the masculine role.[33] Though the angling of the passage from *Coelum Brittannicum* is towards the female gentry, the satire rebounds on the female court: the key participants in culture, the key actors of Amazon examples. This motif of the usurpation of masculine prerogative brings me to Henrietta Maria, and the anomaly of the woman-actor itself.

LADIES ERRANT

At the start of the new reign female acting was stamped in the public mind as a continental phenomonen. English xenophobia came to the fore in 1629, when actresses belonging to a French troupe attempting to play in London were 'hissed, hooted, and pippin-pelted from the stage' in one of their three performances.[34] Prynne wrote them up as 'some French-women, or Monsters rather . . . [who] attempted to act a French play, at the Play-house in Black-friers: an impudent, shamefull, unwomanish, gracelesse, if not more than whorish attempt', to which, as he adds elsewhere, 'there was great resort'.[35] Some mild play on the association between France and women-actors occurs in Shirley's comedy *The Ball* (1632), in which Jack Freshwater, 'a pretended traveller', discoursing on the respective strengths of English and French theatre, drops a reference to women-actors in an effort to appear *au courant*:

> But there be no such comedians as we have here; yet the women are the best actors, they play their own parts, a thing much desired in England by some ladies, inns'o'court gentlemen, and others.[36]

Shirley's allusion suggests that female acting was a topic of the moment in fashionable circles, even before the events of 1633. This suggestion is strengthened by the complex publishing matrix of the first two plays I wish to discuss: Shirley's romantic comedy *The Bird in a Cage* and Ford's tragedy *Love's Sacrifice*. Both of these plays were published in 1633, and together, in their printed form, they situate themselves in a direct relation to the publication of Prynne's *Histrio-Mastix* at the end of the previous year. The timing of Prynne's publication, some five or six weeks before the performance on 9 January of *The Shepheard's Paradise* by Henrietta Maria and her English women, gave Archbishop Laud an excuse to suggest that Prynne's attack on the spectrum of Caroline culture and religion, most especially his attack on women-actors, was a slur cast specifically at the court and on the queen.[37] Though there was a widespread counter-attack on Prynne throughout the drama,[38] Shirley and Ford's plays were unique in that they dramatized the issue of female acting, and were printed with prefatory material which was extremely hostile to Prynne. Moreover, it is likely that each of these plays was written before the performance of *The Shepheard's Paradise* and Prynne's subsequent arrest. *The Bird in a Cage* was entered in the

Stationers' Register on 19 March 1633, and was performed at the Phoenix theatre some time earlier in the year.[39] The play was acted without a licence. Frances Frazier Senescu has made light of this fact by arguing convincingly that *The Bird in a Cage* is identical with a lost play of Shirley's called *The Beauties* (licensed 21 January 1633) and that Shirley renamed this play and provided a dedication, so as both to allude to, and capitalize on the circumstances of Prynne, who was in prison awaiting trial at the time that the play went to press.[40] The dedication is to Prynne, and is bruisingly ironic, reaching its peak at the moment where Shirley declares that the play

> wanteth, I must confess, much of that ornament, which the stage and action lent it, for it comprehending also another play or interlude, personated by ladies, I must refer to your imagination, the music, the songs, the dancing, and other varieties, which I know wou'd have pleas'd you infinitely in the presentment.[41]

Shirley's elaborate framing of this part of the play seems to work implicitly to exonerate the queen's acting. His reference to himself on the title-page as 'Servant to her Majesty' – an allusion to his recent appointment as *valet de chambre* to Henrietta Maria – strengthens the impression that his dedication was indeed aiming to champion the queen. What is astonishing, in the light of this posture, is the clashing tone of the interlude itself, in which a princess and her waiting-women (the 'Beauties' of the former title) pass their confinement in a tower by singing, dancing, and improvising a play around the somewhat risqué myth of Jupiter and Danae. The scene might be read as legitimizing this kind of recreational activity for women, were it not for the fact that the extempore play takes the form of a riotous burlesque, fusing imaginative release with sexual excitement in a way which wholly confirms Prynne's epithet: 'I have known men have been insufficient', declares one of the princess's ladies, 'but women can [always] play their parts' (416).[42] While the behaviour and language of the princess are impeccable, her maids are cast in the comic mould of lustful court women, speaking lines such as, 'Now would I give all my jewels for the sight of a pair of breeches though there were nothing in them' (415). The demurring undertow of Shirley's *The Ball* with regard to female revels is reinscribed in *The Bird in a Cage* as an open contradiction between the text and the playwright's use of the text in the act of publication. Shirley fully exploits the chance to castigate Prynne in his preface, while his play actually illustrates Prynne's notorious equation.

The text of Ford's *Love's Sacrifice* reproduces this double aggravation of Prynne. The play was entered in the Stationers' Register on 21 January 1633 and was printed with commendatory verses from Shirley.[43] Shirley's harassment of Prynne in his second stanza draws out a more discreet allusion in Ford's dedication:

> Look here, thou, that hast malice to the stage,
> And impudence enough for the whole age;
> *Voluminously*-ignorant, be vext
> To read this tragedy, and thy own be next.[44]

The 'vexing' aspect of the tragedy for Prynne lies in its depiction of three court women performing in an antic masque or dumb-show. The 'antic' is suggested by a courtier who describes witnessing a similar entertainment in Brussels, 'Perform'd by knights and ladies of [the] court . . . which', he adds, 'For that I ne'er before saw women-antics – /Was for the newness strange, and much commended' (II.61). In the course of the masque, however, the three women fall upon and stab to death the lecherous Italian courtier who has impregnated them all. They subsequently appear unmasked, '*each with a child in her arms*' (71). As the leader of the murderous trio delivers another vengeful stab, the words of the onlooking duke, 'Forbear, you monstrous women!' (72), write the moral caption to the tableau. Ford's sensational reversed revels go to a further extreme than Shirley's interlude in attributing homicidal tendencies to the actress-whore. The episodes in both the plays thus mirror, indeed elaborate, Prynne's equation.[45] Independently of *Histrio-Mastix*, Shirley and Ford had arrived at the same conclusions about women-actors. Their construction of their own material in concerted warfare against Prynne reveals a tension between allegiance to the theatrical profession – and, implicitly, to Henrietta Maria – and acquiescence with the ideological norm regarding women.

Clearly, of its own accord, the drama was beginning to register and respond to the topic of female acting in England. Shirley and Ford's plays situate their women-actors in Italian courts; a distancing facilitated by genre. Aspects of the plays, however – a reference in *The Bird in a Cage* to the absence of jeering spectators, and Ford's portrayal of women participating in a court entertainment – are suggestive of the cultural climate in England in the early 1630s. The continental context of the plays may be seen as a tacit acknowledgement of the cultural specificity of Henrietta Maria, and the custom she introduced. I would argue further that in the qualities of expressive hilarity and flamboyant violence which characterize the women-actors there are traces of

Henrietta Maria's cultural difference; her particular form of French feminine.[46]

The stigma of whoredom attached to female expressivity is clearly and crudely iterated by the episodes in Ford and Shirley's plays. In opposition to this ideology culture tailored especially for the queen insisted on the legitimacy of women's talents finding expression and being put to view. Thomas Heywood, for instance, wrote a pastoral playlet, *Amphrisa*, clearly designed as a showcase for the female participants' singing, discoursing, and dancing, and in which a queen asserts to a group of innocent shepherdesses that these accomplishments 'may become a Theatre of eyes,/Yet wrest no blushes from you'.[47] For the culture at large, however, Prynne's equation between female performance and sexual immodesty held firm.

Prynne suffered the spectacular disciplinary measures of the state for his apparent imputation of immodesty to the queen. He had his revenge, however, in his 1640 pamphlet, *A New Discovery of the Prelates Tyranny*, in which he gave his own version of the events of 1633, protesting himself innocent of any intentions of slandering the queen. Prynne's minor triumph comes in the form of a marginal aside where he writes that:

> *Mr H. I. that first presented & shewed the book to the King, was a few moneths after committed prisoner to the Tower for begetting one of the actors of this pastorall with childe soone after it was acted, and making a reall commentary on M. *Prynnes* misapply'd text, both the Actresse, and he for this cause becomming M. *Prynnes* fellow prisoners in the Tower, A Strange providence and worthy observation.[48]

For once in his publishing career, Prynne let reality supply the gloss. Henry Jermyn, one of the queen's favourites, did indeed make Eleanor Villiers, one of the platonic brigade who acted in the pastoral, pregnant.[49] The episode makes its own comment on the tenuousness of the platonic ethic at court. However earnestly intended by Henrietta Maria, the cult was not wholly successful in policing female desire.

Prynne's usage of 'actresse' in this note registers the newly compound sense of the word with which this essay began. The perception of the actress as whore is essentially a perception of woman as wrong-doer, as (sexual) malefactor. It is a short step from this notion to the combined threat of female agency and feminine counterfeit or duplicity which informs the model of the politically motivated woman-actor with which I will end.

Cartwright's tragicomedy *The Lady-Errant*, published in his *Works* of 1651, sits in an historical vacuum both with respect to its date of composition and the date and circumstances of its performance. As far as we know it could have been written at any time between 1628 and 1643, the date of Cartwright's matriculation at Oxford and his premature death there from plague.[50] Lines in the prologue, however, suggest that the play was intended to be performed outdoors in front of a courtly audience. Moreover, this performance was to be distinguished by the unusual distribution of parts:

> if you will conceive, that though
> The Poem's forc'd, We are not so,
> And that each Sex keeps to its Part,
> Nature may plead excuse for Art.
>
> As then there's no Offence
> Giv'n to the Weak or Stubborn hence,
> Being the Female's Habit is
> Her owne, and the Male's his.[51]

The natural ordering of parts gestured at here would have been something of a freak occurrence in the Caroline period. Reading these lines in conjunction with the epilogue's reference to the pastoral prowess emanating from 'the neighbouring plain', Cartwright's editor G. Blakemore Evans construes the play and its mode of performance to be a mild reproach and intended corrective from the Oxonian Cartwright, directed at Henrietta Maria's female performance of *The Shepheard's Paradise*, written by the Cantabrigian Montagu.[52] The suggestion that *The Lady-Errant* should be seen as written in the wake of the queen's performance of Montagu's pastoral, in which women had again played men, makes particular sense in the light of the play's subject, which is sexual subversion. Cartwright's prologue calls attention to the contrast between the absence of transvestism in performance, and the transgressive aspect of the play, which depicts women aspiring above their sex in an effort to usurp male power. By drawing a distinction between the forced nature of the play, and the unforced manner of its presentation – 'The Poem's forc'd, *We* are not so' – the prologue states loudly that *here* there is no erring in the acting. In this performative stance Cartwright's play may be seen as legitimating the theatrical notion of the woman-actor *who keeps to her part*, specifically so as to silence her symbolic threat.

The play gives particular emphasis to its comic plot in which 'Three busie factious Ladies' attempt a female *coup d'état* while the men of Cyprus are away at war, a war which has arisen over the decision of the Cretan king to banish his priests. The factious women enlist the eponymous Lady Errant in their cause, a naive girl called Machessa, who traces her descent from the Amazons. In the event, the wilier Eumela, acting for the queen and the princess, manages to dissuade Machessa from assisting 'Rebellious Persons 'gainst their King' (line 1385) and to connive at sending the female rebels' contributory wealth to the king and his army in Crete.

Eumela's foiling of the plot sets up a problematic parallel between her duplicitous counter-contrivance, and the women's subversive scheming. In her role as 'Mistris Speaker' to the newly assembled female parliament she gives an oration deriving women's political astuteness from their acting ability, or skill in the cosmetic arts:

> He that saies Woman is not fit for Policy,
> Doth give the Lie to Art; for what man hath
> More sorts of Looks? more Faces? who puts on
> More severall Colours?
>
> (line 1214)

In her immediate situation of affecting allegiance to the female cause Eumela is implicated by her own rhetoric. In the romantic plot, however, her histrionic dimension works in the interests of love. Two exemplary ladies, 'sadly bearing the Absence of their Lords', relate how Eumela contrived various theatrical devices in an effort to dispel their gloom:

> thy bringing in my Father's Dwarf
> With Bow and Wings, and Quiver at his back,
> Instead of *Cupid*, to conveigh us Letters
> Through th'Air from hence to *Crete* was but a trick
> To put away our sadness.
>
> (line 319)

Eumela's ingenuously amateur theatre clearly models itself on the Caroline masque. Like a number of Caroline texts *The Lady-Errant* condones cultural activity for women in the form of music, poetry, and theatre. Eumela's artifice is a legitimate quantity because it is harnessed to such laudable ends as aiding the path of romantic love and working to avert treason. The play condemns the women's political contrivance while it sanctions Eumela's chicanery. The dramatic text thus reiterates the gesture of the prologue, which presented appropriate female acting as offsetting or neutralizing the more serious active transgression within the text. Eumela represents those ladies 'that would willing/Keep their own Sex and not turn Lords.' (line 220). Her 'keeping her part' within the play functions implicitly as a reproof to the women who impersonated men in Montagu's pastoral, and to any who might be contemplating extending this symbolic subversion into the real world beyond.

In the absence of a firm date *The Lady-Errant* provides fertile ground for speculation about its relation to contemporary cultural and political contexts. The play contains descriptive eulogies of the king in action and the queen as a goddess of love, and it ends in a ritual celebrating the communion of love and wisdom. It opens with a particularly intriguing scene which presents the three women 'busily discoursing' of the response they have had from 'Court-Ladies', 'Countrey-Ladies', 'City-Wives', 'Countrey-Gentlewomen and their eldest daughters', all of whom have subscribed to the 'Rowl of the Asserters of Female Liberty' (line 273) and who are offering 'mony, Plate/Jewels, and Garments' (line 13) as contribution to the cause. This collection might be read alongside the rumour of a private female collection to be sponsored by Henrietta Maria during the First Bishops' War, described by a newswriter as 'a design to send to all the great ladies, as well wives as widows, to contribute out of their allowances towards the charge of the King's army'.[53] On the basis of this rumoured collection one might argue for a later date for *The Lady-Errant* than the mid-1630s, construing the play as alluding to Henrietta Maria's political intervention, or even to the influences to which she was subject, to the possibility of her wandering astray.

I believe it more profitable, however, to situate the play broadly in the cultural and political context of the 1630s. Another mock Lady-Errant, or 'Hercules come from the distaff' appears in Thomas Randolph's academic drama of 1632, *The Jealous Lovers*. Decorous Amazons, or martial women in 'warlike habits' feature in several productions from the middle of the decade, staged either for or by the court, among them Cartwright's *The Royal Slave* (1636) and the last of the Caroline masques, Davenant's *Salmacida Spolia* (1640). These static representations of female valour were perhaps less alarming than the usurpation of masculine roles by women in the queen's pastoral performances. In any case, it is notable that female politicking, or role transgression in the political arena, has become a dramatic *topos* by the end of the decade. In Ford's *The Fancies Chaste and Noble* (1637) a woman remarks to her husband:

> Sure, in some country
> Ladies are privy-counsellors, I warrant ye;
> . . . there the land is doubtless
> Most politicly govern'd; all the women
> Wear swords and breeches, I have heard most certainly:
> Such sights were excellent.[54]

Clearly this *topos* of the insubordinate woman-actor rebounds on Henrietta Maria herself, who in acting politically was judged by Puritan onlookers to be playing boss to her husband.[55] At the outset of the Civil War her lady-errantry took her to Holland, where she stayed for a year, pawning the crown jewels and buying arms and ammunition. Her subsequent Amazonian exploits involved landing in the north at Bridlington Bay, where she was besieged by cannon-fire from parliamentary ships, and then spending five months on the road at the head of an army before meeting Charles at Oxford.[56] It was these activities and her 'actual performances with her popish army'[57] for which the queen was impeached by Parliament in 1643. The publication of her letters to Charles, in 1645, revealed both the extent of her influence over the king and an ironic awareness of the role she was playing. Her fondness for this playful dimension is suggested by her remark, 'In case of a descent, I must act the captain, though a little low in stature, myself' and her jocular description, while itemizing the state of the army she is bringing to Oxford, of 'her she-majesty, generalissima', bringing up the rear.[58] I suggest that in these parts of her letters Henrietta Maria is drawing on the discourse of female performance which her acting helped set in motion, a discourse in which the functional sense of acting is overlaid with a theatrical dimension. This discourse is identifiable in a number of poems addressed to the queen,[59] and may also be at work in Dr Denton's advice to the exiled Sir Ralph Verney, on the political utility of women's histrionic powers:

> I am confident if you were here, you would doe as our sages doe, instruct your wife, & *leave her to act it with committees*, their sexe entitles them to many privileges and we find the comfort of them now more than ever.[60]

I wonder, further, about the application of courtly images to women who were perceived to be engaged in radical political action. Women Levellers petitioning for the release of John Lilburne in 1649 were described in contemporary newsbooks in language which draws noticeably on the satiric lexicon of the woman-actor, being dubbed 'the Ladyes-errants of the Seagreen Order', whose desires were to 'raigne as Queenes'.[61] In his book *Amazons and Warrior Women*, Simon Shepherd has traced this imagery to a broadly Protestant literary tradition of the warrior woman, suggesting a link between the cultural presence of such images and women's active political protest.[62] By way of conclusion I would suggest that the female claim to the rights of a subject may have been further spurred by the fact that women's acting was justified at the Caroline court.

NOTES

1 Stephen Orgel and Roy Strong, *Inigo Jones: The Theatre of the Stuart Court*, 2 vols (Berkeley: California University Press, 1973), vol. I, 24–5; vol. II, 383–8.

2 Alfred Harbage, *Cavalier Drama* (1936; New York: Russell & Russell, 1964), 11–12; Jean Jacquot, 'La Reine Henriette-Marie et L'Influence Française dans les Spectacles à la Cour de Charles I', *Cahiers de l'Association Internationale des Études Françaises* 9 (1957), 128–60 (129–30). T. S. Graves surveys evidence for the exhibition and participation of women in a range of irregular forms of performance before this date: see 'Women on the pre-Restoration stage', *Studies in Philology* 22 (1925), 184–97. For a discussion of women in the Stuart court masque see Suzanne Gossett, ' "Man-maid, begone!": Women in masques', *English Literary Renaissance* 18 (1988), 96–113.

3 G. E. Bentley, *The Jacobean and Caroline Stage*, 7 vols (Oxford: Clarendon Press, 1948–61), vol. IV, 548–9.

4 Bentley, vol. IV, 549 (my italics).

5 Bentley, vol. IV, 548.

6 The date given by the *OED* for the first recorded usage of 'actress' in the theatrical sense is 1700. The generic term 'actor' was used to signify 'player' (from 1581) and 'doer' (from 1603); 'actress' was used in the sense of 'a female doer' from 1589. Henrietta Maria was again called 'the prime actress' in reports about the later court pastoral, Walter Montagu's *The Shepheard's Paradise* (1633), see Bentley, vol. III, 917.

7 Katharine Eisaman Maus, ' "Playhouse Flesh and Blood": sexual ideology and the Restoration actress', *English Literary History* 46 (1979), 595–617.

8 Clifford Leech's thesis, 'Private performances and amateur theatricals (excluding the academic stage) from 1580–1660' (Ph.D. dissertation, University of London, 1935) documents an increasing incidence of female participation in private masques and dramatic entertainments after 1625.

9 William Prynne, *Histrio-Mastix* (1633), sig. 5R4.

10 See 'Précieuses at the court of Charles I', in J. B. Fletcher, *The Religion of Beauty in Woman and Other Essays on Platonic Love in Poetry and Society* (New York: Macmillan 1911), 166–205; and Erica Veevers's revisionist study, *Images of Love and Religion: Queen Henrietta Maria and Court Entertainments* (Cambridge: Cambridge University Press, 1989), 1–74.

11 See Louis Adrian Montrose, ' "Eliza, Queene of Shepheardes", and the pastoral of power', *English Literary Renaissance* 10 (1980), 153–82. Two 'pastoral tragicomedies' by Samuel Daniel, *The Queen's Arcadia* and *Hymen's Triumph* were presented before Queen Anne in 1605 and 1614 respectively; I am grateful to Jonathan Hope for alerting me to Daniel's plays.

12 Harbage, 39–40; Clifford Leech, 'The Caroline audience' in *Shakespeare's Tragedies and Other Studies in Seventeenth Century Drama* (London: Chatto, 1950), 159–81; Andrew Gurr, *The Shakespearean Stage 1574–1642*, second edn (Cambridge: Cambridge University Press, 1980), 205–6; Michael Neill, ' "Wits most accomplished Senate": the audience of the Caroline private theatres', *Studies in English Literature* 18 (1978), 341–60 (341–4).

13 Jacquot, 'La Reine Henriette-Marie'; Martin Butler, *Theatre and Crisis 1632–1642* (Cambridge: Cambridge University Press, 1984); John Peacock, 'The French element in Inigo Jones's masque designs' in David Lindley (ed.), *The Court Masque* (Manchester: Manchester University Press, 1984), 149–68; Kevin Sharpe, *Criticism and Compliment: The Politics of Literature in the England of Charles I* (Cambridge: Cambridge University Press, 1987); Veevers, *Images of Love and Religion, passim.*

14 Butler, chapters 3 and 4, *passim* (35). Cf. R. M. Smuts's comments on the political dimension of the feminine influence at court, where he notes the use of platonic love-codes as a masking device for the political manoeuvring in which powerful women, especially Henrietta Maria, played a focal part; *Court Culture and the Origins of a Royalist Tradition in Early Stuart England* (Philadelphia: Pennsylvania University Press, 1987), 189, 194–6.

15 Butler, chapter 3, *passim*; see also Sharpe, 94–101. Both critics draw on R. M. Smuts's reappraisal of Henrietta Maria's political positioning in the conflicts of the 1630s; see Smuts, 'The Puritan followers of Henrietta Maria in the 1630s', *English Historical Review* 93 (1978), 26–45.

16 In her book *Shakespeare and the Nature of Women* (London: Macmillan, 1975), Juliet Dusinberre touches briefly on the issue of female performance, but only to dismiss the related cults of female acting and platonic love fostered by Henrietta Maria as a debilitating influence on seventeenth-century drama (17–18, 268–71). Because her reading focuses exclusively on the idealized inscription of women in Caroline drama, Dusinberre inevitably by-passes the wider drama or cultural controversy which arose in response to the staging of women at the Caroline court. Erica Veevers's study of Henrietta Maria's influence on Caroline court culture, *Images of Love and Religion* (see note 10) newly assesses the queen's 'social fashions' (2) of platonic love and *préciosité*, but does not recognize female performance as either a fashion or an issue. Veevers's book appeared after this essay was completed.

17 See note 2.

18 R. M. Smuts, 'The political failure of Stuart cultural patronage' in Guy Fitch Lyttle and Stephen Orgel (eds), *Patronage in the Renaissance* (Princeton: Princeton University Press, 1981), 165–87. See also Smuts, *Court Culture and the Origins of a Royalist Tradition*, 53–72.

19 Richard Brome, *The Court Begger, Dramatic Works*, ed. H. Shepherd, 3 vols (London, 1873), vol. III, 206.

20 Natalie Zemon Davis, 'Women on top: symbolic sexual inversion and

political disorder in early modern Europe' in Barbara Babcock (ed.), *The Reversible World: Symbolic Inversion in Art and Society* (Ithaca: Cornell University Press, 1978), 148–83.

21 Richard Braithwait, *The English Gentlewoman* (1631), 48.

22 Davis, 154; Margaret Cavendish, *Poems and Fancies* (1653), 162. Cavendish went into exile as a maid of honour to Henrietta Maria, spending several years with the queen in Paris before meeting and marrying William Cavendish, then the Marquis of Newcastle (*Nature's Pictures* (1656), 373–5). Both liaisons contributed towards the production of Cavendish's own dramatic writing.

23 Bentley, vol. IV, 538–9.

24 William Hawkins, *Apollo Shroving* (1627), 3.

25 ibid., 8.

26 *The Oxford Dictionary of English Christian Names*, ed. Elizabeth G. Withycombe, third edn (Oxford: Clarendon Press, 1976), 190.

27 Ben Jonson, *Complete Plays*, ed. Gerald A. Wilkes, 4 vols (Oxford: Clarendon Press, 1981–2), vol. IV, 248.

28 James Shirley, *Dramatic Works and Poems*, ed. William Gifford and Alexander Dyce, 6 vols (London, 1833), vol. VI, 264.

29 On the furthering of this early seventeenth-century trend in the Caroline period, concomitant with the growth of London as a centre of commercialized leisure and entertainment, see Butler, 102–10, and Smuts, *Court Culture*, 54–8.

30 Prynne, 992.

31 ibid. (my italics).

32 Thomas Carew, *Poems, with a Maske*, third edn (1651), 182.

33 The third term in what I would suggest is an associative chain within satiric discourse is the *hic-mulier* or masculine woman, whose mannered 'masculine' appearance constitutes another prime example of female self-fashioning in this period. In this respect Prynne's *Histrio-Mastix* is exemplary for its triple arraignment of 'female Play-haunters', women-actors, who dare 'to speak publikely on a Stage, (perchance in mans apparell, and cut haire. . .)', and 'our frizled, pouldred, shorne, swaggering Lasses' or 'English Man-women monsters' (341, sig. 5R4, 219, 188). Prynne risks adding as a fourth term 'Popish Nonnes', whose polled heads indicate their espousal to Christ and freedom 'from all subjection to men' (201).

34 Bentley, vol. I, 25.

35 Prynne, 414, 214.

36 Shirley, *Dramatic Works*, vol. III, 79.

37 Although *Histrio-Mastix* is dated 1633, it was published towards the end of 1632. See *Documents Relating to the Proceedings against William Prynne in 1634 and 1637*, ed. S. R. Gardiner (London, 1877), 52; Bulstrode Whitelocke, *Memorials of the English Affairs* (1682), 18; Ethyn W. Kirby, *William Prynne: A Study in Puritanism* (Cambridge, Mass.: Harvard University Press, 1931), 20–5.

38 See E. N. S. Thompson, *The Controversy between the Puritans and the Stage* (1903; New York: Henry Holt & Co. 1966), 222–3.

39 Bentley, vol. V. 1080.

40 Frances Frazier Senescu, 'James Shirley's *The Bird in a Cage*, edited from the

Quarto of 1633, with Introduction and Notes' (unpublished University of Chicago thesis, 1948), xlix–li. Senescu argues against the theory that Shirley added the scenes which dramatize women acting in between the first performance of *The Shepheard's Paradise* (9 January) and the licensing of the play (21 January). On the basis of internal allusions she suggests a composition date between January 1630 and January 1631, construing the scenes at issue as a compliment paid to Henrietta Maria in the wake of the French actresses' performance in November 1629 (li–lv). Bentley does not find the allusions 'definite enough to prove composition such an unusually long time before Herbert's licence' (vol. V, 1081). What seems clear is that Shirley wrote the play at a time when the subject of female acting was in vogue, perhaps (as Bentley suggests in respect of Ford's *Love Sacrifice*) during the period when news of the queen's forthcoming performance was in the air (vol. III, 453).

41 Shirley, *Dramatic Works*, vol. II.sig.2A8v. Further page references are given in the text.

42 Senescu reads this line as pointedly complimenting women-actors (li); ignoring the sexual innuendo in the phrase 'play their parts'. For examples of this pun see T. S. Graves, 193, n.56, and Lisa Jardine, *Still Harping on Daughters: Women and Drama in the Age of Shakespeare* (Brighton: Harvester, 1983), 11–13. Senescu's reading of the 'interlude' as a transparent compliment to Henrietta Maria overlooks its farcical and bawdy aspects.

43 Bentley, vol. III, 451–3.

44 John Ford, *Works*, ed. William Gifford, rev. Alexander Dyce, 3 vols (London, 1869), vol. I, lxxiv. Further page references are given in the text.

45 Bentley construes Ford's initial reference to women-antics at court as a polite allusion to Henrietta Maria's activities, in the period leading up to the performance of *The Shepheard's Paradise* (vol. III, 452–3). But his reading ignores the implications of the subsequent action in which female acting is linked with 'fallen' sexuality and wilful violence.

46 Cf. Smuts, *Court Culture*, 194. I can do no more than gesture here to this particular cultural and sexual difference; numerous contemporary accounts of Henrietta Maria, however, suggest that her behaviour was characterized by an informality, authority, and impulsiveness which initially startled and subsequently alienated the English.

47 Thomas Heywood, *Pleasant Dialogues and Drammas* (1637), 201. I am grateful to Martin Butler for directing me to this play.

48 Prynne, *A New Discovery of the Prelates Tyranny* (1640), 8.

49 Quentin Bone, *Henrietta Maria: Queen of the Cavaliers* (London: Peter Owen, 1973), 84–6.

50 Bentley, vol. III, 128–32 (131).

51 *The Plays and Poems of William Cartwright*, ed. G. Blakemore Evans (Madison: Wisconsin University Press, 1951), prologue, line 21. Further references are given by line in the text.

52 Evans, 83–4.

53 Edmund Rossingham to Edward Viscount Conway, 23 April, *Calendar of State Papers Domestic*, 1639, 73–4. The 'design' is ascribed to Lady Denbigh and Lady Killigrew. This rumoured collection is no doubt related to the appeal to English Catholics overseen by the Papal envoy George Con,

which took the form of a letter drafted by Walter Montagu and Kenelm Digby and sent in the queen's name. See *The letter sent by the Queenes Majestie concerning the collection of the recusants mony for the Scottish warre, April 17, 1639* (London, 1641).

54 Ford, *Works*, vol. II, 252.

55 See Milton's remarks in *Eikonoklastes* (1649); *Complete Prose Works of John Milton*, ed. Don M. Wolfe *et al.*, 8 vols (New Haven: Yale University Press, 1953–82), vol. III, 420–1; and those of Lucy Hutchinson in *Memoirs of the Life of Colonel Hutchinson* (London, 1846), 85, 88–9. Cf. the joke made by Sir Ralph Verney, cit. Bone, 86–7.

56 Bone, chapter 6, *passim*; 'A Short History of the Troubles in England – As it was Related by the Queen of England', in François Bertaud de Motteville, *Memoirs for the History of Anne of Austria*, translated from the French, 5 vols (1725–6), vol. I, 216–21.

57 Perfect Diurnal, 29 May 1643, cited in *Letters of Queen Henrietta Maria*, ed. M. A. E. Green (London, 1857), 214.

58 ibid., 167, 222.

59 See, for instance, the revised version of Townshend's 'Hide not thy Love', discussed in Sharpe, 170–1.

60 Cited in Alice Clark, *Working Life of Women in the Seventeenth Century* (1919; London: Routledge, 1982), 20 (my italics).

61 Patricia Higgins, 'The reactions of women, with special reference to women petitioners', in Brian Manning (ed.), *Politics, Religion and the English Civil War* (London: Edward Arnold, 1973), 179–222 (205).

62 Simon Shepherd, *Amazons and Warrior Women: Varieties of Feminism in Seventeenth-Century Drama* (Brighton: Harvester, 1981), 64–6.

Index